The Art of the Illustrated Book

Haeckel, Kunstformen der Natur. Tafel 8 — Desmonema.

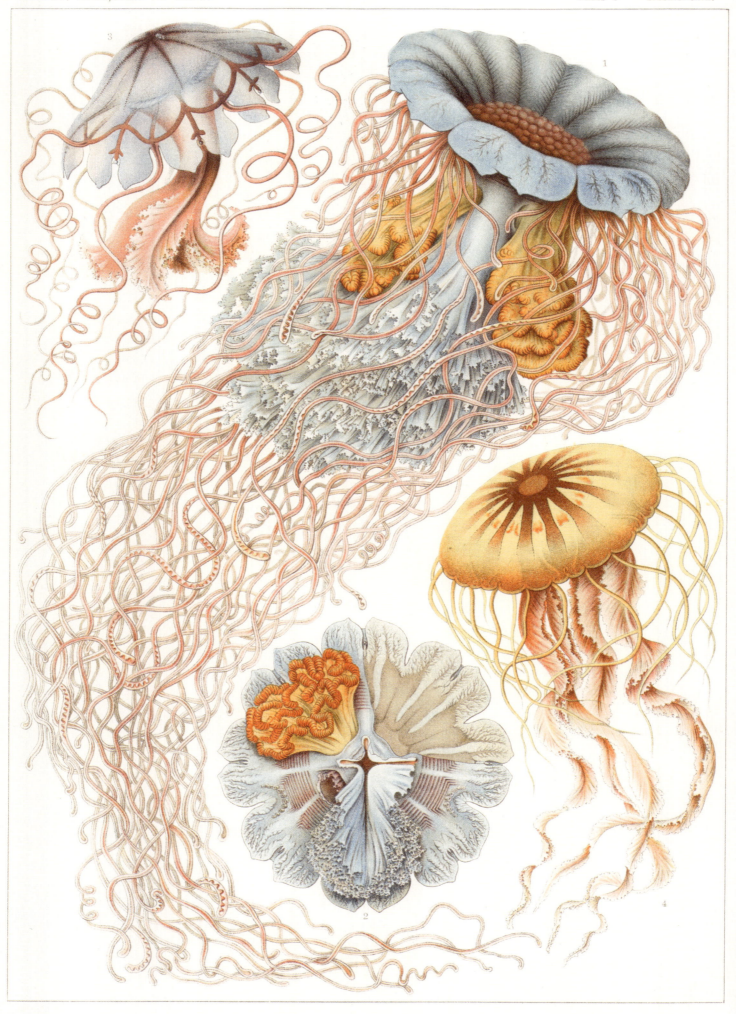

Discomedusae. — Scheibenquallen.

The Art of the Illustrated Book

Edited by JULIUS BRYANT

with ELIZABETH JAMES *and* CATHERINE YVARD

Front cover: Detail from *Kunstformen der Natur*, 1904 (p.60)
Back cover: Detail from *Della magnificenza ed architettura de' Romani*, 1761 (p.170)

Jacket: Details from *Alice's Adventures in Wonderland*, 1865 (p.17); *The Terra-cotta Architecture of North Italy*, 1867 (p.176); *Poissons, écrevisses et crabes de diverses couleurs et figures extraordinaires*, 1754 (p.50); *Les Robes de Paul Poiret racontées par Paul Iribe*, 1908 (p.251); *Darstellung und Geschichte des Geschmacks der vorzüglichsten Völker in Beziehung auf die innere Auszierung der Zimmer und auf die Baukunst*, 1796–9 (p.174); *Dunhuang Tang dai tu an xuan*, 1959 (p.199); *XXIV Fables*, 1959 (pp.96–7); *Edmund Dulac's Fairy-Book: Fairy Tales of the Allied Nations*, 1916 (p.93); *Fresco Decorations and Stuccoes of Churches & Palaces in Italy*, 1844 (p.189); *L'Ornement polychrome*, 1869–87 (p.192); *Collection of Etruscan, Greek and Roman Antiquities from the Cabinet of the Honble Wm Hamilton*, 1801–8 (pp.148–9); *A Second Series of the Monuments of Nineveh*, 1853 (p.151); *Sōmoku kajitsu shashin zufu*, c.1836 (p.57); *Descriptio publicae gratulationis*, 1595 (p.208); and *The International Exhibition of 1862* (p.229).

Frontispiece: Detail from *Kunstformen der Natur*, 1904 (p.60)

EDITORS' NOTE

This book is intended to appeal to a general audience and, we very much hope, to present some unknown details to the specialist; as such, we have chosen to follow certain stylistic conventions for ease of reading. Book titles are given in their original language, but capitalization and older glyphs and allographs have generally been regularized.

Book titles in languages other than English are followed by either the title of a published English translation of the book (given in italic) or a direct translation (given in roman). Where mentioned, popular assumed titles have been given in single quotes: the 'Kelmscott Chaucer', for example.

The captions in this book include the method of illustration used in the featured book: copperplate engravings, steel engravings, etchings, woodcuts, etc. From the beginning of the twentieth century, however, colour offset lithography has been largely ubiquitous in the printing of illustrated books. For this reason we have not listed the printing method for illustrations in most titles published after 1900, but, where this is of particular note, we have detailed the type or source of illustration, such as colour photography, screen-printing and so on.

As the business of book publishing grew across the centuries, the imprint of the publisher took precedence over that of the printer. It is difficult to draw an exact line as to when this transition occurs, but readers will notice that for books from the eighteenth century onwards more captions list only the publisher. However, the printer's details are often given on a publication's imprint page, and readers seeking this or any further information about the titles included are encouraged to visit the National Art Library's online catalogue or visit the library in person at the Victoria and Albert Museum, London.

Full details can be found at:
https://www.vam.ac.uk/info/national-art-library
Explore the Collections at: https://www.vam.ac.uk/collections

First published in 2022 by Thames & Hudson Ltd, London, 181A High Holborn, London WC1V 7QX, in association with the Victoria and Albert Museum, London

First published in the United States of America in 2022 by Thames & Hudson Inc., 500 Fifth Avenue, New York, New York 10110

The Art of the Illustrated Book © 2022 Victoria and Albert Museum, London/Thames & Hudson Ltd, London

Text and V&A photographs © 2022 Victoria and Albert Museum, London
Design © 2022 Thames & Hudson Ltd, London
Designed by Charlie Smith Design

All Rights Reserved. No part of this publication may be reproduced or transmitted in any form or by any means, electronic or mechanical, including photocopy, recording or any other information storage and retrieval system, without prior permission in writing from the publishers.

British Library Cataloguing-in-Publication Data
A catalogue record for this book is available from the British Library

Library of Congress Control Number 2022931896

ISBN 978-0-500-48069-4

Printed and bound in Thailand by Cyberprint Group Co., Ltd

Be the first to know about our new releases, exclusive content and author events by visiting
thamesandhudson.com
thamesandhudsonusa.com
thamesandhudson.com.au

INTRODUCTION

Worlds Beyond Words
The Art of the Illustrated Book
6

—

1. Religion
22

2. Natural History
42

3. Travel
62

4. Fables and Folk Tales
82

5. Literature
100

6. Art Making
120

7. Art History
140

8. Architecture
160

9. Ornament and Pattern
180

10. Festivals
200

11. World's Fairs
220

12. Fashion
240

13. Shopping
260

—

NOTES 278

FURTHER READING 278

CONTRIBUTORS 281

ACKNOWLEDGMENTS AND PICTURE CREDITS 282

INDEX 283

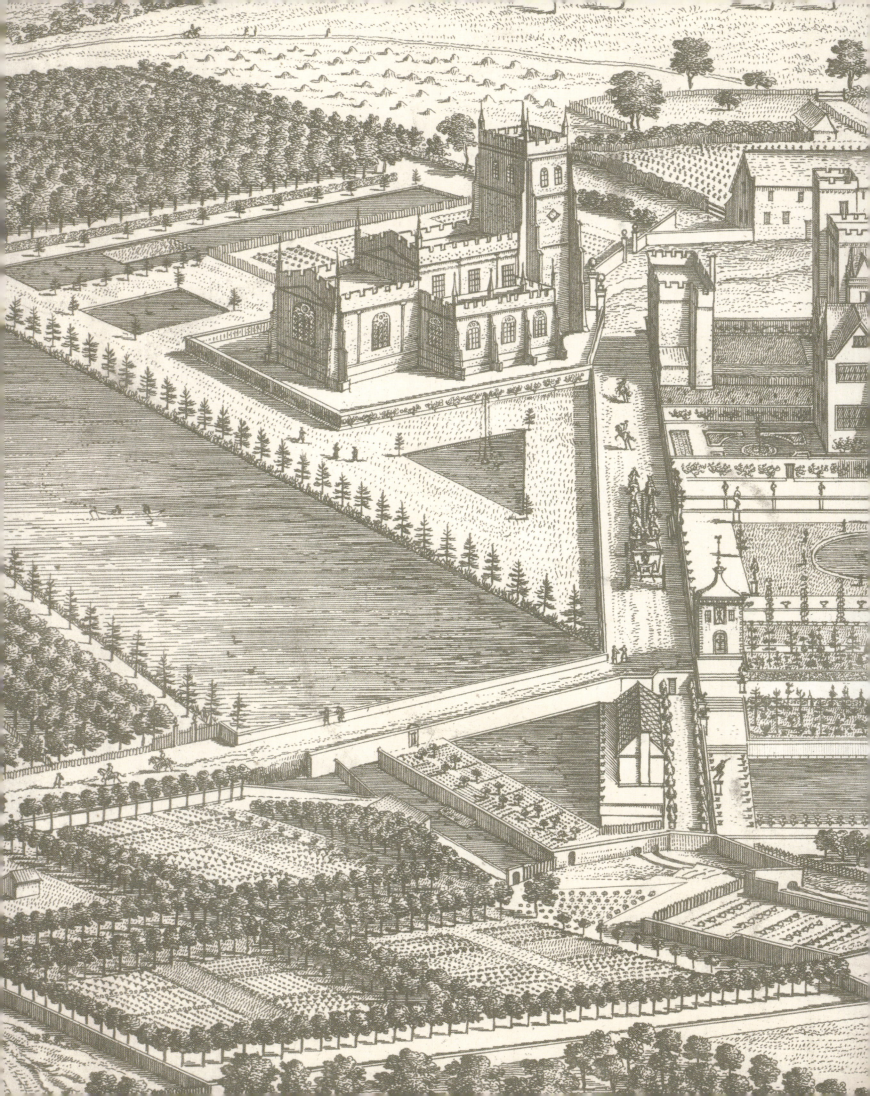

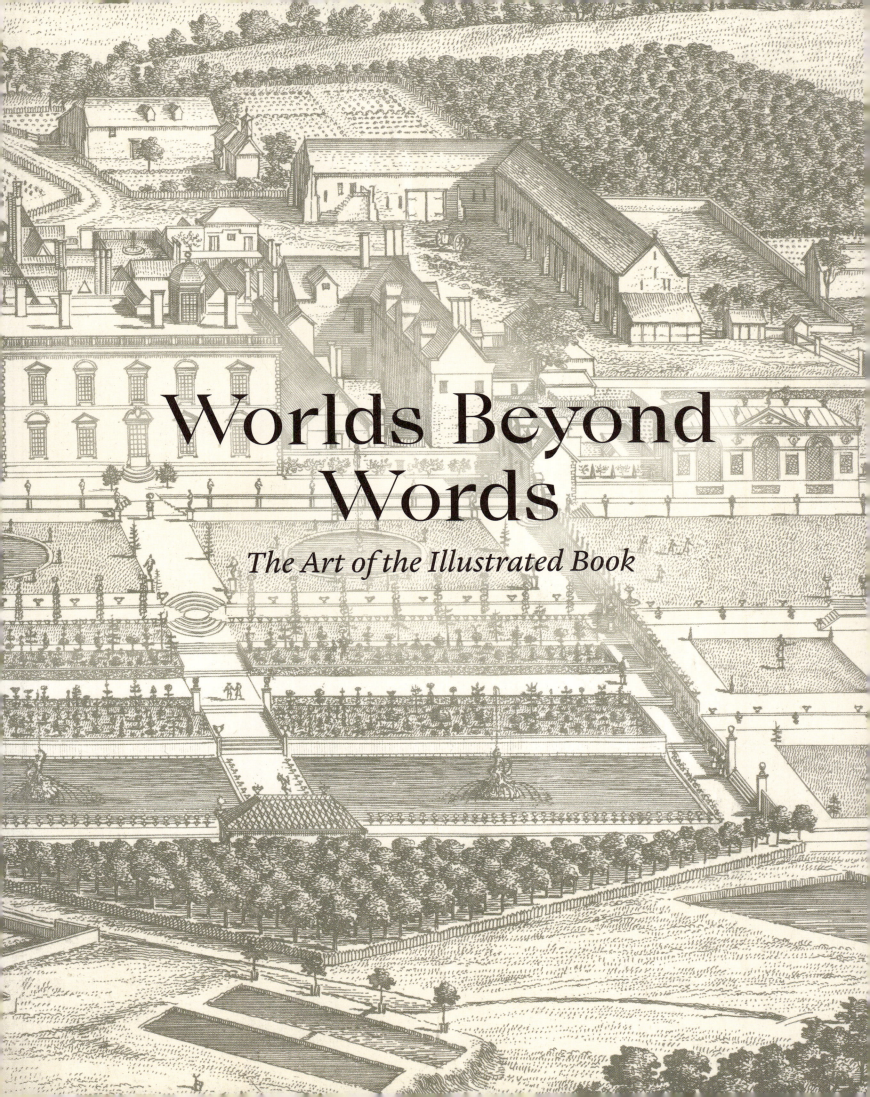

Worlds Beyond Words

The Art of the Illustrated Book

Worlds Beyond Words
The Art of the Illustrated Book

JULIUS BRYANT

In his essay 'The Ideal Book' (1893) the artist and designer William Morris declared that the illustrated book 'gives us such endless pleasure, and is so intimately connected with the other absolutely necessary art of imaginative literature that it must remain one of the very worthiest things towards the production of which reasonable men should strive'.[1] A founder of the Arts and Crafts movement in Britain, Morris established the Kelmscott Press in London in 1891 to revive the art of the book beautiful through illustrations, typefaces, ornamental borders and fine printing. This volume will explore the many roles that images play when they contribute to a book. Of course, not every favourite can be included. Some titles will meet Morris's standards, but beauty (and the attendant luxury of highly expensive art books such as his 'Kelmscott Chaucer', 1896; right) is not the sole reason for inclusion. Rather than an assembly of the usual suspects, gathered here are some of the most innovative, influential, compelling and striking examples of the illustrated book, all chosen from the collections in the National Art Library (NAL) at the Victoria and Albert Museum (V&A) in London.

Our focus is on printed books from the fifteenth century to today, in which illustrations are visual responses to texts.[2] Illustrators are communicators who record real people, places, species, things, and (through diagrams) theories and ideas, and evoke imaginary characters and settings. Illustrators can clarify narratives, and interpret and amplify texts by offering something else to the reader. In their creative responses, illustrators also question, challenge or digress from the texts. For this book we have selected not only books illustrated by graphic artists but also those that use photographs, including reproductions of other works of art. Artists' books (*livres d'artiste*) and photobooks have certainly influenced the way in which texts and images are published commercially, but since they are led by images, they lie beyond the scope of this illustrated book (although the eagle-eyed reader will notice one or two examples that correspond with a chapter theme).[3]

The 153 key examples included here have been brought together by 25 subject-specialist librarians and curators at the V&A. The thematic chapters will lead you through worlds of spirit, nature and human creativity. The book is arranged broadly in chronological order. The first part (Religion, Natural History and Travel) gathers illustrated books that attempt to document, interpret and understand the spiritual and natural worlds as shared knowledge. The second part (Fables and Folk Tales, Literature, Art Making, Art History, Architecture, and Ornament and Pattern) explores the creative response through the worlds of imagination and invention. Finally, the third part (Festivals, World's Fairs, Fashion and Shopping) takes us into the social worlds of celebration, national commemoration and competitive consumption, where the art of illustration continues to play a vital role in global communication.

Contributors selected examples that they admire from as wide a range of periods and places as possible (within the collections of the

ABOVE
William Harcourt Hooper after Edward Burne-Jones and William Morris, 'The Romaunt of the Rose: Richness and Largesse', woodcut from *The Works of Geoffrey Chaucer* ('Kelmscott Chaucer'), London, 1896
V&A L.757-1896

OPPOSITE
Michael Wolgemut, 'The Feast of Herod; Scenes from the Life of the Virgin; Genealogies', woodcuts from Hartmann Schedel, *Liber chronicarum* ('Nuremberg Chronicle'), Nuremberg, 1493
V&A 38041800368516

NAL, which are naturally focused largely upon art and art history) and they reflect on the particular challenges each theme has presented to the illustrator. As mentioned above, not all favourites can be included since each chapter could easily have been a book in itself. Inevitably, some choices, such as Thomas Chippendale's *Gentleman and Cabinet-maker's Director* (1754, see Chapter 13, p.265), could have appeared under several headings, but the reader's understanding is welcomed. Our overall aim has been to convey our fascination with the interplay of texts and images, and help readers understand the myriad ways in which illustrated books contribute to the visual culture of humankind. As such this selection cannot hope to be a comprehensive global survey of all illustrated books,[4] nor will it (or this Introduction) escape a Western perspective. But in keeping with the V&A's founding remit, we hope our choices may inspire writers, illustrators, designers, publishers and printers to create brilliant new books.

The Illustrated Book

A Historical Overview

Major advances in the development of the illustrated book are often linked to the emergence of new printing technologies. It is well known that moveable metal type was perfected in the German city of Mainz about 1450 by Johann Gutenberg, whose Latin Bible was published about 1455. The first printed illustrated books to combine moveable type with woodcut images were published by Albrecht Pfister of Bamberg from 1460 until his death six years later. The Chinese inventor and engineer Pi Sheng, however, had created moveable type using baked clay centuries earlier, between 1041 and 1049, and single-sheet woodblock prints had also been produced in China for many years before that. Thus the marriage of word and image on a printed page was not new to the fifteenth century. Nonetheless, moveable metal type allowed for stronger printing plates that could produce more copies; this led to the radical expansion of the publishing industry. Pfister's new books did not immediately dominate the market, however. They were costly to purchase and had a rival in the less expensive form of 'block books' – traditional short books in which text and image were cut from the same woodblock. The pictures in block books arguably had to work harder as they were hugely popular with a less literate market. As might be imagined, by the end of the fifteenth century the publication of illustrated books had become big business.

The first Englishman to publish a printed book was the merchant William Caxton, who had acquired a printing press and learned how to operate it in Cologne, Germany. Caxton established the first printing press in England, in the precincts of Westminster Abbey, London, about 1476. His first edition of Geoffrey Chaucer's *Canterbury Tales* (1476) lacked illustrations, but Caxton included woodcuts in the second (1482). He published more than one hundred books, including Thomas Malory's *Morte d'Arthur* (1485).

In Nuremberg, Anton Koberger ran 24 presses and also managed binders and booksellers. His best-known production, the *Liber chronicarum* (1493) by Hartmann Schedel, boasts more illustrations than

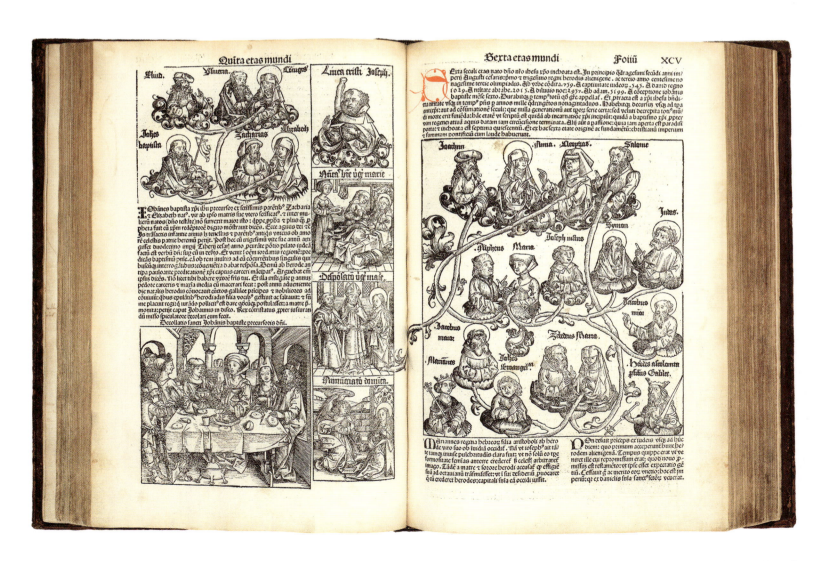

any other fifteenth-century book (previous page). Featuring 1,809 images from 645 woodblocks cut from designs by the painter and printmaker Michael Wolgemut, the 'Nuremberg Chronicle' (as it is also widely known) presents a detailed history and geography of the world from the biblical Creation to 1493. It did not end there, however, since Koberger included blank pages at the end for successive owners to update and illustrate themselves (see Chapter 1, p.29).

One of the artists apprenticed to Wolgemut, who may have contributed illustrations to the 'Nuremberg Chronicle', was Koberger's godson, Albrecht Dürer. As a graphic artist, he is best known for *The Apocalypse* (1498), a series of 15 full-page woodcuts, each with text from the Book of Revelations on the reverse to face the images when published as a book (above). The woodcuts were also sold as single-sheets when Dürer republished the book in 1511. His series of 37 woodcuts known as the *Little Passion* was published in book form in 1511 as the *Passio Christi ab Alberto Dürer Nurenbergensi effigiata* (Christ's Passion as imaged by Albrecht Dürer of Nuremberg). In that same year, his woodcut series the *Great Passion of Christ* was also published in book form, as well as his *Life of the Virgin*, a set of 19 full-page woodcuts, each with text on the reverse. These two sets are among Dürer's most familiar works, as they remained in print almost continually until the eighteenth century and were used as illustrations for prayer books. He also produced diagrams for the technical treatises that preoccupied his later years, on human proportions (1523), practical geometry (1525) and designs for fortifications (c.1527). Dürer's enjoyment of book illustration and decoration is clear from the 45 ornamental margins he drew in the printed prayer book *The Book of Hours of Emperor Maximilian I* (1513, Bayerische Staatsbibliothek, Munich).

Dürer made two visits to Venice (in 1495 and 1505–7), where he was influenced by studies of the human figure and perspective and sketched Venetian dress. Venice was, like Nuremberg, a centre of printing and publishing at that time. The German printer Erhard Ratdolt published in Venice the first mathematics book to be illustrated with diagrams, *Elementa Geometriae* (*Elements of Geometry*, 1482), by the ancient Greek mathematician Euclid. This includes some 400 geometrical shapes along with fine initials and ornamental borders. Aldus Manutius, who ran the Aldine Press in Venice from about 1490, is the most important printer in Western history after Gutenberg. Manutius produced one of the finest illustrated books ever published, Francesco Colonna's *Hypnerotomachia Poliphili* (Poliphilo's strife of love in a dream, 1499, see Chapter 10, p.203). Here 174 woodcuts, probably designed by Benedetto Bordon, accompany a text set in roman type designed by Francesco Griffo. The book was highly influential in spreading a taste for roman (rather than gothic) typography and in its style of woodcuts, which used line, space and architectural settings. The sculptor Gian Lorenzo Bernini used many classical sources quoted in the woodcuts for his fountains and obelisks in Rome, as did the painter and architect Giulio Romano for the Palazzo del Te in Mantua. The book's influence on architecture continued into the eighteenth century through a French translation, *Discours du songe de Poliphile* (1546).

The Protestant Reformation further mobilized the printing presses in the German-speaking states of central Europe. Between 1517 and 1530 a media revolution produced 10 million copies of more than 100,000 religious pamphlets and books. The theologian Martin Luther's translation of the Bible into German (1522–34) was illustrated by his close friend Lucas Cranach the Elder with original woodcuts, several indebted to Cranach's main rival, Dürer. The Swiss city of Basel produced a masterpiece of the history of medicine and the illustrated book, the anatomical treatise *De humani corporis fabrica* (*On the Fabric of the Human Body*, commonly known as Vesalius's 'Anatomy', 1543) by the surgeon Andreas Vesalius. The illustrations, of full-length flayed figures and skeletons in landscape settings, were soon attributed to Titian and his pupils, among whom Jan Stephan van Calcar is now given credit. Other important illustrated scientific treatises published in Basel include the pioneering *De historia stirpium commentarii insignes* (Notable commentaries on the history of plants, often known as the 'Great Herbal', 1542) by Leonhart Fuchs, illustrated by Heinrich Füllmaurer. Basel produced an artist of international stature who also worked for publishers. For Hans Holbein's best-known book, *Les simulachres et historiées faces de la mort* (*The Dance of Death*, 1538), 49 woodcuts and text were printed in Lyon from blocks cut in Basel. The same year the same printers published Holbein's *Icones historiarum Veteris Testamenti* (Images of the Old Testament), in which 92 woodcuts of scenes from the Old Testament each fill a page, with biblical quotations above and verse below.

While in England (in 1526–8 and 1532–43), Holbein designed an elaborate title page for the 'Coverdale Bible' (1535), the first complete translation in modern English and the first to be printed. It was published in Antwerp, which had overtaken Bruges as the centre of book publishing in the Spanish Netherlands of the sixteenth century. Nevertheless, manuscript illustration continued to flourish in Bruges, as it did in England. Colour was a strong advantage of the manuscript, and soon printer–publishers were employing artists and illuminators to decorate and paint miniatures in printed books. Increasing demand for individual reproductions of paintings led to a rise in skilled copperplate engraving in Antwerp. The city's leading publisher, Christophe Plantin, began using copperplate engravings, as well as woodcuts, for illustrated books, beginning with his eight-volume *Biblia polyglotta* (a wildly ambitious Bible in Hebrew, Latin, Greek, Syriac and Aramaic, 1568).

The artist Peter Paul Rubens provided illustrations for his friend Balthasar Moretus, Plantin's grandson, from 1614. The V&A's collections include a superb painted design by Rubens for a title page, showing War and Victory (opposite top), which was engraved for *Le Voyage du Prince Don Ferdinande Infant d'Espagne, Cardinal* (The voyage of Cardinal-Infante Ferdinand of Spain, 1635). Between about 1612 and 1637 Rubens designed nearly 50 title pages for Moretus. The printer noted the artist's requirements to a potential client: 'I must inform him six months ahead that he may think over the title and design it with complete leisure on Sundays; on weekdays he does not busy himself with work of that kind. Also he would ask 100 florins for a single design.'[5] One of Rubens's best-known books, published after his death, the *Pompa introitus ... Ferdinandi* (1641), records his designs for arches and other decorations for the arrival in Antwerp of the new Governor of the Spanish Netherlands in 1634. It belongs to one of the most extravagant forms of publication, the festival book. These lavish souvenirs recorded ephemeral architecture, parade floats and costumes and were produced to impress rival courts (see Chapter 10, p.209).

Engraving and etching on copper plates became the main media for book illustration in the seventeenth century. Woodcuts, however, continued for cheap anonymous literature sold in the streets, such as broadsides (single sheets printed on one side) and chapbooks (single sheets folded and trimmed to form booklets of up to 24 printed pages). Engravings were also needed for the greater detail required in designs for ornament, goldsmithing, lacemaking and other decorative arts (see Chapter 9). As engravings required separate printing presses from moveable type, the medium encouraged full-page illustrations, frontispieces and fine title pages for which the engraver also cut the text. In 1638 Cardinal Richelieu created the Imprimerie Royale at the Louvre in Paris, employing the finest Netherlandish engravers, printers and paper. This increased the quality and quantity of book production and illustration in France. The leading French artist of the age, Nicolas Poussin, was commissioned to design four title pages between 1640 and 1642 for the royal press. Poussin also contributed designs to a book on growing oranges, published in Rome, *Hesperides, sive de malorum aureorum cultura et usu libri quatuor* (Hesperides, or Four books on the culture and use of the golden apples, 1646), for which the Baroque painter Pietro da Cortona designed the frontispiece. The demand for garden books to support the fashionable and highly competitive growing of citrus fruits and tulips was a further stimulus to the art of illustration (see Chapter 2).

Another marked influence on the development of book illustration appeared in two pocket-size books by Jacques Callot, *Vie de la Mère de Dieu* and *Lux claustri* (Life of the Mother of God; Light of the cloister, both 1646). These emblem books, as the genre has come to be known, are collections of succinct allegorical illustrations, each explained by a brief moral text or poem. They were far more popular than illustrated contemporary literature in the seventeenth century and, in some cases, beyond. Francis Quarles's *Emblemes* (1635), for example, remained in print through successive editions well into the nineteenth century. This educational potential of pictures also led to the first illustrated books for children from the seventeenth century (right). Similar to emblem books in format is the first book aimed at teaching children through images, *Orbis sensualium pictus* (The World in Pictures, 1658) by John Amos Comenius. Sold throughout Europe as the standard schoolbook, it became the best-known German publication of the seventeenth century and was much imitated. Within a year, a new edition was published in

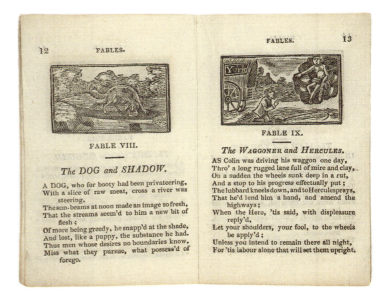

OPPOSITE
Jeronimus Greff after Albrecht Dürer, 'Michael casting out the Dragon', woodcut from *Die heimliche Offenbarung Johannes* ('The Secret Revelation of St John'), Nuremberg, 1498
V&A 25100:5

TOP
Peter Paul Rubens, *War and Victory: Model for a Title Page*, oil on panel, 28.1 × 22.6 cm, 1634–5
V&A D.1399-1891

ABOVE
'The Dog and Shadow' / 'The Waggoner and Hercules' from *A Collection of Fables: For the Instruction and Amusement of Little Misses and Masters*, York, c.1815–25
V&A 38041803198407

WORLDS BEYOND WORDS 11

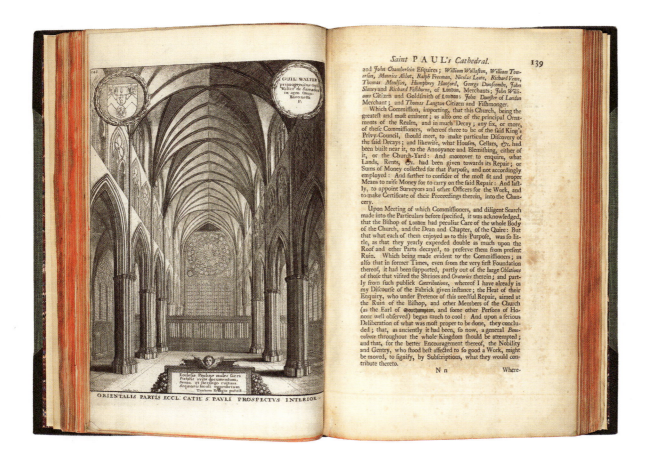

LEFT
Wenceslaus Hollar, 'Orientalis Partis Eccl. Cath. S. Pauli Prospectus interior', engraving from William Dugdale, *History of St Paul's Cathedral*, London, 1658
V&A 38041800392961

OPPOSITE
Johannes Kip after Leonard Knyff, 'Staunton Harold in the County of Leicester', engraving from Kip and Knyff, *Britannia illustrata, or Views of Several of the Queen's Palaces also of the Principal Seats of the Nobility and Gentry of Great Britain*, London, 1707
V&A E.356-1944

London, translated by Charles Hoole as *Visible World* (1659), with Michael Endter's original woodcuts replaced by copperplate engravings.

The most vivid records of seventeenth-century European cityscapes were sketched and etched by Wenceslaus Hollar. Born in Prague, Hollar worked in England for 32 years. He came to London with Thomas Howard, 2nd Earl of Arundel, in 1636 but left for Antwerp in 1644 as the Royalists' prospects in the English Civil War (1642–8) faltered. When he returned in 1652, he lacked the patronage of Lord Arundel, but this was to the benefit of book illustration. Hollar's commissions as an illustrator in his second English period include William Dugdale's *History of St Paul's Cathedral* (1658, above), his etching of 44 full-page plates after Francis Cleyn for an edition of the works of the ancient Roman poet Virgil (1654) by the publisher John Ogilvy, and illustrations to Ogilvy's *Aesopics, or a Second Collection of Fables* (1668). Hollar was one of several artists to illustrate Edward Benlowes's *Theophilia: or Love's Sacrifice, a Divine Poem* (1652), to which the English artist Francis Barlow also contributed. Barlow, who has been called 'the first master of English book illustration',[6] is best known for his *Aesop's Fables* (1666, 1687, 1703, see Chapter 4, p.88).

Other English landmarks in the history of book illustration in the seventeenth century include the 'Cambridge Bible' (1660), published to celebrate the Restoration of the monarchy, and the first illustrated edition of John Milton's *Paradise Lost* (1688), 19 years after the epic poem was first published, with 7 of the 12 engravings signed by John Baptist Medina. Throughout the century scientific publications continued to showcase the potential of the illustrated book in ever more deluxe editions. Robert Hooke's *Micrographia* (1665) records insects, plants and feathers as seen through the compound microscope that he designed. In Isaac Newton's *Philosophiæ naturalis principia mathematica* (Mathematical principles of natural philosophy, 1687), text and diagrams are interdependent. The treatise of Galileo Galilei that confirmed Nicolaus Copernicus's heliocentric theory of the solar system, *Dialogo sopra i due massimi sistemi del mondo, Tolemaico e Copernicano* (The dialogue concerning the two chief world systems, Ptolemaic and Copernican, 1632), has a frontispiece by Stephano Della Bella showing the astronomers Aristotle, Ptolemy and Copernicus standing debating their theories. Despite this tactful visual preface to a hypothetical discussion, the Roman Inquisition banned the book a year later. In Poland, Johannes Hevelius published *Selenographia, sive Lunae descriptio* (Selenography, or A description of the Moon, 1647), the first detailed moon maps made from his observatory. John Flamsteed became the first Astronomer Royal at the Royal Observatory, Greenwich, in 1675 and spent 20 years producing his celestial atlas, *Atlas Coelestis* (1729), published posthumously.

World travel was another factor behind the seventeenth-century appetite for illustrated books (see Chapter 3). Exploration led to travellers' accounts and other books presenting distant lands and cultures, such as Melchisédech Thévenot's *Relations de divers voyages curieux* (Accounts of various curious voyages, 1663), a compilation of descriptions of the East Indies, Middle East and the Pacific. The first major description of Japan to be published in the West, Arnoldus Montanus's *Gedenkwaerdige gesantschappen* (Memorable embassies, 1669), is a collection based mainly on accounts by staff of the Dutch East India Company. Curiosity about newly discovered species of bird, beast and plant, and about people newly encountered in the expanding known world, spurred the publishing of illustrated books of natural history, some with bizarre creatures, such as Edward Topsell's *Historie of Foure Footed Beastes* (1607) and John Jonston's *Historiae Naturalis de Quadrupedipus* (Natural history of the quadrupeds, 1657). Mermaids, unicorns, flying dragons and humans with heads in their chests were all documented in fantastical illustrated books of the seventeenth century.

This age of wonder also saw the first illustrated book of fairy tales, Pierre Perrault d'Armancourt's *Histoires ou contes du temps passé, avec des moralitez* (Stories or Tales from Times Past, with Morals, also known as 'Tales of Mother Goose', now attributed to Charles Perrault, 1697). The theatre also drove illustration in France, in the collected editions

of plays by Corneille (1660), Racine (1676) and Molière (1682). More than half the work of Sébastien Leclerc, *graveur du roi* (Engraver to the King), was as a book illustrator. In the eighteenth century Paris overtook Antwerp and Amsterdam as the European centre of publishing and produced new kinds of books. The Rococo age of recreational reading needed not only intimate-size novels but also smaller, pocket almanacs containing calendars and fashionable new poetry illustrated with tiny engravings. A famous and influential early example was Giovanni Boccaccio's *Decameron* (1759–61), with more than one hundred full-page engravings by François Boucher, his former pupil Hubert-François Gravelot and others, spread over five volumes. Madame de Pompadour, official mistress to King Louis XV and a great patron of the arts, had her own printing press at Versailles and herself engraved illustrations after Boucher's designs for a very limited edition (20 copies) of Corneille's tragedy *Rodogune* (1760).

When Gravelot moved to London in 1732 he introduced the French Rococo style to the circle of artists based in St Martin's Lane, among them William Hogarth, Thomas Gainsborough and Francis Hayman. Gravelot brought a new informality by depicting everyday middle-class interiors, with people in conversation in contemporary dress, as seen in his illustrations to John Gay's *Fables* (1738). Paris and London did not have a monopoly on illustrated novels and almanacs, however. Many of the finest illustrated books were still published in Venice in the eighteenth century; one of the most admired is an edition of Torquato Tasso's *La Gerusalemme liberata* (*Jerusalem Delivered*, 1745), illustrated by Giambattista Piazzetta. Gravelot's German counterpart, Daniel Chodowiecki, had a gift for visualizing characters in their settings, as in his illustrations to Laurence Sterne's *Life and Opinions of Tristram Shandy* (1764) and to a 1785 French translation of Samuel Richardson's *Clarissa*. Such harmony between text and illustration could also see a writer defer to his illustrator, as when the poet Thomas Gray chose to take second place in *Designs by Mr. R. Bentley for Six Poems by Mr. T. Gray* (1753).

The French critics Edmond and Jules de Goncourt described the seventeenth century as the age of the frontispiece and title page; they saw the eighteenth century, when illustration flourished through popular romantic novels, as the age of the vignette.[7] But it was also the age of the Enlightenment, the 'Age of Reason' that produced archaeologically informed surveys of the architecture of ancient Greece and Rome, prestigious retrospectives from living architects, and collections of designs for luxury goods (see Chapters 8 and 9). By far the most ambitious illustrated book of the century was the 28-volume *Encyclopédie, ou Dictionnaire raisonné des arts, des sciences et des métiers* (Encyclopedia, or Systematic dictionary of the sciences, arts and crafts, 1751–72), edited by Denis Diderot and Jean Le Rond d'Alembert. The contributing artists provided 2,883 engravings depicting lucid diagrams of equipment, as well as images of the craftworkers (men, women and children) in their factories, workshops and studios, like actors hard at work on stage (see Chapter 6, p.123).

The Enlightenment appetite for visual communication produced classic monographs in natural history, archaeology, topography, contemporary architecture and design. Books with global ambition include Johann Bernhard Fischer von Erlach's first pictorial history of world architecture, *Entwurff einer Historischen Architectur* (*Outline of Historical Architecture*, 1721). Britain's pride in its country houses as centres of culture and design, both in buildings and gardens, led to Leonard Knyff's illustration of 69 stately homes in bird's-eye views, engraved by Johannes Kip for their *Britannia illustrata, or Views of Several of the Queen's Palaces also of the Principal Seats of the Nobility and Gentry of Great Britain* (1707, above).

George Stubbs's *Anatomy of the Horse* (1766) was engraved by the painter from his dissections. The same obsessive scrutiny and accuracy were brought to the ruins of ancient Greece by the painter and architect James 'Athenian' Stuart and his co-author, Nicholas Revett, in their *Antiquities of Athens* (1762–1816). Their measured drawings of monuments accompany evocative topographical views and anecdotal descriptions of their discoveries.[8] The market for souvenirs of the Grand

Tour to Italy and beyond produced luxurious books of engravings for collectors. Thomas Chippendale translated the formula of architectural survey publications to more affordable books of designs for furniture, as in his *Gentleman and Cabinet-maker's Director* (1754, see Chapter 13, p.265). Even more affordable and portable were the many small illustrated topographical guides for tourists travelling in their own land (see Chapter 3).

Illustrated guides to nature also proved popular in this more middle-class market for smaller books. Thomas Bewick is best known for his series *A General History of Quadrupeds* (1790, see Chapter 2, p.53), *A History of British Land Birds* (1797–1804) and *Water Birds* (1804). In the eighteenth century woodblock declined as a printing medium, but it survived mainly for chapbooks, where Bewick first started as an engraver. Taking the copperplate engraver's burin to the woodblock, he cut into the end grain, rather than cutting the wood's surface with a knife in the traditional way. Copper plates could wear out after 100 impressions, but Bewick calculated that one of his engraved woodblocks had produced 900,000 impressions and remained fit to use. Bewick brought about the revival of woodblock printing in time for its use in industrialized mass production and had an influence from western Europe to North America.

In the industrial age of commercial publishing, another artist–craftsman, trained as an engraver, experimented with his materials and techniques with very different results. Two years younger than Bewick, William Blake produced hand-coloured, hand-printed books that integrated his own compositions as a poet with illustrations and marginal embellishments in the tradition of medieval book illumination (see Chapter 1, p.36). He developed a method of printing his 'illuminated books' in the 1780s, at a time when text and image were not usually printed from the same plate. His illuminated books were published in limited editions; only 28 copies are known of his most numerous, *Songs of Innocence and Experience* (1794). But Blake also worked to commission; his *Book of Job* (1826, right) was published by his friend the landscape painter John Linnell in an edition of 315 and proved a critical success. In his day Blake's art was admired by John Flaxman, Henry Fuseli, Thomas Stothard and other members of the Royal Academy, and later Dante Gabriel Rossetti led his rediscovery by the Pre-Raphaelites. But Blake owes his position in the art history of book illustration more to twentieth-century scholars than to the immediate influence of his work.[9] The major publishing project to which British artists of Blake's era contributed was the Shakespeare Gallery, established by the publisher John Boydell to demonstrate British art's mastery of history painting. In addition to the actual gallery of paintings, opened in London in 1789, Boydell planned a grand illustrated edition of Shakespeare's plays and commissioned 96 artists to contribute – including leading painters of the day Joshua Reynolds, Benjamin West and George Romney.

The French Revolutionary and Napoleonic Wars from 1792 to 1815 led to the collapse of the European market for art publishers such as Boydell. With the Grand Tour to Italy off-limits, travellers and artist–illustrators turned to their own countries' picturesque sights and antiquarian sites. The painter J.M.W. Turner began making regular sketching tours for publishers of illustrated books in 1792, and this remained a steady source of income throughout his life.[10] Mezzotint, the preferred reproductive medium for painters, could translate colour into monochrome with the subtlest tonal range, but it was unsuitable for book illustration as the copper plates soon wore out. Steel plates were developed in the United States for printing banknotes and about 1822 the first mezzotints from steel made it possible to print up to 30,000 impressions. An early example is William Cullen Bryant's *The American Landscape* (1830), with steel engravings by Asher B. Durand. Turner's international reputation was based not on exhibitions of his paintings but on prints, as illustrations to the poetry of Lord Byron and Samuel Rogers (opposite top), the novels of Walter Scott and a new kind of image-led publication, gift books. The

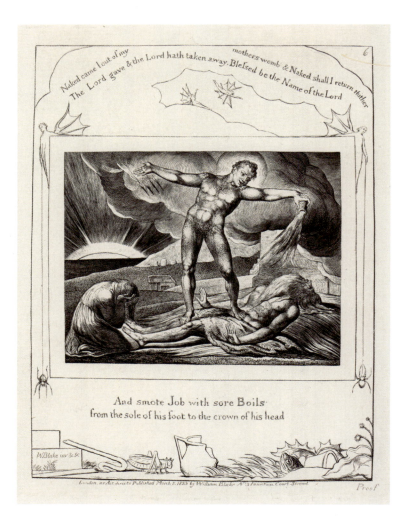

series *Turner's Annual Tour* (1833–5) began as a book commission to paint 'The River Scenery of Europe' along the Seine and Loire.

Turner's greatest publishing project was a visual catalogue of his own oil paintings. He began his *Liber studiorum* (Book of studies) in 1806 but abandoned it in 1819 after the 71 plates he etched in outline himself had been completed by engravers working in mezzotint. Turner was emulating the studio records of Claude Lorrain, the seventeenth-century French artist whose 'Liber veritatis' (Book of truth) gave security against forgeries. Turner may have also had in mind the tradition of illustrated publications by architects, such as Colen Campbell's *Vitruvius Britannicus* (1715–25) and William Kent's *Designs of Inigo Jones* (1727). John Constable devoted considerable time in his final years to his paper retrospective, *English Landscape Scenery* (1855), a book of mezzotint engravings on steel made after his paintings by David Lucas. Begun by 1829, the first edition was a set of 22 prints published in five parts by the artist (1830–2), but Constable's perfectionism left him unable to delegate to his engraver and the collaborative project became a major frustration.

In 1828 a French translation of Johann Wolfgang von Goethe's *Faust* was published in Paris with 17 illustrations by Eugène Delacroix, printed as lithographs (opposite bottom). As crayon drawings made direct on polished slabs of limestone, lithographs much reduced the printer's role. The medium had been discovered in Munich by the actor and playwright Alois Senefelder in 1798 and was used initially to reproduce the scripts of his plays. Many French artists became, in effect, painter-lithographers, a tradition that continued well into the twentieth century. Great artists realized the potential of monochrome mezzotint and lithography to capture the subtlest tonal range, from the sunshine and sparkle of nature to the mysterious deep, velvety blackness of the Romantic imagination. But none could stop the hunger for colour, which led to the development of stipple engraving and hand-coloured tonal etchings, known as

aquatints. Rudolph Ackermann, Britain's leading publisher of aquatints in books, periodicals and as decorative prints, opened his fashionable gallery in The Strand in London in 1794 and ran a team of about 50 artists colouring prints and decorating furniture.

In 1837 Gottfried Engelmann patented a high-quality chromolithographic process, which had the capacity to overprint up to 20 individual colours to achieve a remarkable chromatic range. When one of Ackermann's rivals, Charles James Hullmandel, published *Picturesque Architecture in Paris, Ghent, Antwerp, Rouen* (1839) by the artist Thomas Shotter Boys, with 26 colour plates, the introduction claimed it as 'the first attempt to imitate pictorial effects of Landscape Architecture in Chromalithograph' [sic]. The new medium of chromolithography proved popular in Germany for children's books, such as *Struwwelpeter* (1845), written and illustrated by Heinrich Hoffman. As industrialized mass production spread throughout the nineteenth century, colour became more commonplace.

Along with the expansion of literacy came a more democratic visual culture. The UK especially demonstrated a commitment to visual education, developing the art of seeing through the establishment of new museums, exhibition halls and art schools. Publishers responded to this need to see more by including images in the new illustrated press, such as *The Illustrated London News* (founded in 1842), where pictures could take pride of place. Charles Dickens was commissioned to write *Posthumous Papers of the Pickwick Club* (1836–7) to link a set of humorous drawings by an illustrator, Robert Seymour. Other illustrators who helped inspire and visualize Dickens's characters include George Cruikshank, H.K. Browne ('Phiz'), John Leech, Daniel Maclise and William Makepeace Thackeray. The last also illustrated his own novels, such as *Vanity Fair* (1847), which first appeared in monthly serial form. Many novels were originally issued this way, with their illustrations pasted up in print shop windows as advertisements, alongside political caricatures and engravings of paintings. In France, the works of Victor Hugo, Honoré Balzac and Alexandre Dumas invited illustration. The most ambitious is the 1838 edition of Bernardin de Saint-Pierre's *Paul et Virginie* (1789) with wood engravings after Tony Johannot, Ernest Meissonier and other artists.

With the invention of photography (announced in both France and the UK in 1839), photographs could contribute to illustration directly by being pasted into books, as in William Henry Fox Talbot's pioneering publication *The Pencil of Nature* (1844). Photography also contributed to the revival of wood engraving, since a method of developing photographic images directly onto woodblocks was discovered in 1839; soon after, it became possible to create metal printing blocks via chemical processes (known as electrotypes). The revival also rested on an unbroken tradition, for Thomas Bewick's pupil Charles Thompson had moved to Paris in 1817 to train French wood engravers for the publishing family Didot. Other English wood engravers soon followed him.

TOP
John Henry Le Keux after J.M.W. Turner, 'Sunrise', steel engraving from Samuel Rogers, *Poems*, London, 1834
V&A Dyce 8290/1

LEFT
Eugène Delacroix, 'Méphistophélès apparaissant à Faust', lithograph printed by François Le Villain, from Johann Wolfgang von Goethe, *Faust Tragédie*, Paris, 1828
V&A Circ.603-1968

OPPOSITE
William Blake, 'Satan Smote Job with Sore Boils', engraving from William Blake, *Illustrations to the Book of Job*, London, 1826
V&A E.5342-1903

Celebrated examples include the 1839 edition of Jean de La Fontaine's *Fables* with wood engravings after the popular illustrator and caricaturist Jean Ignace Isidore Gérard (known pseudonymously as 'Grandville') and the same artist's *Un autre monde* (1844). At about this time the wood engravings of the German Adolph Menzel caught the eyes of the brothers George and Edward Dalziel. They founded Dalziel Brothers in 1839 and soon led the revival of wood engraving in the UK as illustrators, engravers and publishers.

The classic period of British printed book illustration is known as the 'Eighteen Sixties', but stretched from about 1855 to 1875, when the Pre-Raphaelite artists and their followers were encouraged by the Dalziels.[11] The illustrated edition of Tennyson's poems, published by Edward Moxon in 1857 (see Chapter 5, p.104), has 54 woodcut illustrations. Most were cut by the Dalziel brothers, after drawings by Rossetti, John Everett Millais, William Holman Hunt, William Mulready, J.C. Horsley, Thomas Creswick and Clarkson Stanfield. The Dalziels planned an illustrated Bible, and leading artists were commissioned from 1863 onwards, including Ford Madox Brown, Frederick Leighton and G.F. Watts. The project proved overambitious, however, and the resulting 62 wood engravings were published with just a title page accompanying them as *Dalziel's Bible Gallery* nearly 20 years later in 1881 – and even in this reduced format it proved too expensive to sell. By contrast, after the French painter Gustave Doré published his Bible in 1865, it sold so well in England that he opened the Doré Gallery in New Bond Street, London (see Chapter 1, p.37). Doré went on to produce illustrated editions of Dante's *Inferno* (1862), Cervantes' *Don Quixote* (1863), Milton's *Paradise Lost* (1866) and Tennyson's *Idylls of the King* (1868–9). His *London: A Pilgrimage* (1870) is his most familiar work today, especially for its graphic record of slum life in the metropolis.

The most familiar product of the 'Eighteen Sixties' is a children's book with illustrations cut by the Brothers Dalziel: Lewis Carroll's *Alice's Adventures in Wonderland* (1865, opposite). The author (whose real name was Charles Dodgson) chose as his collaborator a leading artist, who was also the most popular illustrator of the day, John Tenniel. As the manuscript reveals, the book was conceived through text and images, with the author adding his own illustrations.[12] In the first paragraph of Chapter One he introduces Alice, bored by the book her sister is reading, with her question: 'and what is the use of a book ... without pictures or conversations?'[13] The sources for Tenniel's 42 illustrations (and the 50 for its sequel, *Through the Looking-Glass and What Alice Found There*, 1871) ranged from Renaissance portraits to the proto-Surrealist illustrations of his French contemporary Grandville. Tenniel's *Alice* is a perfect example of how an inspired artist can go beyond the clues provided by an author to flesh out classic characters.

The revival of wood engraving in the 1860s was not all black and white. As a reaction against the dazzling excesses of chromolithography, Edmund Evans used colour printing from woodblocks to produce nursery rhymes and fairy tales for children in 'toy books'. Walter Crane contributed to 37 of Evans's books (1865–75). The influence of Japanese prints can be seen in Crane's use of flat areas of colour and in his decorative compositions, several of which were later reproduced to illustrate accounts of the Aesthetic Movement. Crane became a leading Arts and Crafts designer of wallpapers, textiles and ceramics, while his rival illustrators made children's books their speciality. Crane, Kate Greenaway and Randolph Caldecott were admired in France and the United States, as illustrations proved to appeal to adults as buyers, givers and readers of children's books.

Japan's influence on book illustration had increased after the country was forced to trade with the West from 1854. During its period of self-isolation (from 1639 to 1854) Japan had rejected the printing press and moveable type to return to traditional hand-printing in colour from woodblocks. Japan's urban middle class sought novels set in the world of transient pleasures, fashionable courtesans and celebrated kabuki actors. A type of painting, printmaking and illustrated book evolved in Japan to celebrate this love of living for the moment, known as *ukiyo-e*, 'the floating, fleeting world'. Hishikawa Moronobu illustrated more than 150 books and claimed to be the father of *ukiyo-e*, but more familiar today are the *Picture Book: Selected Insects* (1788) and the graphic erotica *Poem of the Pillow* (1788) by Kitagawa Utamaro. Katsushika Hokusai illustrated 500 books, specialized in landscape and is best known for his *One Hundred Views of Mount Fuji* (3 vols, 1834–49). His rival, Andō Hiroshige, also produced colourful picture books devoted to landscapes and the lives of celebrities in Edo (present-day Tokyo).

In the nineteenth century many French artists, including Edgar Degas, Henri de Toulouse-Lautrec, Vincent van Gogh and Paul Gauguin, recognized the power of Japanese prints and illustrated books. The use of flat colour and innovative ways of composing female figures also influenced the colour etchings of Mary Cassatt. However, when Oscar Wilde saw the 17 illustrations Aubrey Beardsley made for his play *Salome* (1894, see Chapter 5, p.110) he described them as too 'Japanese'.[14] Beardsley had an international influence on illustration, arguably greater than any British rival, and on artists from Edvard Munch to Pablo Picasso and Serge Diaghilev, thanks partly to his contributions to two new periodicals, *The Yellow Book* (1894–5) and *The Savoy* (1896–8).

William Morris's Kelmscott Press ran for only seven years (1891–8) but its influence on the idea of 'the book beautiful' spread through the private press movement. Lucien Pissarro, son of the French Impressionist Camille Pissarro, established the Eragny Press in London in 1895. The movement included Charles Ricketts's Vale Press; C.R. Ashbee's Essex House Press; the Doves Press, founded by Thomas J. Cobden-Sanderson and Emery Walker; and the Golden Cockerel Press. Artists commissioned by the Golden Cockerel Press included Edward Bawden, Eric Ravilious and John Nash. The Nonesuch Press, founded in 1922, brought the private press movement to the high street and commissioned various artists and techniques – from woodcuts by Paul Nash to stencil-coloured illustrations by Edward McKnight Kauffer, from wood engravings by Ravilious to Stephen Gooden's revival of seventeenth-century line engraving.

The influence on publishing of Morris and the woodcut (rather than wood engraving) remained strong in Germany. German Secessionist painters such as Lovis Corinth and Max Slevogt had used lithography for book illustration, but it was the Expressionist sculptor Ernst Barlach and painter and printmaker Ernst Ludwig Kirchner who revived woodcut with a Gothic spirit. The Cranach Presse was founded in Weimar by Harry Graf Kessler in 1913 and continued the influence of the English private press movement, balancing artistic originality with book design, typography, quality paper and high production values. In New York the Limited Editions Club (founded in 1929) promoted equally high standards by commissioning not only recognized artists such as Picasso, Henri Matisse, Salvador Dalí, Jacob Epstein and Graham Sutherland but also European émigrés, including Hans A. Mueller and Fritz Eichenberg, and Americans, most notably McKnight Kauffer, who brought his experience in advertising graphics. Today the Folio Society (founded in London in 1947) continues this tradition of marrying texts, artists and printing techniques.

Histories of the art of the illustrated book often focus on the private press movement in preference to mass-produced commercial publications. The exception is children's books, or rather, illustrated books for adults to read to children, while the pictures hold their young listeners' attention. (Today this branch of publishing fills the largest market for illustrated books, especially at Christmas.) In the nineteenth century children's books evolved from didactic texts to artists' evocations of idyllic worlds. Beatrix Potter distinguished herself from her forebears in her first book, *The Tale of Peter Rabbit* (1902), through her understanding of the true appearance of animals and in the scientific accuracy of her observation in watercolours of birds, insects

LEFT
The Brothers Dalziel after John Tenniel, 'A Mad Tea-Party', engraving from Lewis Carroll, *Alice's Adventures in Wonderland*, London, 1865
V&A Forster 1428

The Hatter opened his eyes very wide on hearing this; but all he *said* was, "Why is a raven like a writing-desk?"

"Come, we shall have some fun now!" thought Alice. "I'm glad they've begun asking riddles.—I believe I can guess that," she added aloud.

"Do you mean that you think you can find out the answer to it?" said the March Hare.

"Exactly so," said Alice.

and plants. There was realism too in the way her flopsy bunnies could end up in a pie, reflecting a darker side of books for children. Kenneth Grahame's *Wind in the Willows* (1908), a thinly veiled polemic on Edwardian society's failure to protect country houses, was illustrated by Ernest H. Shepard (1931) and by Arthur Rackham (1940). Grahame's classic inspired A.A. Milne's *Winnie the Pooh* (1926), for which Shepard, as collaborator, evoked a safer world through sketchy suggestions that integrate word and image. Magical lands could also be revealed and explored in vivid detail, thanks to new colour photographic printing processes, in annual deluxe gift books that became instant classics, such as *Stories from the Arabian Nights* (1911) and *Stories from Hans Christian Andersen* (1911) – both illustrated by Edmund Dulac – and in Arthur Rackham's illustrations to James Barrie's *Peter Pan in Kensington Gardens* (1906).

Jean de Brunhoff drew with a far less polished, almost naive style for his *Histoire de Babar* (1931). The artist–author adopted a format that had come to France from eastern Europe in large, mass-produced colour-lithographed toy books that were more affordable than deluxe annuals. A popular classic written by Diana Ross and illustrated by the Polish graphic artists Jan Lewitt and George Him was *The Little Red Engine Gets a Name* (1942), published in a large oblong format. Several émigrés from the Soviet Union illustrated the *90 Albums du Père Castor* (1931–46), including Feodor Rojankovsky, who illustrated over 100 books, including John Langstaff's *Frog Went A-Courtin* (1955). The success of these cheap and colourful children's books led the publisher Penguin to launch Puffin Picture Books in 1940 (see Chapter 2, p.61).

A streak of Surrealist eccentricity runs through illustrated books aimed at older children and adults alike. A sense of playing close to the edge, between innocence and the unconscious, can be found in, for example, Maurice Sendak's *Where the Wild Things Are* (1963) and in Quentin Blake's illustrations for novels by Roald Dahl. No one can forget the nightmarish pictures by Mervyn Peake for his *Gormenghast* novels (begun 1946) or to Lewis Carroll's *Alice's Adventures in Wonderland* and *Hunting of the Snark* (1941). Raymond Briggs's graphic novel *When the Wind Blows* (1982) describes a retired couple experiencing a nuclear attack with dark humour and agonizing pathos. Edward Gorey, creator of an Edwardian Gothic realm, was an American but was often assumed to be a British illustrator, not only from his imagery but also from his absurdist sense of humour. This he shared with the British artist-author Glen Baxter, who is a regular contributor to the *New Yorker*, as Gorey had been. With bizarre reciprocity, Gorey was enamoured of the imagery of Edwardian England just as Baxter is of the American Wild West.

Like fantasy worlds, the prospect of escape to a clean and comfortable country life is an enduring theme through the history of illustrated books. Country books feed the spirit through the promise of holidays and day trips, or simply armchair travel. The English poet John Betjeman conceived the Shell Guides to Britain, a series that ran for 50 years from his first volume, *Cornwall* (1934, see Chapter 3, p.66), illustrated with drawings and photographs by John Piper and the brothers John and Paul Nash. Through these handbooks and commissioned posters, the petrol company Shell was a major patron of artists, including Rex Whistler, McKnight Kauffer, Sutherland and Ben Nicholson (see Chapter 3). In their innovative design Shell Guides were indebted more to trade literature (see Chapter 13), manuals and European Modernism than to traditional illustrated travel guides. Aimed at young urban motorists on weekend drives, they offered a nostalgic vision of Britain at a time of unrest, the texts peppered with more critical remarks on recent changes. From 1936 to 1952 Batsford published a more commercially successful topographical series, The Face of Britain, which helped spread a sense of national identity through text, quality photographs and line drawings, and 150 colourful dust jackets, which were designed by Brian Cook Batsford. Likewise, Batsford's British Art and Building series included classics such as *English Church Monuments*

ABOVE
'Amritsar: The Golden Temple', from *DK Eyewitness Travel: India*, Dorling Kindersley, London, 2011 (third edition)

OPPOSITE
Tom Phillips, 'Canto IX/2' from Tom Phillips (trans.), *Dante's Inferno*, Thames & Hudson, London, 1985
V&A L.173-1986

1510–1840, by Katharine Esdaile (1946), and *The Age of Adam*, by James Lees-Milne (1947). From 1951 both the Shell and Batsford series were gradually superseded by the Buildings of England series, conceived and edited with a more systematic, documentary approach, by the German art historian Nikolaus Pevsner.

Alongside escapism and patriotic nostalgia, a key factor in the development of illustrated books in the 1930s was the move to London from central and eastern Europe of publishers, graphic designers, artists and art historians seeking to escape from the Soviet Union or fascism. The Viennese publisher Wolfgang Foges founded Adprint in Britain in 1937, initially to print advertising material, hence its name. It soon became a pioneer producer ('packager') of illustrated books for publishers. Its Britain in Pictures series, printed in Glasgow by William Collins, was based on patriotic photographic books published in Germany from 1907 by K. Langewiesche. The 126 titles published (1941–50) included *British Photographers* by Cecil Beaton, *English Country Houses* by Vita Sackville West, *The English People* by George Orwell and *English Women* by Edith Sitwell. Produced in a slim and affordable small format with black-and-white and colour photographs between hardcovers, they were designed to sell throughout the British Empire and the United States. Allen Lane launched Penguin Books in 1935 and, two years later, Foges and Walter Neurath proposed to him the King Penguin series of small factual books inspired by the example of one of Germany's leading publishers, Insel Verlag. The series included *Caricatures* by Ernst Gombrich and E. Kris (1940).

In 1949 Neurath (who had fled Vienna in 1938) and his future wife, Eva Feuchtwang (who had escaped from Berlin in 1939), left Adprint to form Thames & Hudson; they targeted markets in London and New York (as the namecheck to the rivers in the two cities suggests). An early

WORLDS BEYOND WORDS

classic that later joined their World of Art series of affordable illustrated surveys aimed at a wide readership was *English Cathedrals* (1950), with photographs by Martin Hürlimann. Phaidon Press had been founded in Vienna in 1923 by Béla Horovitz, Ludwig Goldscheider and Fritz Ungar but transferred to the UK in 1938, only a year after its launch of affordably priced, large-format art books. In 1950 Phaidon Press published the bestselling art survey, Ernst Gombrich's *Story of Art*; key to its success was not only the fluent, concise narrative but also the way in which its illustrations were integrated with the text (see Chapter 7, p.155). Like Thames & Hudson, Phaidon Press tackled the technical challenges of colour printing to make fine art more widely accessible, beyond the traditional market for luxurious art publications.

Paul Hamlyn had been born Paul Hamburger in Berlin in 1926, but moved to London with his parents in 1933. He also recognized the need for higher standards in colour reproduction, and made the most of new developments in printing in Czechoslovakia. Hamlyn published well-illustrated 'coffee-table' books on cookery, lifestyle and other non-literary subjects for sale in alternative outlets, such as supermarkets and department stores. Following Hamlyn's example, a major innovator in producing boldly designed educational illustrated books for the mass market is Dorling Kindersley (DK), founded in 1974. DK's Eyewitness Travel Guides follow the company's distinctive house style of integrated annotated maps with bird's-eye views of streets, cutaway architectural drawings and vivid, almost three-dimensional, colour photographs (p.18).

In the twenty-first century when smartphones put multiple libraries into people's pockets, certain fields continue to appeal to the creators of books. For example, Taschen, founded in Cologne in 1980, has published its series of slim artist monographs from 1985 but is now best known for its 'Sumo' limited editions. The series began with *Helmut Newton* (1999), a hefty tome 50 × 70 cm (19½ × 27½ in.) in size and 30 kg (66 lbs) in weight, sold with a stainless-steel stand designed by Philippe Starck. The 10,000 copies were numbered and signed by the photographer, like a *livre d'artiste*. Strictly speaking, this is a photobook, for Newton's photographs are the primary subject and are not illustrations to a text. Working on a more intimate scale, Tom Phillips is an artist who has integrated images and texts, as in his classic work, *A Humument: A Treated Victorian Novel originally by W.H. Mallock* (1976, sixth edition 2016, published as an app in 2019).[15] By painting and drawing over the pages while leaving some of the novel's text clear, he created another story through his art. Phillips used the same technique for some of his illustrations in *Dante's Inferno* alongside his own translation. First published in a limited edition by the Talfourd Press (1983), it was later reproduced by Thames & Hudson (p.19), who also published *A Humument* in facsimile.

A further field of publishing that has driven the development of more affordable illustrated books is museum and gallery exhibition catalogues. Since the 1970s they have grown in ambition with the success of international blockbusters and have set new business models for publishing illustrated books. Recent bestselling examples from the V&A include *David Bowie Is* (2013, above), *Alexander McQueen* (2015) and *Wonderful Things* by Tim Walker (2019, see Chapter 12, p.259). Similarly, scholarly sales catalogues published by the major art auction houses and private galleries have evolved, many becoming standard books of reference in their specialist subjects and collectors' items in their own right. Like contemporary photography, art and architecture continue to inspire publishers to set new standards for the illustrated book.

OPPOSITE
[Masayoshi] Sukita, David Bowie, 1973, photograph from Victoria Broakes, Geoffrey Marsh and Martin Roth, *David Bowie Is*, V&A Publishing, London, 2013
V&A 38041013011044

RIGHT
Charlie Mackesy, '"Cake" said the mole', illustration from Charlie Mackesy, *The Boy, the Mole, the Fox and the Horse*, Ebury Press, London, 2019

Illustration has always been vital to the evolution and endurance of the book, embracing new and revived technologies, from wood engraving to chromolithography and photography. From the 1980s floppy disks, CDs and then DVDs offered publishers an affordable way to include more images when they were sold with books, in a compromise that could have threatened the future of the illustrated book printed on paper. Since then the acceleration of the digital age, with websites, apps and sharing platforms, has redefined publishing. Once online, anyone can feel empowered as an imagemaker and graphic designer, whether publishing their research and hobbies or illustrating their lives, for universal reproduction to innumerable followers worldwide. The traditional distinction in standards between amateur and professional publishing seems less clear. Major museums are publishing digital catalogues that can be printed on demand, and academic sponsors increasingly require new research to be made swiftly and freely available through open access online. Now that an infinite number of the highest-quality digital images is available on the web, no illustrated book need be self-sufficient – including this one. But there are also signs that, beyond the luxury market for major works in art and architecture, for limited editions and facsimiles, the art of the illustrated book for general readers is not a thing of the past.

During the Covid-19 pandemic between 2020 and 2022 (when this book was written), there was a surprise publishing phenomenon. *The Boy, the Mole, the Fox and the Horse* by Charlie Mackesy is a modest fable illustrated with simple truths in the tradition of *Winnie the Pooh* that began as an Instagram post (above). Once published as a book it featured in the top ten 'general hardbacks' in Britain during the pandemic and afterwards, mostly at number one.[16] Its success as a book may be an example of how, while reading online posts on a screen mediated to a mass audience is excellent for rapid reference communication, it is not enough for everyone's needs. Many readers still value the sense of intimacy, authenticity and even identity that owning a physical book can bring, along with the sheer delight of turning paper pages to discover, in illustrations, visual ideas that speak beyond the written word.

Another sure sign that the art of the illustrated book will continue to flourish is the annual competitions that recognize artists and publishers. One of these, the V&A Illustration Awards, has invited new judges and entries since its foundation in 1972. As well as an overall winner, prizes are awarded for the best illustrated book, book covers and illustrated journalism and to the Student Illustrator of the Year. Each year the judges are always spoilt for choice. For this book, V&A staff have faced the challenge of choosing from the history of publishing, and hope that this selection may help to inspire the art of the illustrated book for many years to come.

An entire history of art could be told through illustrated books. From the drolleries drawn in the decorative margins of illustrated manuscripts by medieval monks to noble title pages by Rubens, from Delacroix's tenebrous lithographs for Goethe's *Faust*, to Tom Phillips's reconstructive treatment of a Victorian novel, the histories of patronage, cultural movements, publishing and consumerism are all here. What makes the art of the illustrated book different from painting, sculpture, architecture, design and the applied arts is the immediate relationship between word and image. Illustration is often described as subordinate to painting, as a secondary, reproductive and more overtly commercial art form, but it may be closer to theatre, opera and choral music in the challenges it faces. At its best, illustration communicates a text while also affording a creative response, one that surpasses literal description and evokes levels of content that an artist can perceive, without overwhelming the text. For this reason, whatever the threats and opportunities of new forms and practices of communication, the art of the illustrated book is sure to thrive.

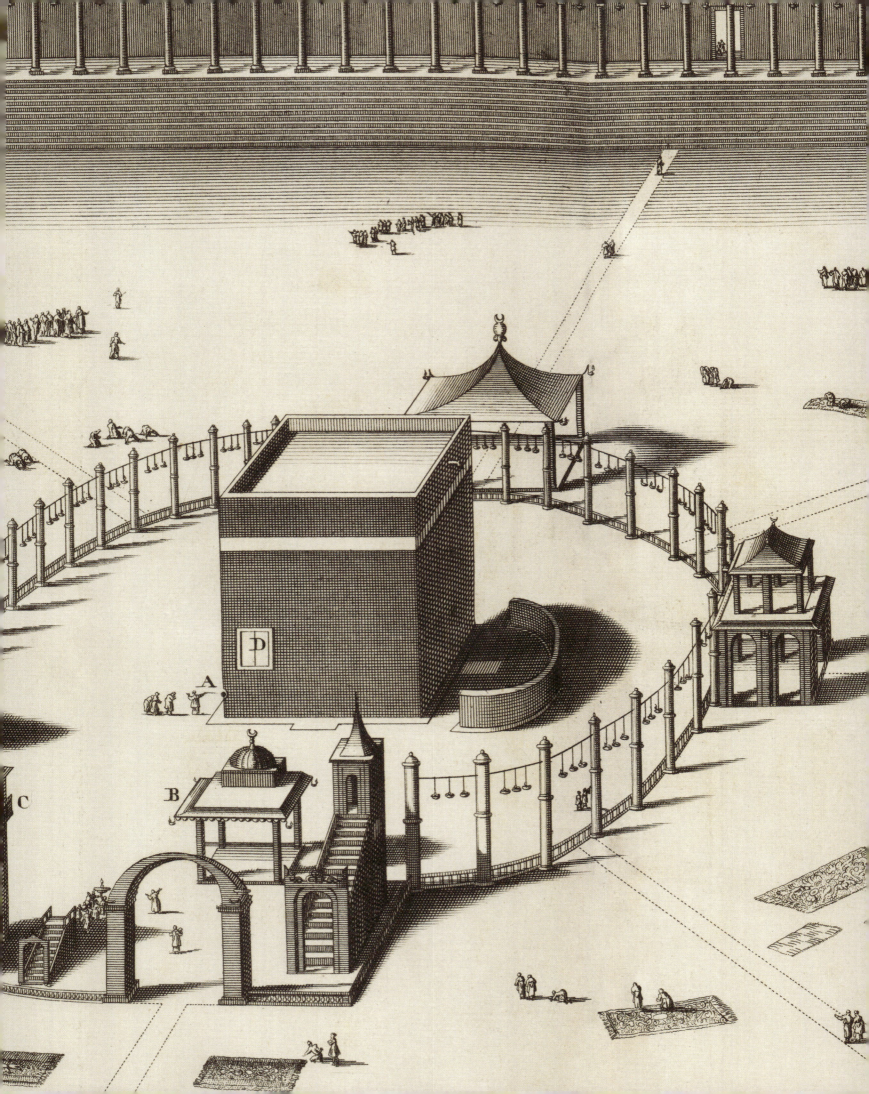

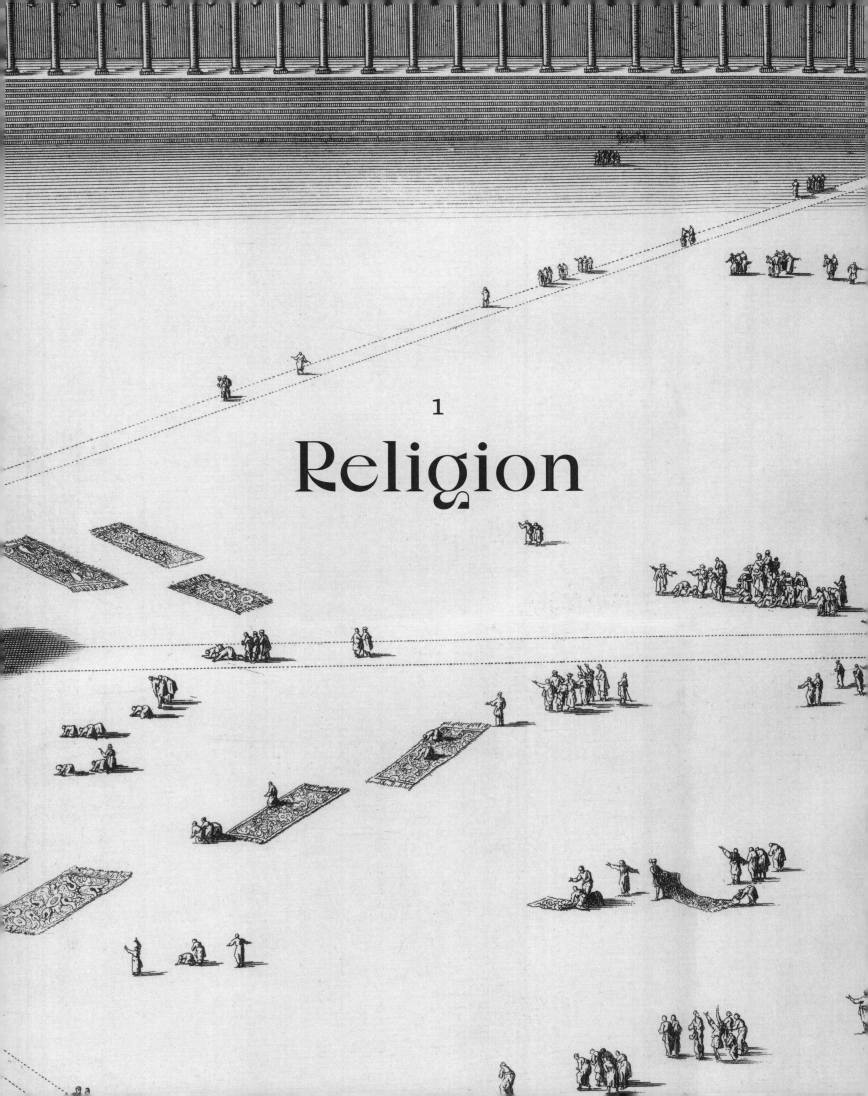

1
Religion

Religion

Catherine Yvard

It would be impossible to consider the illustrated book in a religious context without an emphasis on manuscripts, because of the importance of traditions that long predate print and which, in some cases, have continued to the present day. It is also crucial to reflect on the power of images when allied with a sacred text. The combination of the two is often imbued with special powers: in ancient Egypt, for instance, the dead were buried with what came to be called in the nineteenth century the 'Book of the Dead', a varying collection of spells often illustrated with depictions of the deceased in the company of the gods. Initially written on papyrus scrolls during the New Kingdom (sixteenth to eleventh centuries BCE), a thousand years later it was commonly found on bandages of Egyptian mummies (opposite left). This shroud of spells and images was believed to have the power to protect and guide the deceased into the afterlife.

The dynamic between image and text is intensified in a religious context, as the image can be seen as conjuring up the deity's presence. In some Indian manuscripts the representations of a divinity or holy figure do not serve to illustrate the text, but rather to guard the scriptures, as in an early twelfth-century Buddhist manuscript of the 'Perfection of Wisdom in 8,000 Verses' sutra (above). Conversely, depictions of the devil in medieval Christian prayer books and bibles were often defaced, as if harming the image could hurt the evil foe: in a fifteenth-century Flemish book of hours someone has scratched out the demon at St Michael's feet (opposite right).

The importance of the written text in Islam, Judaism and Christianity is so central that they are commonly known as the 'religions of the book', respectively the Koran, the Hebrew Bible and the Bible. The Torah, a part of the Hebrew Bible, is believed to have been directly dictated by God to Moses, and the Koran is, to Muslims, the word of God as revealed by the Archangel Jibril (Gabriel) to the Prophet Muhammad between 610 and 632 CE. The Bible's New Testament is mainly an account of the life of Christ and his teaching as relayed by his followers. The appearance of a book containing the sacred scripture is therefore no trivial matter. As the physical vessel for the word of God it must be produced with the utmost care and its copying is often equated with an act of devotion, but should it be decorated or even illustrated?

Images, because of their ability to represent the world, have often generated mistrust or defiance when the artist was seen as sacrilegiously 'playing god'. Furthermore, images can be deceitful and lead the faithful to worship representations of the divinity rather than the divinity itself. This concern was rooted in the biblical Second Commandment:

Thou shalt not make unto thee any graven image, of any likeness of any thing that is in heaven above, or that is in the earth beneath, or that is in the water under the earth.
(Exodus 20:4)

This prohibition has had lasting consequences on artistic production in Jewish and Muslim religious contexts, leading to an avoidance of figurative representation. The Torah scroll, hand-written on parchment, is entirely devoid of decoration, the perfection of its calligraphy being a tribute to the holiness of the words. In Islam letterforms became, through virtuosic calligraphy, a way to decorate the text (p.27); this also occurred in Judaism, with text occasionally transformed into image by shaping diminutive script into Old Testament scenes.

Of course, every rule has its exceptions. The Book of Esther, read every year at the Jewish spring festival of Purim, is plain when intended for the rabbi at the synagogue, but Esther scrolls used by worshippers can be decorated or illustrated. Some beautiful examples survive, dating from the sixteenth century onwards; they were made not only in the Netherlands and Germany, but also the Middle East and North Africa (p. 26, bottom). In the Islamic world, although the Koran is never illustrated, books depicting episodes from the life of the Prophet were made from the thirteenth century onwards for courtly audiences in countries with a strong pictorial tradition, such as Persia or Turkey.

Christianity did not shy away from images – quite the contrary, which accounts for its strong presence in this chapter's selection. Among the earliest-known surviving illuminated biblical books are the Garima Gospels (between the fifth and seventh centuries). Made at the Abba Garima monastery in Ethiopia (where they remain today), they contain vibrant full-page paintings showing St Mark the Evangelist and the Temple at Jerusalem. This appetite for illustrating the Bible endured through the ages, leading to a profusion of Christian imagery, both in books and beyond them. In the fifteenth century the first volumes to be printed in the West were religious block-books, in which the text and images are carved out of a single wood block, such as the *Biblia pauperum*, a picture book in which episodes from the Old Testament announce the New (p. 26, top).

ABOVE
Leaf from the *Asthasahasrika Prajnaparamita* ('Perfection of Wisdom in 8,000 Verses'), ink and gouache on palm leaf, Bengal, c.1112
V&A IS.9-1958

OPPOSITE LEFT
Book of the Dead, ink and pigments on linen bandage, Egypt, c.100 BCE–100 CE
V&A 2177A-1900

OPPOSITE RIGHT
Book of Hours, ink, gold and tempera on parchment, Flanders, c.1460–70
V&A MSL/1902/1674 (Reid 30), f.77v

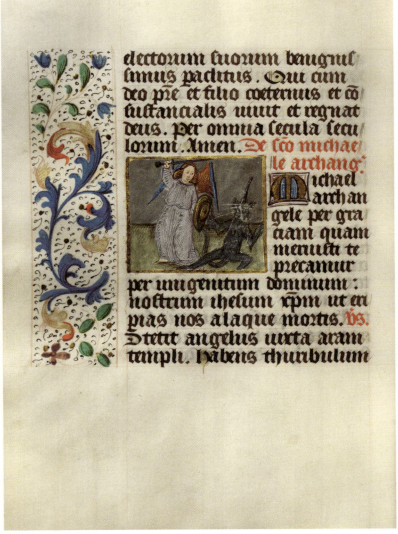

ABOVE
Leaf from the *Biblia pauperum*,
ink on paper, Netherlands, *c*.1465
V&A E.687-1918

Images have been periodically criticized and even physically targeted. In the early twelfth century the Cistercian order was founded to return to a simpler monastic life, closer to that recommended by the original Rule of St Benedict. To comply with this vision, it advocated greater austerity in artistic creation, including the appearance of books, and in 1152 the order statutes recommended that 'letters should be of one colour, and should not be figurative'. The most extreme exponents of the Reformation in sixteenth-century Europe returned to the Second Commandment to launch an attack on images, but this was mainly directed at statues and church furnishings. Book illustration was neither shunned nor incriminated, and Martin Luther's German translation of the New Testament (1522) contained woodcut illustrations, especially in the Book of Revelation. This section's 21 full-page images designed by Lucas Cranach the Elder and assistants included visual attacks on the papacy. Both reformers and their opponents greatly exploited this kind of provocative imagery for propaganda in pamphlets and publications, using the relatively recent medium of print.

The selection that follows is necessarily shaped by, on the one hand, the multifarious relationships between different religions and images and, on the other, pragmatically, by the museum's holdings. Not all religions could be given justice in such few pages. The choice was influenced by the visual qualities of the book, but also by the ways in which text and image combined to serve the book's main function, whether it was devotional, ritual, propagandist, instructional, artistic or subversive.

RIGHT
Esther and Mordecai in Esther
scroll (Megillat Esther), ink on
parchment, Amsterdam, 1643
V&A MSL/1879/36

OPPOSITE
Manuscript leaf from a Koran,
ink, gold and tempera on paper,
probably Mamluk, Egypt,
late 15th century
V&A MSL/1910/6099

Bible

BOLOGNA, 1260–70

ILLUMINATED MANUSCRIPT ON PARCHMENT

V&A MSL/1902/1696 (Reid 55)

The turn of the thirteenth century is a crucial landmark in the making of bibles, when all the books that comprised the Old and New Testaments were gradually brought together into one volume, according to a set order. This development originated in France but soon spread to the rest of Europe. This Bolognese Bible is a representative example: compact, written in a small script on thin parchment, its books are each introduced by a historiated initial, containing a scene relating to the ensuing text. Here Ahaziah, King of Israel, is shown in the initial 'P' falling from the top of a tower at the beginning of the second Book of Kings, where this accident is recounted (2). The iconography became largely standardized, repeated from one manuscript to another. The Book of Psalms was, for instance, commonly introduced by a depiction of its alleged author, King David, playing the harp. Franciscan friars appear on several pages (1, 3), indicating that this Bible was made for members of this order. The Dominican and Franciscan orders, founded in the early thirteenth century, greatly contributed to the success of these bibles, whose portable format suited the friars' need to travel and preach. [CY]

1.

2.

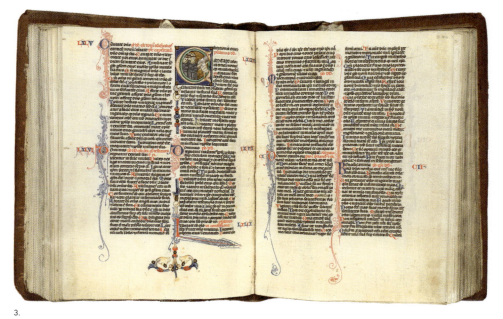

3.

Bible

PRINTED AND PUBLISHED BY ANTON KOBERGER, NUREMBERG, 1483

2 VOLUMES, WOODCUTS, ILLUMINATED BY HAND

V&A A.L.793:1 to 2-1894

From the mid-fifteenth century large bibles, also called 'lectern bibles', usually in two volumes, came back into fashion (having last been favoured in the twelfth century) among monastic communities, especially in northern Europe. There was a wish to return to the biblical text and an emphasis was put on its accuracy – two major principles of the later Protestant Reformation. It is, therefore, no surprise that the first book printed using moveable type by Johann Gutenberg in 1453–5 was a Bible: large and expensive to print, but with a guaranteed audience. Anton Koberger began his career as a printer–publisher in Nuremberg about 1470–1 and had produced 220 to 250 editions by the end of 1500, operating on a European scale. Best known for his involvement in the 'Nuremberg Chronicle', an illustrated world history, he also published 12 editions of the Bible, including this one in German. It is generously illustrated with woodcuts reused from an earlier edition that Koberger had helped to finance. As printing in colour was a challenge, illuminators were often hired to heighten early printed books with colours and gold. Copies from the same edition could look radically different, depending on how much expense had gone towards their illumination or colouring, as well as their binding. [CY]

1.

2.

RELIGION 29

Kalpasutra

GUJARAT, c.1500

ILLUMINATED MANUSCRIPT ON PAPER

V&A IS.46:1 to 92-1959

The Kalpasutra, or 'Book of Rituals', is the most important canonical text in Jain literature for the Shvetambaras, one of the two main sects of Jainism. Numerous Kalpasutra manuscripts were made, especially between 1450 and 1500, to preserve and propagate the doctrine, and because commissioning and then donating them to a temple was a meritorious act that would gain the donor better prospects in the next life. The text is recited every year at the important Paryushan festival. Originally written on palm leaf, these manuscripts retained the leaf's elongated format, opening along a horizontal axis even after the use of paper was adopted (2). The largest part of the text deals with the lives of the 24 Jinas, the Jain spiritual teachers, all royal or privileged people who renounced their comfortable lives to become wandering ascetics. By 1500, when this example was made, the cycle of illustrations had become largely standardized. Gold and expensive pigments were used extensively, as the greater the expense, the greater the merit attached to such a donation. The majority of illustrations typically depicted the Jinas and episodes from their lives, with a focus on Mahavira, the 24th Jina. [NB/CY]

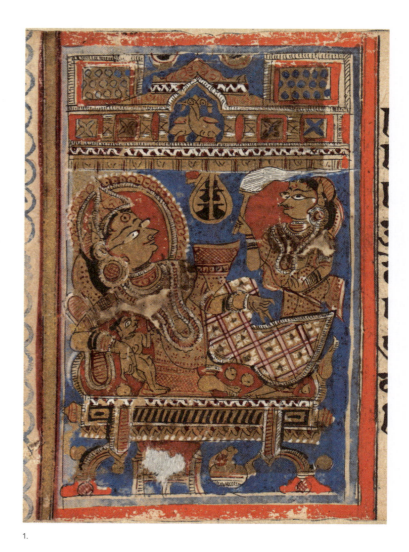

1.

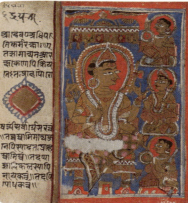

2.

Book of Hours

PRINTED BY SIMON VOSTRE, PARIS, c.1515

METALCUTS, SOME COLOURED BY HAND

V&A 38041800159204

Books of hours were the most common type of Catholic prayer book in the late Middle Ages in western Europe: thousands of them survive, dating from the thirteenth to the sixteenth centuries. In their manuscript form, they were beautifully illuminated, with painted scenes and borders. Printed books of hours appeared in the mid-1470s and multiplied in the following decades. Paris became the main centre of production of such books, even catering for an international market. The profuse imagery of Parisian books of hours was a major selling point and greatly influenced decorative arts in different media. The main illustrations introduced the sections and supported the owner's devotions, while the borders offered additional narratives, sometimes with captions, competing with the main text. New features included a title page with the printer's mark (1) and a page providing medical advice, with a 'planetary man', or skeleton illustrating the supposed influence of planets on parts of the body (2). The first owners of this book, members of the Lorraine nobility, inscribed their names in the margins: Eve de Ligniville; her husband, Gaspar de Hassonville (also spelt Haussonville); and their daughter Renée. It was common for such prayer books to be treasured and passed on from generation to generation. [CY]

1.

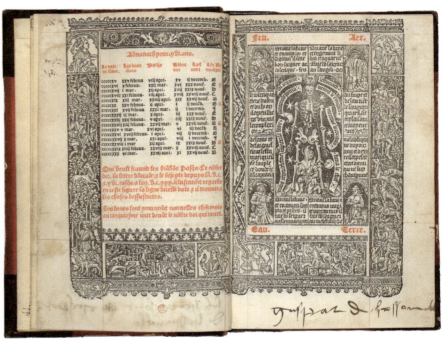

2.

3.

RELIGION

Passional Christi und Antichristi

(Passion of Christ and Antichrist)

MARTIN LUTHER, PHILIP MELANCHTHON AND JOHANN SCHWERTFEGER

EXTRACTED FROM *DER [ERSTE] THEIL DER BÜCHER, SCHRIFFTEN, UND PREDIGTEN ...* (THE [FIRST] PART OF BOOKS, WRITINGS AND SERMONS ...)

PRINTED BY URBAN GAUBISCH, EISLEBEN, 1564

26 WOODCUTS AFTER LUCAS CRANACH THE ELDER

V&A 965-1879

At the time of the Reformation, print was used as a weapon of propaganda by both Catholics and Protestants. This pamphlet was first published in 1521 under the reformer Martin Luther's supervision. It aimed to shock and educate the reader through 26 woodcuts, each accompanied by a paragraph of text. These illustrations, devised by the prominent painter and printmaker Lucas Cranach the Elder, were arranged in pairs, contrasting the deeds of Christ with those of the Antichrist represented as the Pope. Christ crowned with thorns faces an enthroned Pope being crowned with the papal tiara (1); Christ chases the moneylenders from the Temple, while the Pope receives payment for letters of indulgences, a practice that pardoned sinners in exchange for money and was severely criticized by reformers (2). The series concludes with a striking depiction of the Pope being hurled into hell by fantastical demons, while Christ ascends into heaven surrounded by cherubs (3). The theologian Philip Melanchthon and the lawyer Johann Schwertfeger wrote the text in German rather than Latin, including the biblical passages, so that it would be understood by the people and not just the clergy. This later edition was embellished with a decorated border around each woodcut. [CY]

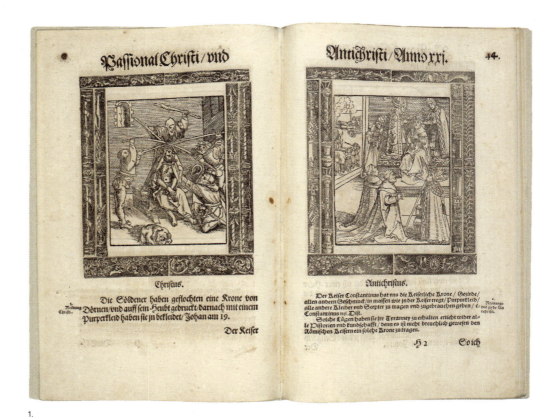

1.

2.

3.

Rhetorica Christiana ad concionandi et orandi usum accommodate ...

(Christian rhetoric for use in praying and preaching)

DIEGO VALADÉS

PRINTED AND PUBLISHED BY PETRUS JACOBUS PETRUTIUS, PERUGIA, 1579

17 COPPERPLATE ENGRAVINGS BY THE AUTHOR

V&A 24-1891

1.

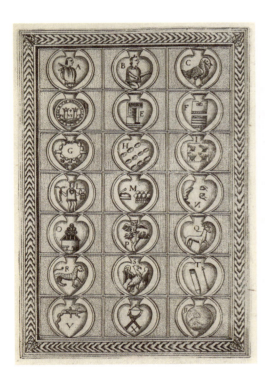

2.

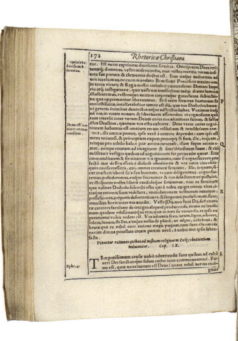

3.

Long believed to be the son of a Tlaxcaltec mother and a Spanish father, Diego Valadés was in fact born in Spain but emigrated aged four to Mexico (then part of New Spain). There he was educated by the Franciscans and subsequently joined their order, but also learned three indigenous languages. In 1570 he was sent to Spain, then Rome, where he became close to Pope Gregory XIII. *Rhetorica Christiana* is a theological treatise promoting the Franciscan missionary endeavour in New Spain, but it sits at the juncture between two worlds. Valadés not only expounded on the importance of rhetoric in the dissemination of the Catholic faith, but also shared his knowledge of indigenous cultures. He carefully devised the illustrations to present complex concepts and world views. His 'Great Chain of Being', for instance, represents a hierarchy of life on earth, from plants to humans, with the Holy Trinity in heaven at the apex and hell in the lower register (1). Three plates show mnemonic alphabets, which spoke to local pictographic traditions (2), while a fold-out view of Mexico provides an overview of indigenous customs, rituals (including a human sacrifice at the centre of the composition), activities and flora (3). [CY]

Cérémonies et coutumes religieuses de tous les peuples du monde

(Religious ceremonies and customs of all the peoples of the world)

JEAN-FRÉDÉRIC BERNARD

PUBLISHED BY JEAN-FRÉDÉRIC BERNARD, AMSTERDAM, 1723–43

9 VOLUMES (BOUND IN 8 VOLUMES), ENGRAVINGS BY BERNARD PICART

V&A 38041800167330, 38041800760449, 38041800760456, 38041800760464, 38041800760472, 38041800760480, 38041800497687 and 38041800760498

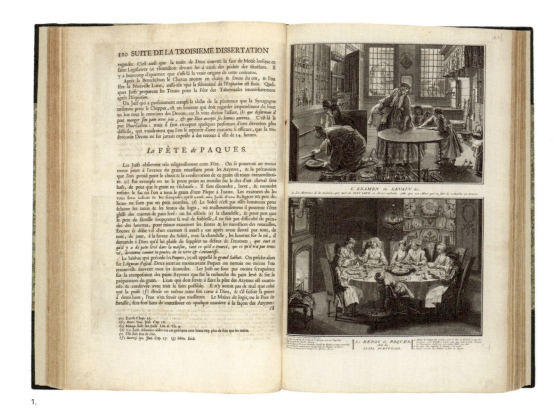

1.

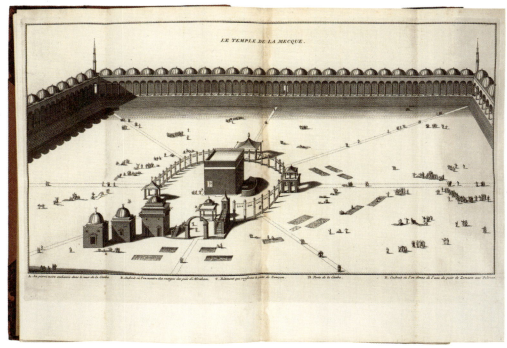

2.

This substantial work was the first publication to provide an illustrated survey of world religions and their customs, endeavouring to present them all on an equal footing. It encouraged comparative study, inviting readers to distance themselves from their own beliefs to achieve a better understanding. It advocated for religious tolerance and radically distanced itself from previous publications by, for instance, presenting Islam and Judaism in a positive light. It resulted from a collaboration between two French Protestants living in the Netherlands: the publisher Jean-Frédéric Bernard, who compiled, edited and wrote the text, and the engraver Bernard Picart. The illustrations, when drawn from first-hand observation, have a remarkable documentary quality, as in the case of the rituals of the Amsterdam Jewish community (1). However, to account for Muslim or Hindu traditions, for instance, Picart had to rely on secondary sources such as travel accounts and numerous visual sources including artworks and manuscripts (2, 3). Certain plates were clearly copied from an album of Mughal miniatures. This unprecedented book had a long-lasting influence on Western understanding and representations of the world's religions. [CY]

Premiere jncarnation.

Seconde jncarnation.

Troisieme jncarnation.

Quatrieme jncarnation.

3.

There is No Natural Religion

WILLIAM BLAKE

PRINTED BY WILLIAM BLAKE AND CATHERINE BLAKE, LONDON, c.1794

RELIEF ETCHINGS, COLOURED BY HAND

V&A E.365 to 375-1956

Though William Blake made his living as an engraver and designer of illustrations for others, he is celebrated today for the highly individual, very rare books in which he illustrated, printed and published his own writings. His lyric and epic texts are infused with a personal theology influenced by nonconforming sects of the period. Blake adapted the techniques of his trade to the production of what he called 'illuminated books', closely integrating text, decoration and images etched in relief on copper plates. To him, this process itself was of spiritual significance: he later wrote, 'the notion that man has a body distinct from his soul, is to be expunged; this I shall do by printing in the infernal method, by corrosives ... displaying the infinite which was hid'. A similar message is communicated in *There is No Natural Religion*, one of Blake's earliest experiments, designed and etched in 1788 but printed over a later period. A series of remarks, derived from John Locke's empirical philosophy, is countered with assertions of the mind's intrinsic ability to apprehend realities transcending sensory experience and learned concepts. Notwithstanding its small, chapbook-style size and simplicity, this is a mature Blake book, and as such a small treasure. [EJ]

1.

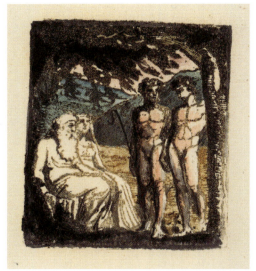

2.

3.

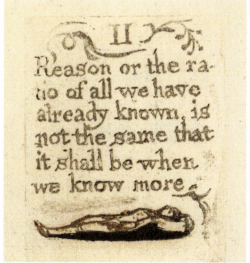

4.

La Sainte Bible. Traduction nouvelle selon la Vulgate

(The Holy Bible. New translation after the Vulgate)

PUBLISHED BY ALFRED MAME ET FILS, TOURS, 1866 (SECOND EDITION)

2 VOLUMES WITH 230 WOOD ENGRAVINGS AFTER GUSTAVE DORÉ BY MORE THAN 30 ENGRAVERS, INCLUDING HÉLIODORE JOSEPH PISAN, ADOLPHE FRANÇOIS PANNEMAKER, ANTOINE ALPHÉE PIAUD; ORNAMENTATION BY HECTOR GIACOMELLI

V&A 846-1888 and 847-1888

1.

The nineteenth century saw the publication of several large illustrated bibles, but none had the impact of the so-called 'Doré Bible', the only one named after its illustrator. Gustave Doré, a precocious and prolific French artist, produced his 228 illustrations between 1862 and 1865 to accompany a recent new translation of the Bible. The first edition, released in time for Christmas 1865, was an instant success and was followed by countless editions in various formats and languages. While Doré fed on a long tradition of biblical imagery from Raphael and Michelangelo to Rembrandt, he also renewed the repertoire, drawing from his vivid imagination to create powerful visions. This superlative style was not to everyone's taste and the novelist Émile Zola wrote in 1865: 'all is light or all is darkness … the engraving has no resemblance to life as we know it … it looks like the design for a stage set.' It is no coincidence that Doré's plates were subsequently produced as magic-lantern slides and later became (and still are) a major source of inspiration for film directors, among them Cecil B. DeMille, whose *Ten Commandments* has been described as 'Gustave Doré in Technicolor'. [CY]

2.

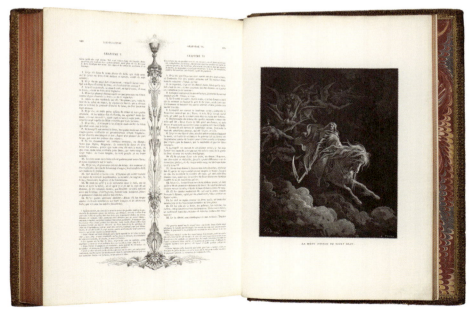

3.

RELIGION 37

Haggadah shel Pesach

(Haggadah for Passover)

PUBLISHED BY TRIANON PRESS, PARIS, 1966

FACSIMILES OF WATERCOLOURS AND CALLIGRAPHY BY BEN SHAHN, PRINTED AS COLLOTYPE WITH HAND-STENCIL, LITHOGRAPH AND HAND-STENCIL FRONTISPIECE

V&A L.4486-1966

1.

2.

The Jewish festival of Passover commemorates the liberation of the Jews from slavery in Egypt, as recounted in the Book of Exodus. Central to this celebration is the Seder, a ritualized meal during which the story is recited from a book called the Haggadah ('telling'). Ben Shahn, a Lithuanian-born American artist, had not yet achieved success when he created his *Haggadah* series in 1931. Inspired by the long tradition of illuminated manuscripts of the Haggadah, he wrote the text in an unconventional Hebrew script and framed it with watercolour borders. Failing to find a publisher to issue his 12 compositions as a book, he abandoned the project. It was revived in 1959, when Shahn, by then famous, encountered the Trianon Press, a Parisian facsimile publisher. The result was this lavish bilingual edition whose accurate reproductions were obtained by collotype and hand-stencil. For each plate an average of 34 colours were applied by hand. The 'mighty hand' and 'outstretched arm' motifs, symbols of divine liberation, are recurrent, and Shahn broke the ban on figurative representations of God in the composition entitled 'God's Mighty Arm' (3). He also chose to illustrate at length the song 'Chad Gadya' ('One kid' or 'One little goat'), sung at the end of the Seder (2). [CY]

Amar Chitra Katha: The Glorious Heritage of India

PUBLISHED IN MUMBAI, 1967–

ISSUES: VOL. 505: *THE GITA*, 1996; VOL. 529: *KARTTIKEYA. A SON OF SHIVA*, 2010

V&A 38041800379315 and 38041800379323

Amar Chitra Katha (ACK), or 'immortal picture stories', has long served as an entry point for many to episodes from Hindu mythology. The comic book series was launched in Mumbai (then Bombay) in 1967 by its founding editor, Anant Pai, to bolster the connection to Indian stories in the face of increasing Western influence on education and media. While initially it drew on tales from Hindu mythology (1), this was later broadened to include Indian history and literature.

Predominantly published in English, the series borrowed from American comic books, particularly the educational series Classics Illustrated, but also brought India's long history of narrative art into comics storytelling. It succeeded in serving the rise of a growing educated middle class in India after independence in 1947. To those who had moved to the cities and abroad, often using English for work but with little knowledge of Sanskrit, ACK provided a bridge back to traditional sagas: as one advertising campaign put it, 'the route to your roots'.

ACK has been criticized for conflating Indian and Hindu identity, but its popularity has embedded the comics in the affection of many in the Indian diaspora. [MW]

1.

2.

Holy Bible

PUBLISHED BY MACK/ARCHIVE OF MODERN CONFLICT, LONDON, 2013

ARTISTS' BOOK BY ADAM BROOMBERG AND OLIVER CHANARIN, EPILOGUE BY ADI OPHIR

V&A 38041013047741

This Bible looks at first glance like any other, with its unassuming black cover inscribed with gold lettering, but one only needs to open the book to understand that something is amiss. An ominous black mass obscures the title page (1) and, on every spread, photographs are superimposed onto the text, making parts unreadable. Whole sections of text disappear behind images of war, upheaval, humanmade and natural disasters, violence (3). The photographs all come from the Archive of Modern Conflict, an organization founded in 1991 that collects vernacular images, objects and ephemera documenting conflict.

Text passages are outlined in red to interact with the image; the biblical words are thus repurposed and function like powerful captions. In the Book of Genesis, a photograph of a Native American man faces a page where the recurring words 'and he died' are underlined (2). Throughout this book artists Adam Broomberg and Oliver Chanarin explore philosopher Adi Ophir's central belief that 'God reveals himself predominantly through catastrophe'. Ophir's short essay 'Divine Violence', printed on red paper, is pasted inside the back cover and acts as a postscript: it is the only text that is fully legible and free from disruptive images. [CY]

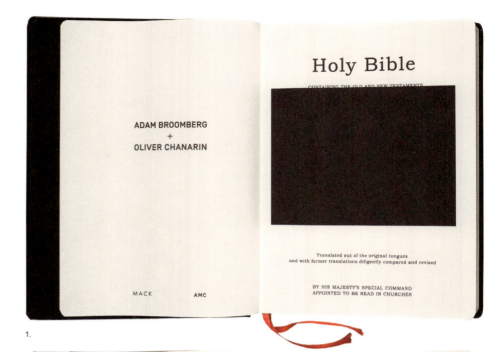

1.

2.

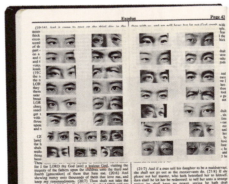

3.

RELIGION 41

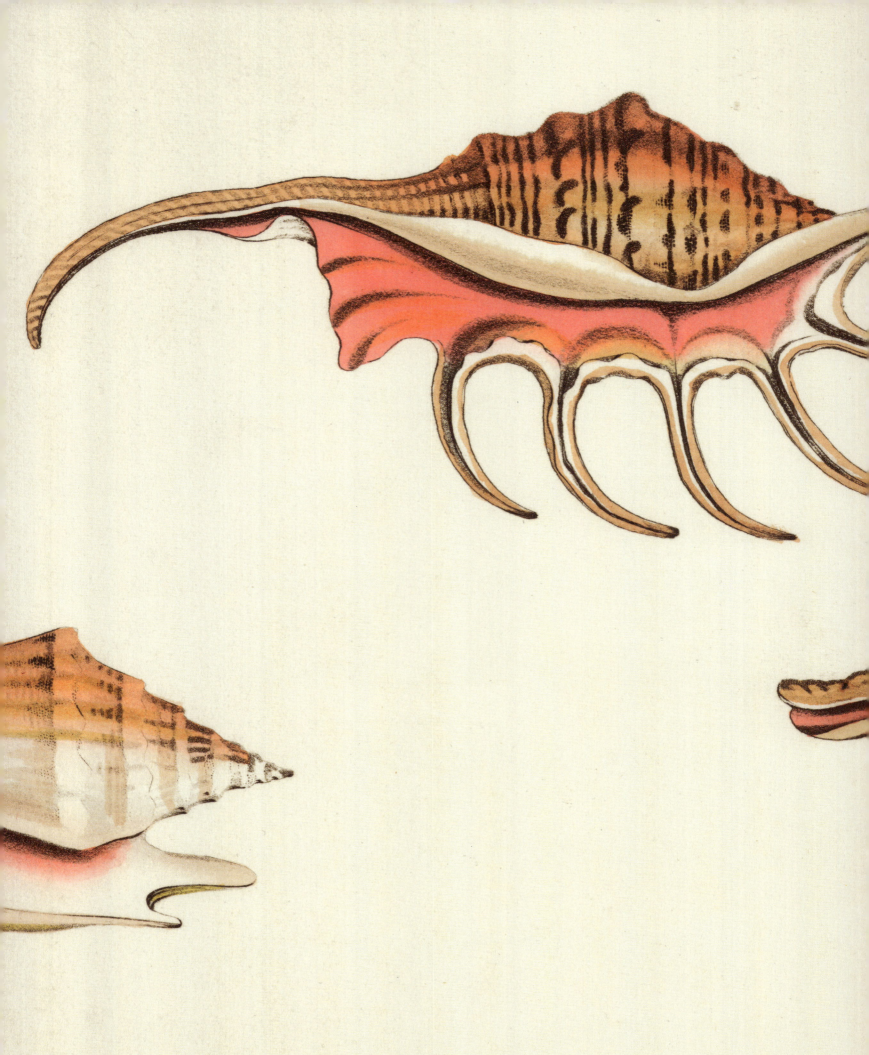

2
Natural History

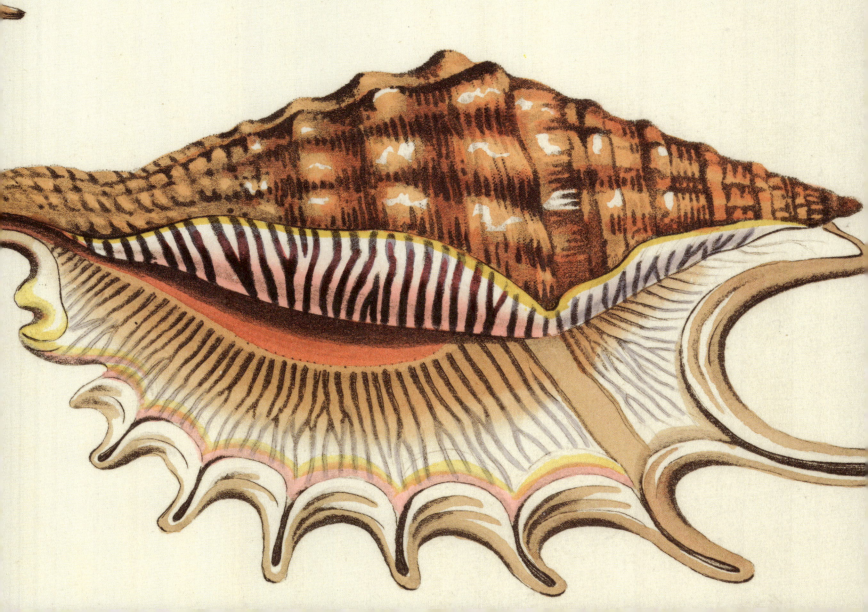

Natural History

GILL SAUNDERS

The illustrated book has been fundamental to developing and disseminating knowledge about the natural world since the late fifteenth century. As Leonardo da Vinci, whose work was informed by natural science, wrote: 'The eye is the chief means whereby the understanding may most fully and abundantly appreciate the infinite works of nature.' Nevertheless, it took many decades for the value and primacy of illustrations to become generally accepted, and for studies from life to supplant images based on hearsay or copying (and distorting) earlier examples. The mythical gradually disappears, replaced by images based on specimens studied at first hand. Tracing the development of natural history illustration through seminal publications on botany, zoology, ornithology or entomology is to chart a meandering but irreversible course from the fantastic and fanciful to the authoritative and verifiable.

The illustrations, and the books that contain them, were designed for various purposes and audiences. Some were compendia codifying received knowledge or identifying and classifying newly discovered species. Others were published versions of the 'cabinets of curiosities' amassed by wealthy collectors or decorative records of fragile, ephemeral living things. Monographs were published documenting everything from butterflies and birds' eggs to seashells and spiders (right). In addition to these lavish and costly books, there were also modest field guides for the amateur and picture books for children. Another category, though scientifically accurate, was designed primarily to highlight patterns in nature, as inspiration for designers in the arts and crafts. One such is Ernst Haeckel's *Kunstformen in Natur* (1904, p.60), with its Art Nouveau styling of sea creatures and other natural forms.

The changing relation between text and image in natural history books reveals their respective status. A shift can be observed from figures in the text to full-page plates once illustrations were recognized as the paramount carriers of information. The graphic conventions of the time, the book's purpose, the current state of scientific knowledge, the print medium employed, the page size and the addition (or lack) of colour have all shaped the character, use and value of the illustrations.

The cramped woodcuts cluttering the encyclopedic *Ortus sanitatis* (*c*.1488, opposite top left), for example, are at best crude approximations of their subjects – charmingly naive, but of little use for identification. These were succeeded by more expansive woodcuts drawn from direct observation, exemplified by the feathery, wilting pasque flower in Otto Brunfels' *Herbarum vivae eicones* (1530–2, opposite bottom left). With the invention of engraving, finer lines and greater detail were achievable – as is clear from the magnificent uncoloured pages of the *Hortus Eystettensis* (1613, pp.48–9), a decorative record of plants in the gardens of the Prince-Bishop of Eichstätt. Another celebrated garden, that of Josephine Bonaparte, Empress of the French, lives on in the exquisitely delicate colour stipple engravings in *Les Liliacées* (1802–16, p.54), the masterwork

ABOVE
Carl Clerck, Eleazar Albin and John Martyn, engraved frontispiece, coloured by hand, from *Aranei: or, Natural History of Spiders*, London, 1793
V&A 38041800392045

BELOW LEFT
J.W. von Cube, 'Elephant' and 'Fennel', woodcuts, coloured by hand, from *Ortus sanitatis* (Garden of health), Augsburg, c.1488
V&A 38041800392243

BOTTOM
Otto Brunfels after Hans Weiditz, 'Pasqueflower', woodcut from *Herbarum vivae eicones* (Herbarium of images from life), Strasbourg, 1530–2
V&A 596-1879

BELOW RIGHT
Maria Sibylla Merian, 'Water Hyacinth with Veined Tree Frog and Giant Water Bugs', engraving, coloured by hand, from *Over de voortteeling en wonderbaerlyke veranderingen der Surinaamsche insecten* (On the reproduction and wonderful metamorphosis of the insects of Surinam), Amsterdam, 1730 (third edition)
V&A 38041800554677

of the renowned botanical artist Pierre Joseph Redouté. Despite the invention of such nuanced colour printing, the practice of hand-colouring engraved or etched plates continued well into the nineteenth century. A fine example of the colourists' art, allied to well-observed drawing, can be seen in William Curtis's *Flora Londinensis* (1777–98, p.52), whose studies of British wild plants have never been surpassed.

Illustrations based on first-hand observation were essential to the recording and classifying of new species as they arrived in European menageries and gardens or during expeditions. Maria Sibylla Merian's renowned images of the insects of Surinam represent another style of natural history illustration – the group portrait comprising multiple specimens together with their food plants and habitat (above right). This convention was still thriving in the 1760s, when Moses Harris published his first edition of *The Aurelian*, illustrating British butterflies and moths in decorative vignettes, yet adhering to properly scientific standards of accurate observation (pp.58–9).

The standard convention for natural history illustration was to lay out specimens in rows or groups on a white page, as in George Perry's *Conchology* (1811) or William C. Hewitson's *British Oology* (c.1833–8, p.46, top). Sometimes they are presented as flat objects, as in Louis Renard's *Poissons* (1754, p.50), but artists often chose to suggest volume and solidity by adding shadows, as seen in Johann Hermann Knoop's

RIGHT
William C. Hewitson, 'Eggs of the Common, or Foolish Guillemot', lithograph, coloured by hand, from *British Oology*, Newcastle upon Tyne, *c.*1833–8
V&A 38041800014904

BELOW
Eleazar Albin, 'Cock and Hen Yellow Water Wagtail', engraving, coloured by hand, from *A Natural History of Birds*, London, 1738
V&A 38041800997819

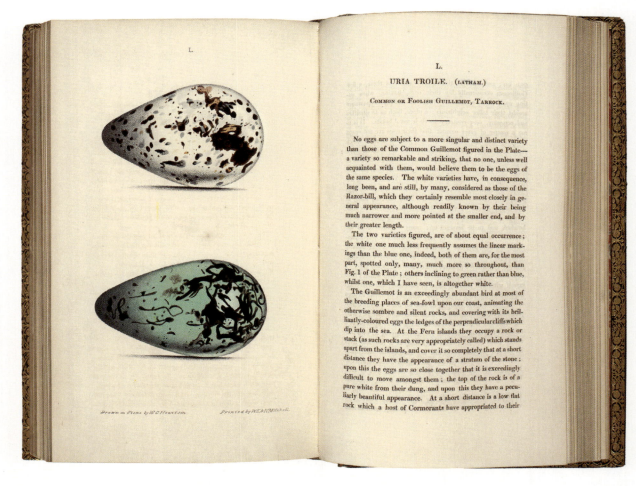

luscious *Pomologia* (1758, p.51), where apples and pears sit plumply on the page.

For birds, the practice of picturing stiff specimens posed on a rudimentary branch or patch of ground – as seen in Eleazar Albin's *A Natural History of Birds* (1738, opposite bottom) and many more – was comprehensively superseded by the innovations of John James Audubon. The richly coloured aquatint engravings in his sumptuous magnum opus, *The Birds of America* (1827–38, p.56), show the subjects in lifelike poses, set in a fully realized landscape or among foliage. A similar naturalism characterizes the plates in bird books compiled by John Gould in Australia (1840–8) and the Himalayas (1830–2), and by Edward Lear in his magnificent work on the parrot family (1832). The illustrations to Thomas Bewick's *A History of British Birds* (1797, 1804) were also based on accurate study, but his popular miscellany *A General History of Quadrupeds* (first published in 1790, p.53), with its miniature wood-engraved illustrations, is a backward-looking curiosity. Bewick used second-hand sources for animals he had never seen, such as the kangaroo and the polar bear. As a result they are cartoonish characters exhibiting multiple inaccuracies.

Other modes of illustration proliferated in the nineteenth century but were of limited application. They included 'nature printing', which involved making a printing plate from an actual specimen, used to represent plants such as ferns and seaweeds (below right), and cyanotype, a white silhouette of a plant 'printed' by the sun onto blue-toned paper.

Photography was rarely used: while useful for popular books and field guides, photographs rarely give enough detail for scientific purposes, and several are required for a complete account of the plant or animal. One notable instance of the use of photography was Charles Darwin's *The Expression of the Emotions in Man and Animals* (1872, below left).

The rise of the amateur naturalist in the nineteenth century saw a concomitant increase in the demand for illustrated manuals as aids to identification. These in turn spawned the spotter's guides to wildlife, intended for children, which were a popular publishing phenomenon in the mid-twentieth century. The pocket-sized picture books of the Ladybird series employed noted artists such as Charles Tunnicliffe, and Puffin Books commissioned the landscape painter Stanley Roy Badmin to produce lively lithographed pictures for *Trees in Britain* (first published in 1943, p.61).

Illustrated printed books of natural history are largely a product of Europe and the United States. Only in the mid-nineteenth century did such publications begin to appear in Japan, China and India, under the influence of Western botanists and plant collectors, or prompted by trading links. Typically, volumes such as Kawahara Keiga's modest herbal (1842, p.57) combined indigenous artistic mannerisms with Western descriptive conventions.

BELOW LEFT
'Examples of Sneering and Defiance', heliotypes, from Charles Darwin, *The Expression of the Emotions in Man and Animals*, London, 1872
V&A 38041800392102

BELOW RIGHT
W.G. Johnstone and A. Croall, nature print, coloured by hand, from *The Nature Printed British Sea-Weeds*, London, 1859
V&A 38041800554586

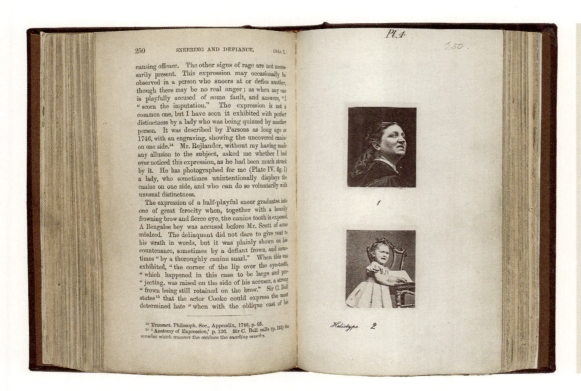

Hortus Eystettensis

(The garden at Eichstätt)

BASILIUS BESLER

PRINTED IN NUREMBERG, 1613

2 VOLUMES, 366 ENGRAVINGS

V&A 38041800377400 and 38041800377418

Hortus Eystettensis is a *florilegium* (meaning 'gathering of flowers', although the term was originally applied to all kinds of compilation or anthology) recording more than a thousand flowering plants in the magnificent gardens of the Prince-Bishop of Eichstätt, Bavaria. Boasting 366 engraved plates arranged by the season of flowering, it is one of the most ambitious and beautiful botanical books ever published. The volume was compiled over 16 years under the supervision of Basilius Besler, a Nuremberg apothecary, who also advised on the design and planting of the gardens. He had boxes of fresh flowers sent to the team of artists for them to work from, yet the specimens here appear rather stiff and are arranged with an emphasis on decoration rather than naturalism. This was one of the first botanical books published with engraved illustrations, which allowed finer detail than woodcuts did. It appeared in two editions, coloured and uncoloured or 'white'. The first copper plates were engraved in the Augsburg workshop of Wolfgang Kilian, but the work was later transferred to a team of engravers in Nuremberg. [GS]

1.

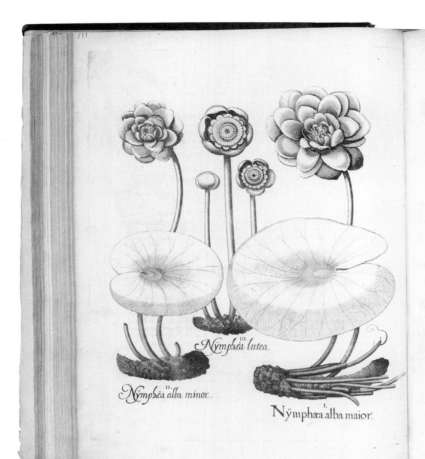

Septimus Ordo. Fol. 3
CELEBERRIMI EYSTETTEN-
sis horti, Icones plantarum Vernalium.

I
Nymphæa alba major. Nenufar, Lotus Ægyptia Prosp. Alpini. Foliis constat amplis, glabris, crassis, tantum non orbiculatis, virescentibus, & ad exortum pediculi sinuatis, rotundis scilicet, & intus porosa medulla farcti, longissimi, altitudinem paludis seu stagni natalis excedentis, quali etiam singuli florum nituntur, numerosa foliorum candidorum, acuminatorum congerie stamina meditullii stipantes: radix crassitudine brachium superat, scabra, nodosa, longa, clavæ similis (unde etiam planta Clavæ Herculeæ nomine indigitata fuit) intus fungosa, foris nigricans, crebris acetabulis, seu foliorum vestigiis insignita, oblongis fibris se in fundo limoso firmans.

Dodon. 575.
Cœsalp. lib. 15. cap. 7. fol. 569.
Clus. LXXVII.
Lobel. Obs. 324. Adv. 257. fol.
Lugdunens. 1008.
Matth. Epit. Cam. 654.
C. Bauh. Matth. 643. & 644.
Phytopin. 361.
Germ. Grosse weisse Seeblumen/Haarwurtz.
Trag. cap. 48. lib. secundo.
Fuchs. 203. cap.
Tabern. 413. fol. lib. secundo.
Cam. Matth. Germ. 305. fol.
Durant. 659.

II
Nymphæa alba minor. Nullatenus priori dissimilis, nisi quòd omnia duntaxat minora habeat.
Germ. Kleine weisse Seeblumen.

III
Nymphæa lutea, cujus flos Dioscoridi ... dicitur. Foliorum paulò oblongiorum florúmq; (præter angulos) pediculis Nymphææ majoris albæ æmulatrix est: flores nonnihil minores, quinis rotundis, crassis, luteis foliis singulatim capitula herbacei coloris, quodammodò Papaveris in morem turbinata, frequentibus concoloribus staminulis coronant: radices priorum æmulatione foris intúsq; candicant.
Autores priores, locis designatis consulendi.
Germ. Gelbe Seeblumen/Wassermohn.

C XXXXXX 1

III Nymphæa lutea.
II Nymphæa alba minor.
I Nymphæa alba maior.

Quintus Ordo. Fol. 14
CELEBERRIMI EYSTETTEN-
sis horti, Icones plantarum Vernalium.

I
Respondet hic Hyacinthus serotinus descriptioni diligentissimi Clusii, L. 11. Rarior. Plant. fol. 177. exaratæ, nisi quòd erecta habeat folia, imbricata, saturatè viridia, eaq; duo potissimùm, in quorum divaricatione ascendit cauliculus rotundus, ex utroq; latere floribus subfuscis vel obsoletis ornatus.
Germ. Spater Hyacinth.

II
Rarioris & insolitæ aliàs magnitudinis, est Ornithogalum lacteum spicatum maximum, in hoc perquàm celebri horto, bicubitale prosiliens: caule multùm erecto, rotundo, ex foliis protensis, superiùs flexuosis, angustioribus, porraceis. Supra medium caulis, flores, ad cacumina usq;, radiatim prodeunt, quilibet, ex suis pediculis uncias longis, foli: sex foliolis interiùs, lacteis, exteriùs verò lacteo herbaceis conspicui, capitulo luteo, staminibus purpureis. Bulbus ex cæpaceis tegumentis & tunicis albicantibus, filamentis crassioribus, pro plantæ magnitudine robustis, circumsparsis, nutrimentum humi petit.
Germ. Weisse grosse Feld-Zwibel.

III
Ornithogali lactei species Major (comosum quis dicere posset) ex duobus bulbis connatis, cum suis capillamentis, effunditur foliis angustis, crassis, porraceis, reflexis; caulibus assurgentibus, prope superiores partes, floribus lacteis undiq; stipatis, medicati odoris, quorum stamina cum luteis apicibus sunt purpurea.
Germ. Ein andere art der grossen weissen Aderzwiebeln.
Pleniorem horum qui desiderat delineationem, Autores consulere potest, quorum in præcedenti Ornithogalum adumbratione facta est mentio.

O XXXX 1

I Ornithogalum lacteum majus.
II Hyacinthus Serotinus obsoleto colore.
III Ornithogalum Spicatum maximum.

Poissons, écrevisses et crabes de diverses couleurs et figures extraordinaires, que l'on trouve autour des Isles Moluques et sur les côtes des terres australes

(Fish, crayfish and crabs of various colours and extraordinary shapes, found around the Maluku and on the coasts of the French Southern Lands)

LOUIS RENARD

**PRINTED IN AMSTERDAM, 1754
(SECOND EDITION, FIRST PUBLISHED c.1719)**

ENGRAVINGS, COLOURED BY HAND

V&A 38041800805954

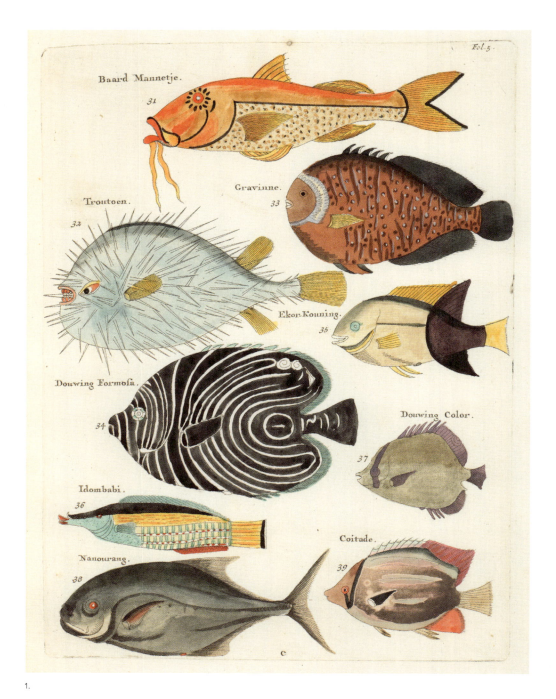

1.

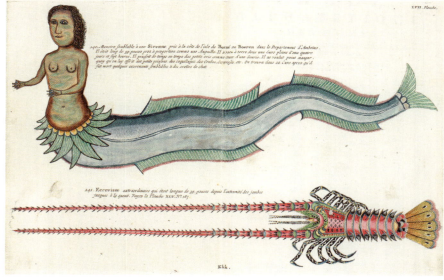

2.

This rare book is an account of the fish, crayfish and crabs native to the seas around the Indonesian islands of the Maluku (then the Moluccas). The sea creatures crowding its pages are extravagantly embellished, implausibly coloured and in some cases entirely fanciful. Louis Renard, publisher, book dealer and allegedly a spy for the British, never visited the islands, but he cited eyewitness accounts in defence of the accuracy of the pictures. He stressed that the brilliant colouring – questioned by those who had previously seen only dried and faded specimens – was true to life. Certainly, the majority of the fishes and crustaceans featured in the first volume are identifiable species, 'copied exactly' from drawings commissioned by Baltazar Coyett, Governor of Ambon and Banda. Plate five, for example, includes the black-and-white striped emperor angelfish and a spiny porcupine fish (1). In volume two, however – which features illustrations based on drawings by the Dutch artist Samuel Fallours made for Coyett's successor Adriaen van der Stel – there is evidence of considerable artistic licence in the fish shown with bizarre markings or human faces, and, in the final plate, an eel-like mermaid (2). [GS]

Pomologia

Bound with *Fructologia* and *Dendrologia*

JOHANN HERMANN KNOOP

PUBLISHED BY ABRAHAM FERWERDA,
LEEUWARDEN, 1758–63

ENGRAVINGS BY JAN CASPER PHILIPS
AND JACOB FOLKEMA AFTER SKETCHES
BY JOHANN HERMANN KNOOP,
COLOURED BY HAND

V&A 991-1882

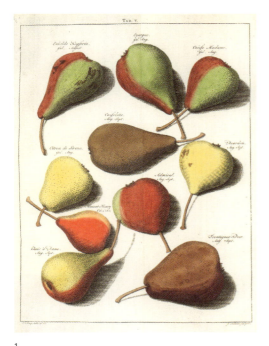

1.

2.

The lush illustrations to Johann Hermann Knoop's *Pomologia* record the best varieties of apple and pear then grown in Germany, the Netherlands, France and England. Engraved at life-size, they were then hand-coloured by the daughters of the publisher, Abraham Ferwerda. The skilful use of cross-hatched shading, combined with *trompe l'oeil* shadows and carefully modulated colouring, creates the illusion of real plump fruits scattered across the page. Knoop was born in Kassel, Germany. Trained by his father, he became head gardener to Marie-Louise, Princess of Orange-Nassau, at Marienberg, near Leeuwarden in the Netherlands. It was here that he cultivated the fruits that he would later describe in his books. However, he also distilled gin from these fruits, and he was dismissed from his post because of drunkenness. Thereafter, he supported himself by writing. The *Pomologia* (one of his several works on botanical subjects) is regarded as the founding text of the science of 'pomology' (the study of apples and pears), to which it gave its name. [GS]

NATURAL HISTORY 51

Flora Londinensis

Or plates and descriptions of such plants as grow wild in the environs of London …

WILLIAM CURTIS

PRINTED IN LONDON, 1777–98

6 PARTS IN 3 VOLUMES, 432 ENGRAVINGS, COLOURED BY HAND

V&A 38041800586893, 38041800586638 and 38041800586547

1.

William Curtis, a renowned botanist, had intended the *Flora Londinensis* as the first instalment of a comprehensive account of British wildflowers, but this was never realized. The illustrations were the work of the finest botanical artists and engravers of the time – notably William Kilburn, James Sowerby and Sydenham Edwards – and they achieved a level of exquisiteness and accuracy that has rarely been surpassed, before or since. Many are unsigned, but we know that Kilburn drew the majority of the illustrations to the first volume; lamenting his subsequent departure, a subscriber wrote to praise 'the uncommon taste in his drawings'. The *Flora* engravings synthesize the naturalistic and schematic approaches to botanical illustration. As Curtis explains, they were 'drawn from the living specimens most expressive of the general habit or appearance of the plant as it grows wild', but he was equally attentive to the scientific value of including dissections of 'the several parts of the flower and fruit'. All the plants are shown life-size and, following earlier practice, most are shown with their roots (1). The hand-colouring of the engraved plates, copied from the original watercolours and closely supervised, is unusually delicate and skilful (2). [GS]

2.

A General History of Quadrupeds

THOMAS BEWICK AND RALPH BEILBY

PRINTED IN NEWCASTLE UPON TYNE, 1790

WOOD ENGRAVINGS

V&A 38041800702524

Thomas Bewick first intended his book for the 'pleasure and amusement of youth'. He remembered his anticipation and subsequent disappointment when, as a child, he opened a book on animals with illustrations so poor that 'even at that time, I thought I could depicture much better'. When *Quadrupeds* was published in 1790, however, it was aimed at a general audience, with scholarly information taken from various sources interspersed with local anecdotes. Bewick and his co-author, Ralph Beilby, eschewed scientific classifications, preferring a hierarchy favouring familiar British animals. The challenge for Bewick in Northumberland was to find specimens of foreign fauna to illustrate. He took advantage of travelling menageries but sometimes copied from existing sources, including the comte de Buffon's *Histoire naturelle* (Natural history, 1749–1804) and the paintings of George Stubbs. He drew animals he knew, such as the stag, from observation and set them in the landscapes of his beloved Tyne Valley (1). Most innovative were his page-filler images of human 'common and familiar life, such as have not been touched on'. His practice of finely engraving into the woodblocks, to create white alongside traditional black lines, adds a sense of depth to the diminutive scenes, opening them up and drawing in the viewer. [AB]

1.

2.

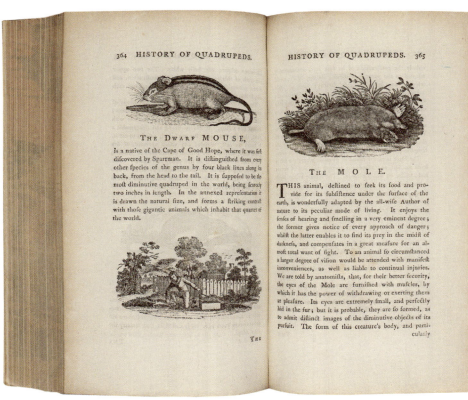

3.

Les Liliacées

(The Liliaceae)

PIERRE JOSEPH REDOUTÉ

PRINTED IN PARIS, 1802–16

3 VOLUMES, STIPPLE-ENGRAVINGS, PRINTED IN COLOURS AND FINISHED BY HAND WITH WATERCOLOURS

V&A 38041800393746, 38041800554628 and 38041800377541

As flower painter to Josephine Bonaparte, Empress of the French, Pierre Joseph Redouté enjoyed access to rare and fine plants in the gardens at her home in Paris, the Château de Malmaison. He illustrated several botanical publications in the early nineteenth century, but *Les Liliacées* is his masterpiece. An account of the Liliaceae family (including lilies, tulips and crocuses), the book features fragile, fleshy plants that were difficult to preserve as dried specimens. The original watercolours were reproduced as stipple engravings printed in colour – a technique characterized by fine lines and subtle dotted shading, which Redouté had learned from the engraver Francesco Bartolozzi in England. In a synthesis of naturalism and science, the prints perfectly capture the delicate sheen of petals and leaves. Some plates, such as the saffron crocus (1), are conventional studies complete with bulb and roots; others, notably the bird-of-paradise (3), show only the flower alongside the detailed dissections that were commonplace in botanical illustration following the general adoption of the Linnaean system of classification. The difficulties of making accurate colour illustrations of these plants were well understood, and after his death Redouté was acclaimed as 'a man of genius' for his achievements in this book. [GS]

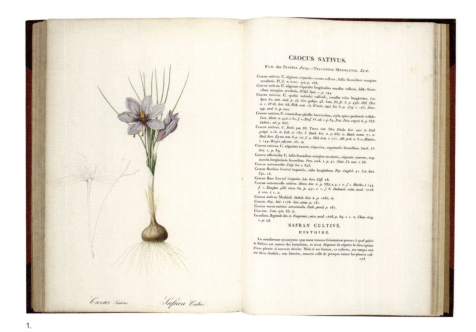

1.

2.

3.

4.

Conchology, or the Natural History of Shells

Containing a new arrangement of genera and species

GEORGE PERRY

PRINTED IN LONDON, 1811

AQUATINTS, COLOURED BY HAND

V&A 38041800500233

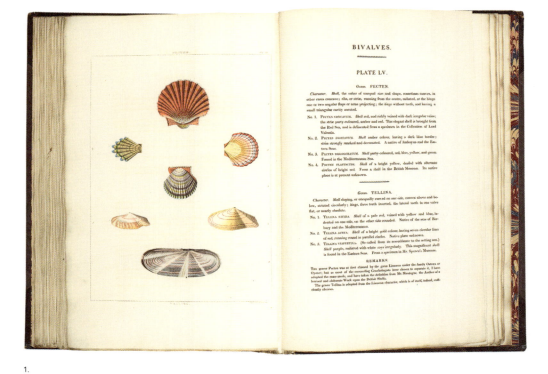

1.

2.

3.

George Perry's *Conchology* is notable for some of the finest renderings of seashells published in the nineteenth century. The plates are aquatint etchings, delicately coloured by hand to record the subtle tints and detailed patterns of the specimens, arranged in spare groups of five or six per page. Perry trained as an architect and became an avid conchologist – his collection, a veritable 'cabinet of curiosities', held shells acquired second-hand from various global expeditions – but otherwise little is known of his life beyond his natural history publications. Evidence suggests that John Clarke engraved the 61 plates after drawings made by Perry. The specimens illustrated came mostly from the British Museum in London and from private collections, including that of Elizabeth Bligh, whose husband (William Bligh of HMS *Bounty*) had brought back many rare and attractive shells from the South Seas. Initially, Perry's work was criticized by some of his rivals in the field – notably G.B. Sowerby – who accused him of publishing fanciful images with erroneous nomenclature. However, the book was later acknowledged as a landmark in conchology, with many of his new generic and specific names accepted. [GS]

The Birds of America

From original drawings by John James Audubon

JOHN JAMES AUDUBON

PUBLISHED BY THE AUTHOR, LONDON, 1827–38

4 VOLUMES (BOUND IN 8 VOLUMES), ETCHINGS WITH ENGRAVING AND AQUATINT, COLOURED BY HAND

V&A 38041800159832, 38041800159899, 38041800159931, 38041800159881, 38041800160004, 38041800160111, 38041800160012 and 38041800160061

Born in Haiti and raised in France, Audubon became an American citizen in 1812. Previous business ventures having failed, he was prompted to publish a book of illustrations of all the birds in 'the United States and its territories'. Ambitious in scale and scope, the resulting work – comprising 435 plates issued in 87 parts – was a masterpiece, generally regarded as the finest ornithological book ever published and the most naturalistic for its time. Frustrated by the challenges of painting a lifelike portrait from a dead specimen, Audubon devised a method of supporting the birds (most of which he had recently killed himself) with an armature of wires pinned to a board marked with a grid. They were shown in their natural habitat, engaged in characteristic behaviour (1). The plates were printed, without text, in London (after a false start with the Edinburgh printer Lizars) by Robert Havell Jr, a landscape painter and printmaker who added many of the plants and landscape backgrounds (2). The engraved plates are monumental – 99 × 66 cm (39 × 26 in.) – to accommodate every bird at life-size. Even so, artful contortions of posture were required to fit the largest birds, such as flamingos and herons, onto the page. [GS]

1.

2.

Sōmoku kajitsu shashin zufu

(A collection of plants, trees, flowers and fruits, faithfully rendered)

KAWAHARA KEIGA

PUBLISHED BY MAEKAWA ZENBEI, OSAKA, c.1836

4 VOLUMES, WOODBLOCK PRINTS, COLOURED BY HAND

V&A L.1254 to 1257-1939

Kawahara Keiga's book is a remarkable synthesis of Japanese and Western observation and illustration. Kawahara, a painter of the late Edo period (1603–1867) was permitted to document local life for the Dutch East India Company's trading post at Dejima, an artificial island in Nagasaki harbour, at a time when Japan was closed to foreigners. He worked there from 1811 to 1842, in close association with the German physician and natural historian Philipp Franz von Siebold, who commissioned Kawahara to paint the native plants he had collected. In the process Kawahara learned Western conventions of botanical illustration, which he adapted in a distinctly Japanese manner, with stylized, asymmetric compositions, flat colours and black outlines. The plates are elegantly expansive, with many illustrations running across two blocks printed on facing pages (1). This allowed for a diagonal emphasis on stems and branches that mimics the spreading habit of plants such as trumpet vine (2) and wisteria (3), with its pendulous flower clusters. Floral details feature in some of the plates, and the names in English have been added throughout in an italic hand. [GS]

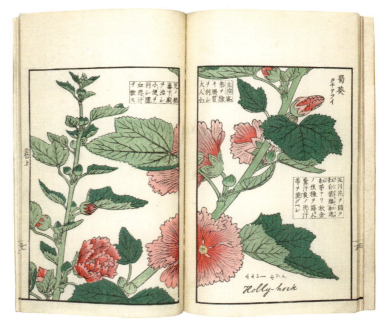

1.

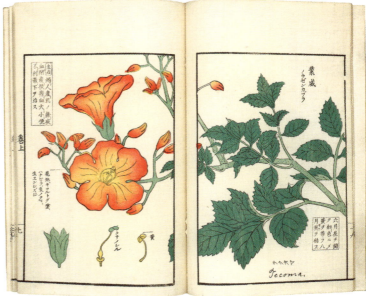

2.

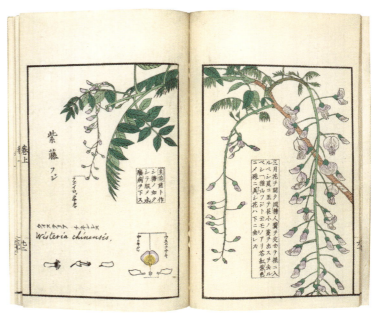

3.

NATURAL HISTORY 57

The Aurelian, or Natural History of English Insects

Namely moths and butterflies. Together with the plants on which they feed

MOSES HARRIS

PUBLISHED BY HENRY G. BOHN, LONDON, 1840

46 ENGRAVINGS, COLOURED BY HAND

V&A 38041800989006

Moses Harris, a leading entomologist, first published *The Aurelian* in 1766. The title refers to the Aurelian Society (later the Entomological Society of London), established about 1745 for the study of insects. The book contains some of the finest illustrations of English butterflies and moths (as well as dragonflies and beetles) ever published, and it was the first to give us the names of certain species, including the skipper, the speckled wood, the purple emperor and the Camberwell beauty. Though arranged in decorative groupings reminiscent of early *florilegia* (botanical anthologies), the plates show the insects with a high degree of accuracy and naturalism, together with the flowers and plants of their habitat. The work was so highly regarded that this new edition overseen by the lepidopterist J.O. Woodward, published in 1840, simply reprinted Harris's plates and text, adding only the current scientific names and synonyms. Woodward praised Harris for 'the grace with which he delineated the difficult and varied positions of insects while on the wing … and above all the correctness of his figures'. Harris's achievements were founded on close study of his subject, his knowledge of natural science and his noted skills as a painter of portrait miniatures. [GS]

1.

2.

3.

Kunstformen der Natur

(*Art Forms in Nature*)

ERNST HEINRICH PHILIPP AUGUST HAECKEL

PUBLISHED BY BIBLIOGRAPHISCHES INSTITUT, LEIPZIG AND VIENNA, 1904

100 LITHOGRAPHS

V&A L.1075-1941

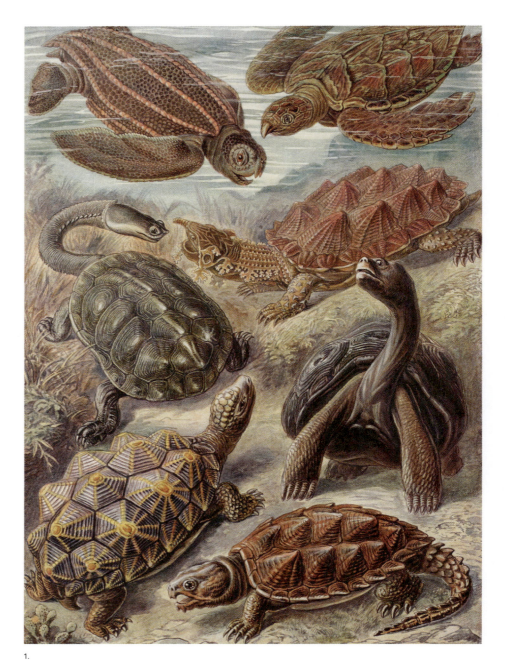

1.

Ernst Haeckel was a reluctant medical student, more inspired by the advancements offered by the microscope than his future practice. Expeditions took him to islands in the North Sea and Italy, where he discovered his passion for marine life, especially the single-celled organisms radiolarians, which he helped to bring to public attention through the stunning *Kunstformen der Natur*. Based on Haeckel's drawings and watercolours, the illustrations were originally printed and issued as lithographs by Adolf Giltsch, and published together in book format in 1904. It follows the established atlas model, with lithographic plates separated from notes, though some have protective overlays printed with a key. The illustrations emphasize the ornamental patterns and symmetries found in the natural world, reflecting Haeckel's enthusiasm for the work of Charles Darwin. Some creatures, such as turtles and tortoises (1), are depicted in landscape settings, but the majority, such as protozoa, algae and lichens, are arranged in ordered decorative compositions against a blank ground. Though the subjects in many of Haeckel's illustrations appear fantastic, they are all scientifically accurate. Evocative of the Art Nouveau aesthetic of their time, certain images such as the Medusae (jellyfish) have served as sources of inspiration for artists and designers of the era and beyond (2). [FW]

2.

Trees in Britain

S.R. BADMIN

PUBLISHED BY PENGUIN BOOKS,
WEST DRAYTON, MIDDLESEX, 1943

V&A 38041997109277

Trees in Britain was one of three educational Puffin Picture Books for children illustrated by Stanley Roy Badmin. Slim and inexpensive, this popular title was reissued several times. It has been described as one of the most attractive illustrated books of the twentieth century, and, though it was intended for children, its clarity, detail and accuracy were such that it was also used by students studying agriculture. Badmin was a skilful and prolific watercolourist, illustrator and printmaker, whose primary subject was the English countryside. His work featured in several of the Shell Guides and on posters too.

His illustrations for *Trees in Britain* include portraits of mature specimens set in charming vignettes: the elms alongside barns, a windmill and a farm cart (1); the horse chestnut giving shade to a horse and foal (2); the oak with a frieze of motifs explaining the various uses of its timber. Noel Carrington, editor of the Puffin series, encouraged the use of autolithography because the artists could draw the illustrations directly onto the printing plates, which gave them a lively immediacy as well as ensuring accuracy. The Puffin books were printed by W.S. Cowell of Ipswich, specialists in colour lithography. [GS]

1.

2.

3
Travel

Travel

CATRIONA GOURLAY

Travel books feed our fascination with the human world, from our first glimpses of newly explored lands and their people to personal encounters with unfamiliar cultures. They encompass a wide range of content – from scientific discoveries to poetic interpretations, on-the-spot reporting to retrospective reflection – and written descriptions are often enriched by illustrations.

A peak in the production of printed travel books, including many illustrated examples, occurred in the eighteenth century – a period dominated by warfare, empire-building and revolution. Major wars carved up the maps of Europe and the Americas, and the vast colonial expansion that would dominate the next century had begun. But this was also the age of the Enlightenment, which coincided with a rapid growth in print culture that enabled fast and widespread exchange of written and visual knowledge.

Titles recording expeditions were a key strand of the eighteenth-century travel-book boom, as imperialists raced to claim lands uncharted by Europeans. One of the most notable examples was Captain James Cook's *A Voyage Towards the South Pole and Round the World*, the official description of his second voyage onboard the HMS *Resolution* between 1772 and 1775. The expedition artist was William Hodges, whose drawings were later converted into print and published alongside Cook's written account. Thanks to the book's illustrations, views of the Pacific islands and portraits of their inhabitants, plants and animals could be seen for the first time in the Western world (right).

Travel illustrations were essential in recording expedition findings before the advent of photography, but unsurprisingly they were not always entirely reliable. The Neoclassical style of Hodges' depiction of 'The Landing at Middleburgh', engraved by John Keyse Sherwin (opposite top), for example, was condemned by Georg Forster, one of the ship's scientists, for its 'Greek contours and features', which he considered to be a step too far in artistic licence.

Another category of travel book developed from an eighteenth-century fashion for cultural pilgrimages, most notably the Grand Tour, a rite of passage for wealthy Europeans. The trip across the continent, typically two to four years long, was undertaken in the company of a cicerone (a knowledgeable guide). Early writing on the Grand Tour appeared as travel journals, but a market soon developed for guidebooks. These publications provided tips on the 'must-see' sights and advice on which souvenirs to buy and where, but they tended to be sparsely illustrated, if at all.

With European travel disrupted by the French Revolution from 1789, Britain saw an upsurge in domestic tourism in the late eighteenth century. Improved roads, the development of the railways, health benefits and the excitement of discovering unfamiliar parts of the country all stimulated travel for pleasure. Publishers such as John Murray specialized in guidebooks that stoked this emerging trend.

ABOVE
John Hall after William Hodges, 'The Chief at Sta [Santa] Christina', copperplate engraving from Captain James Cook, *A Voyage Towards the South Pole and Round the World*, 1777
V&A 38041800377624

OPPOSITE TOP
John Keyse Sherwin after William Hodges, 'The Landing at Middleburgh, one of the Friendly Isles', copperplate engraving from Captain James Cook, *A Voyage Towards the South Pole and Round the World*, 1777
V&A 38041800377624

OPPOSITE BOTTOM
Francis Jukes after William Gilpin, 'Tintern Abbey', aquatint with colour wash from William Gilpin, *Observations on the River Wye*, 1789 (second edition)
V&A L.860-1914

The Handbooks for Travellers series began in 1836, inspired by Murray's own experiences of travelling in Europe, but it also came to cover all of Britain and influenced other guidebook series such as that of German publisher Karl Baedeker.

Likewise, the Reverend William Gilpin undertook an artistic pilgrimage of 'picturesque' views in his tours of England and Wales from 1768 and produced guidebooks based on his travels. His *Observations on the River Wye* (right), first published in 1782, is illustrated with his watercolours reproduced by Francis Jukes as aquatints, a new printing technique that replicated the atmospheric effects of watercolour. The aquatints were accompanied by Gilpin's instructions to professional and amateur artists on which routes to take, where to stand for the best view and even what sentiments to feel when confronted with picturesque scenes.

Until the mid-nineteenth century, travel illustration had, paradoxically, been the product of urban and largely immobile printing processes, often involving multiple makers. The advent of photography meant that accurate and trustworthy representations of other lands could be seen for the first time, largely unmediated by the artist's hand. Despite this change, innovative approaches to travel illustration continued into the twentieth century, often incorporating photography.

In the 1930s the writer (and later Poet Laureate) John Betjeman conceived an ambitious series of guidebooks on the counties of Britain, illustrated with artworks, including many photographs, commissioned from artists such as John Piper, Roger Mayne, and John and Paul Nash (pp.66, 78). Beginning with *Cornwall* in 1934, the project was sponsored by the oil company Shell and was aimed at the growing number of British car owners. Shell Guides were short and informal but informative. They were an alternative to antiquarian guides and contemporary series such as H.V. Morton's *In Search of England* (1927) and Nikolaus Pevsner's Buildings of England series, published from 1951. As Betjeman explained to his contributors, 'The value of the Shell Guides is to tell people what places are really like … Don't bother too much about dates and styles … and don't be too frightened of saying that a place is hideous if you don't

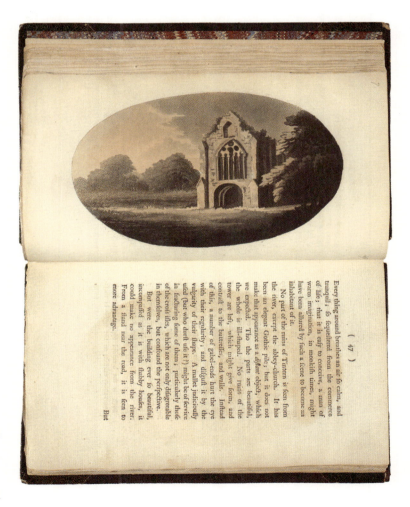

TRAVEL 65

like it.' Full-page reproductions of photographs and other artworks were printed on coloured papers, and techniques such as photomontage were employed (above). A volume on *The West Coast of Scotland* was the only area outside England to be covered when the Second World War brought a halt to the series for over a decade. With its full-page photographs of Highland life and landscape all tinted a vivid, otherworldly magenta, it is a reminder of the continued tendency of travel books to mystify or romanticize their subjects (right).

The publisher Dorling Kindersley's Eyewitness Travel Guides changed travel books in the 1980s by creating more of a picture-book aesthetic and bringing imagery to the fore over textual description (p.18). While practical guidebooks have since become the domain of mainstream publishing and online platforms, illustrated travel accounts have continued to thrive in print.

Rockwell Kent was one of the United States' best-known illustrators in the 1930s and 1940s, and his books on Greenland record his three visits to the island between 1929 and 1934. In *Salamina* (1935) Kent's map of Greenland mocks the absurd renaming of land masses by early explorers: he jokingly calls locations after his artist friends and his dealer, and even names 'General Electric Co. Ice Cap' after his corporate clients (opposite bottom).

Kent was philosophically a socialist, and he saw the community of Greenland as a utopian model of absolute equality. The book is illustrated with his bold, heroic portraits of the islanders, including Salamina, his housekeeper during his second stay, with whom he developed a relationship (opposite top). Personal and affecting responses such as Kent's have invigorated the genre of travel publications and continue to inspire some of the most innovative and popular illustrated books.

TOP
'The Road to Cornwall', from John Betjeman (ed.), *Cornwall*, Shell Guide, The Architectural Press, 1935 (second edition)
V&A L.933-1935

ABOVE
Niall Rankin, 'Glencoe', from Stephen Bone, *The West Coast of Scotland: Skye to Oban*, Shell Guide, Faber and Faber, 1939
V&A L.1972-1938

OPPOSITE TOP
Rockwell Kent, 'Salamina', lithograph from *Salamina*, Berlingske, 1936 (Danish edition)
V&A L.4062-1978

OPPOSITE BOTTOM
Rockwell Kent, 'Discoveries of the Kent Greenland Sub Polar Expedition', lithograph from *Salamina*, Harcourt, Brace & Co., 1935
Senate House Library, University of London

at der var nogen, der plejede at gaa til Vandhullet ad denne besværlige Vej.

Da mit Hus endelig var færdigt, begyndte jeg at leve; jeg lærte Mennesker at kende, inviterede dem til at komme og besøge mig og aflagde ogsaa Genvisit. Jeg fik Venner.

En Dag kort før Jul var jeg sammen med min Husholderske Salamina (som denne Bog er opkaldt efter) hos vore fælles Venner Rudolf og Margrete. Rudolf sad og spillede Harmonika, og jeg spillede Fløjte. For dem, der holdt af det, var det yndigt at høre. Og Salamina og Margrete sad og sludrede.

— Hvad er det for en Justina, I taler om? sagde jeg og sænkede min Fløjte.

— Hvad for noget! raabte de begge to. Kender du ikke hende? Hun er jo forelsket i dig. Og de brast i Latter.

Og saa fortalte de, omtrent saaledes som jeg her har genfortalt den, Justinas Historie.

— Lad os saa faa fat i hende! sagde jeg. De lo igen, og Rudolf gik hen for at hente hende.

Puh! hvor var hun snavset, som hun stod der i det skinnende rene Hus. Hendes Tøj var ikke andet end beskidte Laser. Stakkels Barn! — Og hvor hun tog det pænt. Hvor hun fandt sig i deres Latter og Haan. Hun var naturligvis vant til det. Var hun genert? — Ja. Men samtidig mærkelig rolig, som om hun, midt iblandt de andre, stod i Forbindelse med en indre Verden, der helt og holdent var hendes egen. Vi lo, og hun smilede tilbage. Hun havde kun en fjern Anelse om, at det var hende, vi lo af.

Nu fik de hende til at vise sine Kunster.
— Hvem elsker du? spurgte de.
— Kinte, mumlede hun.
— Tæl saa for os.

Justinas Uddannelse havde ikke været meget omfattende; i Regning var hun aldrig kommet længere end til tyve. En, to, tre, fire, fem — paa den ene Haand (saadan tæller Grønlænderne), seks, syv, otte, ni, ti paa den anden. Men her standsede Justina.

48

Dette er Salamina. Det ser ud, som om hun hun hænger nogle Klemmer op; men hvis hun havde hængt Tøj op, vilde det have skjult hendes Hænder. Det var Arbejdshænder, og hun prøvede altid paa at skjule dem. Men jeg tillader ikke at noget bliver skjult i denne Bog.

Les quatre premiers livres des navigations et pérégrinations orientales

(*The Navigations, Peregrinations and Voyages, Made into Turkie*)

NICOLAS DE NICOLAY

**PRINTED BY GUILLAUME ROUILLÉ, LYON, 1568
(SECOND ISSUE OF FIRST EDITION, 1567)**

60 COPPERPLATE ENGRAVINGS, COLOURED BY HAND

V&A 310-1884

1.

2.

Nicolas de Nicolay's drawings for this book were based on observations and sketches he made while part of a French embassy to Istanbul in 1551. Reproduced as copperplate engravings by Léon Davent and accompanied by descriptions of local customs, the illustrations were among the earliest first-hand images of people in the Middle East.

Nicolay states that he intended to promote mutual understanding between nations, but the text and illustrations still reflect European prejudices of the time. While images of women and children in the Middle East might encourage empathy in the minds of a European audience, exaggerated facial expressions and more lurid depictions, such as the self-mutilating dervishes who have consumed a herb that 'drives them mad', are designed to provoke shock and revulsion (3). The book's commercial success is evidenced by the numerous reissues and translations into other languages that followed the first edition. Nicolay's figures were archetypes for European artistic depictions of the Middle East well into the nineteenth century, despite their problematic nature. A clear reference to his veiled Turkish woman on her way to the baths (2) appears, for example, in the background of Jean-Auguste-Dominique Ingres' *The Turkish Bath* (1862, Paris, Musée du Louvre). [CG]

3.

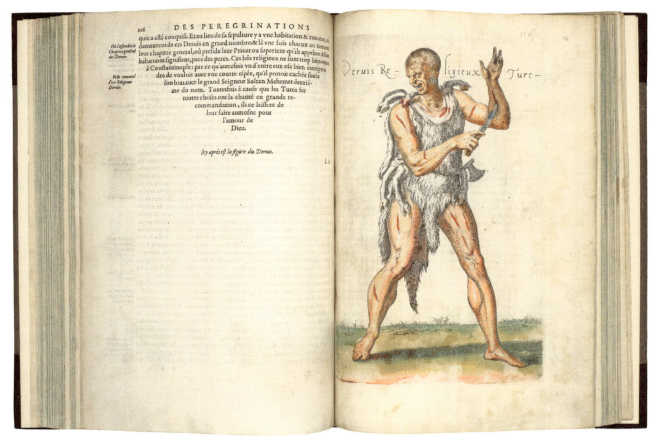

4.

5.

TRAVEL 69

Description géographique de la Guiane

(Geographical description of Guiana)

JACQUES-NICOLAS BELLIN

PRINTED BY FRANÇOIS-AMBROISE DIDOT, PARIS, 1763

30 COPPERPLATE ENGRAVINGS BY P. CROISEY

V&A 648-1889

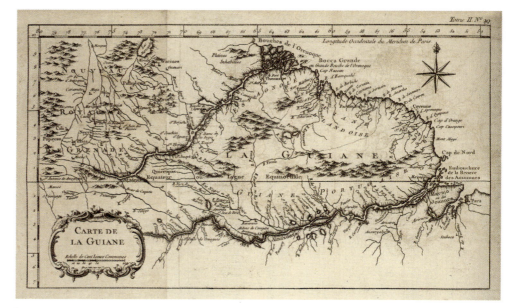

1.

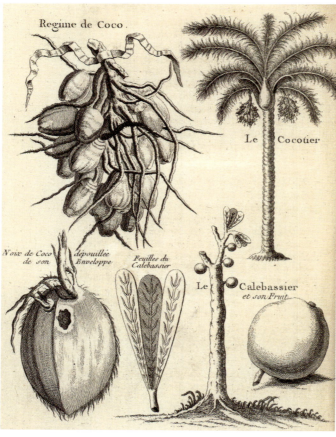

2.

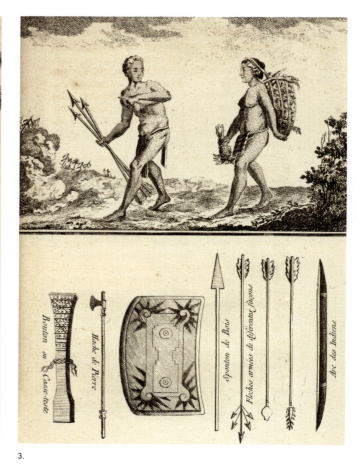

3.

The 1763 Treaty of Paris concluded the fighting of the Seven Years' War and required France to relinquish much of its territory in the Americas to the British. France retained a foothold in Guiana, however, and the publication of this book coincided with its first unsuccessful attempt at wider colonization of the area. With 20 of the 30 copperplate engravings devoted to impressive maps charting the region (1), the book's emphasis is on practicality. Alongside the maps, the text highlights local dangers and provides information on the terrain, vegetation (2) and wildlife, as well as useful food sources.

Jacques-Nicolas Bellin was a respected French hydrographer and geographer. He stated that the prowess of *Description géographique* was achieved by closely studying previous maps of the area – evoking parallels with his evidence-based contributions to Denis Diderot's groundbreaking *Encyclopédie* (1751–72). In a reflection of the times, however, impressions of the Indigenous people of the Guianas receive short chapters compared with those on the wildlife or exploitable natural resources. An indicative illustration of 'Indiens de la Guyane Françoise' (3) gives their weapons prominence. Similar dispassion is shown for enslaved Africans on an indigo plantation in Cayenne. [FW]

The Romantic and Picturesque Scenery of England and Wales

PHILIP JAMES DE LOUTHERBOURG

PRINTED FOR ROBERT BOWYER BY
THOMAS BENSLEY, LONDON, 1805

18 AQUATINT ENGRAVINGS BY WILLIAM PICKETT
AFTER PHILIP JAMES DE LOUTHERBOURG,
HAND-COLOURED BY JOHN CLARKE

V&A 38041800922015

1.

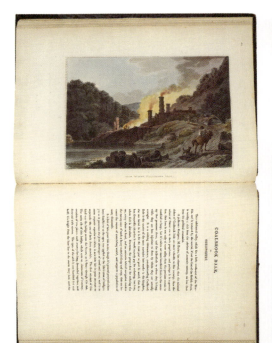

2.

3.

Alsatian painter Philip James de Loutherbourg specialized in landscape and naval battle scenes. In 1771 he settled in London and, having been introduced to the actor–manager David Garrick, started to paint spectacular stage sets for the Theatre Royal in Drury Lane. His interest in technical innovation led to him inventing the Eidophusikon, a small-scale stage set through which he created illusions of sunsets, storms and volcanoes using mechanical effects accompanied by music. As well as fine-art painting and stage design, de Loutherbourg produced drawings that were converted into print for book illustrations, most notably in two large volumes: *The Picturesque Scenery of Great Britain* (1801) and *The Romantic and Picturesque Scenery of England and Wales* (1805). The latter, pictured here, contains engravings alongside texts describing the history and appearance of each location. De Loutherbourg's views take inspiration from William Gilpin's *Observations on the River Wye* (1782) in their picturesque style but they are also suffused with elements of the Sublime, an eighteenth-century aesthetic ideal that aimed to inspire a sense of awe in the viewer, expressed here by de Loutherbourg through the drama of nature. [CG]

Vues des Cordillères, et monumens des peuples indigènes de l'Amérique

(Views of the Cordilleras, and monuments of the Indigenous peoples of America)

ALEXANDER VON HUMBOLDT AND AIMÉ BONPLAND

PRINTED BY JOHN HURFORD STONE, PUBLISHED BY FRÉDÉRIC SCHOELL, PARIS, 1810

69 AQUATINT ENGRAVINGS BY LOUIS BOUQUET IN PARIS AND JOHANN FRIEDRICH ARNOLD IN BERLIN, SOME COLOURED BY HAND

V&A 38041800377426

This very large volume records the German scientist Alexander von Humboldt and the French botanist Aimé Bonpland's expedition to Central and South America between 1799 and 1804. The text is followed by a set of prints, mainly after Humboldt's sketches, some were hand-coloured under his supervision. The book contains a mass of information relating to the area's geography, natural history, archaeology and local customs, but most notable are the reproductions of surviving pre-Columbian and immediately post-Columbian indigenous manuscripts and codices. Humboldt had acquired some of these during his travels and studied others in the libraries of Paris, London, Rome and Dresden. Included is the first publication of any part of the 'Dresden Codex' (4), the oldest surviving book written in the Americas, dating to the eleventh or twelfth century. Also illustrated is the 'Codex Mendoza', dating from about 1541, which contains a history of the Aztec rulers and their conquests. Humboldt's inclusion of them in this landmark publication was influential in the rediscovery of pre-Columbian civilizations and led to this book being considered the founding work of American anthropology. [CG]

1.

2.

3.

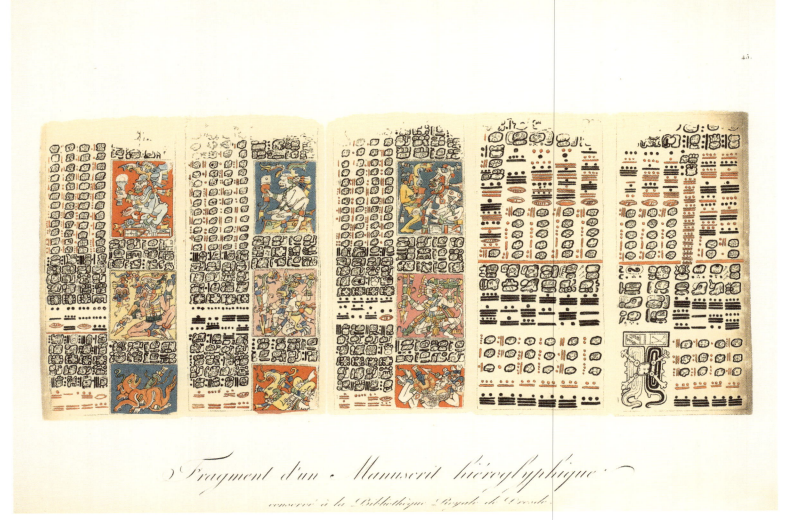

4.

TRAVEL 73

Italy: A Poem

SAMUEL ROGERS

PRINTED BY THOMAS DAVISON, PUBLISHED BY T. CADELL, JENNINGS AND CHAPLIN AND E. MOXON, LONDON, 1830

55 STEEL ENGRAVINGS AFTER THOMAS STOTHARD, J.M.W. TURNER AND OTHERS

V&A 38041800374928

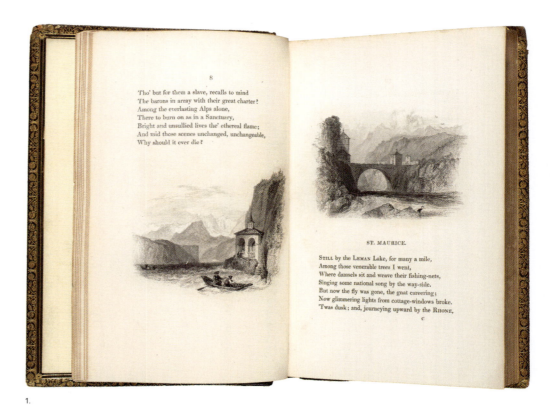

1.

2.

3.

The first part of Samuel Rogers's topographical poem *Italy* was published between 1821 and 1822 and combines his personal experiences of touring the Continent in 1814–15 with sentimental storytelling and musings on history. Unillustrated, it received a lukewarm reception, but, undeterred, Rogers issued revised editions and a second part. Eventually, in 1830, he published this luxury version of the complete work, for which he commissioned vignettes from the painter J.M.W. Turner and Thomas Stothard, a renowned illustrator of literary works. These were then rendered into steel engravings, a technique that had come into use in the 1820s and allowed for finer lines and a larger print run because of the durability of the metal over copperplate. The illustrated version was an instant success, selling 6,800 copies in just two years, with five reprints by 1859. The writer John Ruskin received a copy for his thirteenth birthday and later attributed to this gift 'the entire direction of my life's energies'. For some, however, the jewel-like illustrations outshone the text. The politician and witty poet Henry Luttrell waggishly rhymed: 'Of Rogers's *Italy* Luttrell relates, That 'twould have been dished, were it not for the plates!' [CG]

Hokuetsu seppu

(Snow stories of the north country)

SUZUKI BOKUSHI

PUBLISHED BY BUNKEIDŌ, KAWACHIYA MOHEI, OSAKA, AND CHŌJIYA HEIBEI, EDO (PRESENT-DAY TOKYO), 1835–41

PAPERBACK WITH *FUKUROTOJI* (POUCH BINDING), ISSUED AS 7 VOLUMES, WOODBLOCK PRINTS BY IWASE KYŌSUI

V&A E.2625 to 2631-1925

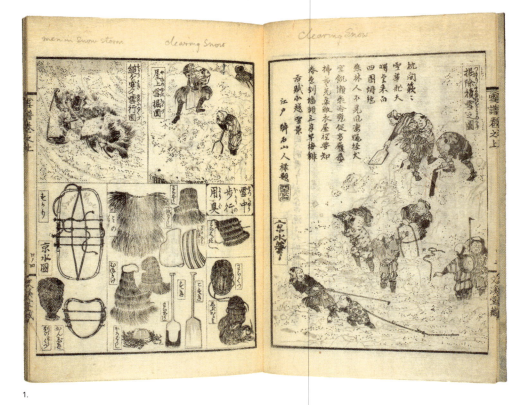

1.

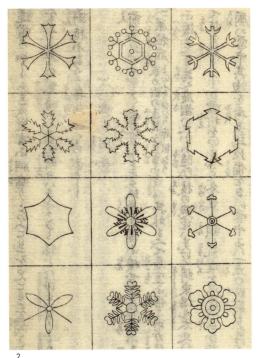

2.

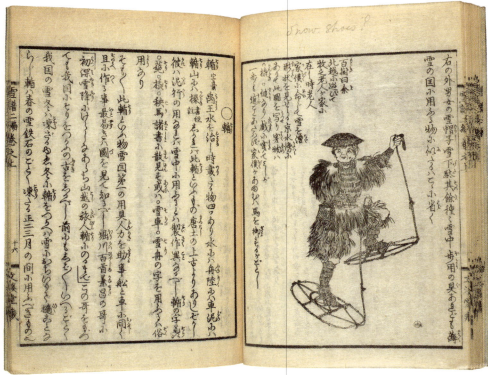

3.

Hokuetsu seppu is an extensive work on life in the former Echigo province of Japan, known for its long winters. It was written by the textile merchant Suzuki Bokushi, originally from Echigo, who wished to convey the realities of life there to his compatriots in the milder regions of Edo, Osaka and Kyoto. Of the woodblock illustrations by Iwase Kyōsui, the most celebrated are the 86 sketches showing different types of snowflake crystals (2). As well as being of scientific interest, these illustrations led to the adoption of the snowflake as a popular motif on kimono and tea bowls. The book covers a wide range of local topics, from the varieties of snow to the customs, lifestyles, regional dialects, industries and folk tales of the area. Bokushi describes how the residents of Echigo spend their short summers preparing for snowfall that can last up to eight months of the year, how they dig tunnels through it to get out of their houses (1) and how they manage to grow their crops. He gives practical advice to the reader, too, such as tips on what to do if caught in a blizzard or avalanche. [CG]

TRAVEL 75

Yokohama kaikō kenbunshi

(Observations on the opening of Yokohama Harbour)

UTAGAWA SADAHIDE

PUBLISHED IN JAPAN, 1862–5

PAPERBACK WITH *FUKUROTOJI* (POUCH BINDING), ISSUED AS 6 VOLUMES, WOODBLOCK PRINTS

V&A E.2805-1925

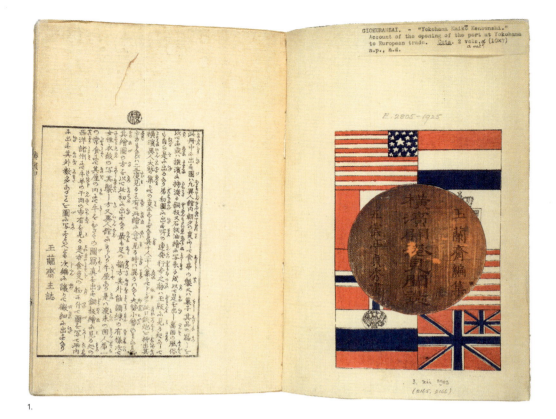

1.

2.

3.

Following the end of Japan's self-imposed isolation in 1854, the port of Yokohama opened to foreign trade in 1859 and quickly established itself as a major international harbour. Publishers in Edo (present-day Tokyo) sent artists to Yokohama to make prints of the appearance and habits of the newly arrived European and American traders. These journalistic prints were popular from about 1860 and eventually became known as *Yokohama-e* (pictures of Yokohama). Some of the prints were published in books, and one of the bestsellers was *Yokohama kaikō kenbunshi*, a guide to the port city, written and illustrated by the artist Utagawa Sadahide. Published from 1862, during the peak of *Yokohama-e*'s popularity, it shows Westerners as the Japanese perceived them, not only emphasizing the differences between the two peoples but also dispelling some myths. For example, Sadahide notes that not all foreigners are tall, despite the stereotypes, and not all of them have long noses. His respectful, often touching observations played an important role in informing the Japanese of foreign culture at a profoundly transitional time. [CG]

The Gossiping Photographer at Hastings

FRANCIS FRITH

PRINTED BY JAMES SPRENT VIRTUE, PUBLISHED BY FRANCIS FRITH & CO., REIGATE, 1864

ILLUSTRATIONS FROM 16 ALBUMEN PRINTS

V&A 38041800766602

Francis Frith was a pioneer of travel photography. His career began with three trips between 1856 and 1859 to Egypt and the Middle East, where he made photographs of landscapes and monuments that were later exhibited to great acclaim. His images were issued in albums by established printing companies, but Frith realized he could profit further from their popularity by founding his own company, Francis Frith & Co., in 1859. Frith & Co.'s prints, albums, publications and postcards of views of Britain appealed to the domestic tourist market (which boomed in the mid-nineteenth century, thanks to inexpensive rail travel) and sold in great numbers. *The Gossiping Photographer at Hastings* was loosely based on informal travel books known as 'gossiping guides', popular in the 1860s. Here, the guide and illustrator is Frith himself, taking us on a humorous tour of Hastings (3, 4), St Leonards, Rye (2) and Winchelsea. The title page features a group of women on the seafront at Hastings and below it, two photographs of Frith, one with his camera and the other seated at a writing desk (1). Frith & Co. dominated the photographic publication industry in nineteenth-century England and continued to be run as a family business until 1971. [CG]

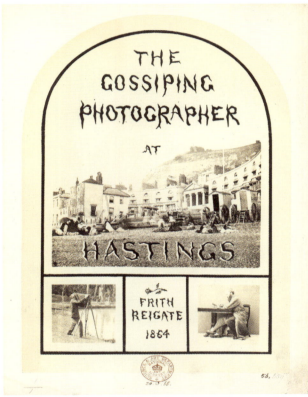

1.

2.

3.

4.

TRAVEL 77

Dorset Shell Guide

PAUL NASH

PUBLISHED BY THE ARCHITECTURAL PRESS, LONDON, 1936

WATERCOLOUR ILLUSTRATIONS AND PHOTOGRAPHS COMPILED BY PAUL NASH

V&A L.956-1936

1.

2.

3.

During the 1930s British artist Paul Nash became increasingly interested in Surrealism. In 1935 the writer John Betjeman commissioned Nash to compile a guidebook on the county of Dorset as part of Betjeman's Shell Guide series. The resulting book is widely considered to be the most experimental in the series, focusing on the primeval history of Dorset, which Nash described as a source of 'natural surrealism'. This focus is made clear from the start with the book's title page displaying a photographed model of the dinosaur *Scelidosaurus harrisonii*, which Nash labels as a 'former native' of Dorset (1). On the endpapers is a collage of photographs depicting fossilized fish specimens from Dorchester Museum and images of Dorset's coastline (2). Both the authenticity of the guidebook and photography's perceived association with the truth are thrown into question by this mismatch of pictures. Rather than provide guidance the book disorientates the reader. [CG]

The Silent Traveller in London

CHIANG YEE

PUBLISHED BY COUNTRY LIFE LTD, LONDON, 1938

ILLUSTRATIONS FROM 14 HALF-TONE PLATES,
18 LINE BLOCK ILLUSTRATIONS

V&A L.53-1939

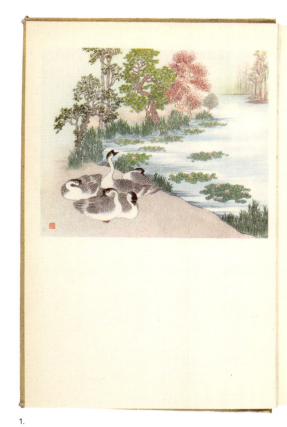

1.

The author and artist Chiang Yee was commissioned by Country Life Ltd to write a series of popular travel books, beginning in 1937 with *The Silent Traveller in Lakeland*. The structure of this second book in the series is more experimental than that of the first; impressions of London are split by seasons and weather types, followed by a consideration of its people, customs, pastimes and entertainments.

Chiang accompanied his writing with his own illustrations, using materials and techniques from Chinese tradition. External and internal stimuli are interwoven in a conversational, poetic manner, imbued with a sense of wonder. The self-styled 'Silent Traveller' makes parallels with the Chinese culture of his upbringing or transports the reader far from metropolitan London, likening, for instance, the movement of umbrellas on Westminster Bridge to 'the waves of the sea washing back from where I stood' (2).

The book is aimed at a British audience, allowing readers to see their surroundings anew from the perspective of a Chinese emigrant as he first experiences British culture. Chiang spent 22 years in Britain, a third of them in London, but in 1955 settled in the United States, teaching Chinese and poetry, while continuing to travel and write. He returned to China for the final two years of his life. [FW]

2.

TRAVEL 79

South Africa

LIU XIAODONG

PUBLISHED BY LOUIS VUITTON,
PARIS, 2016

V&A 38041019029628

South Africa by Chinese artist Liu Xiaodong comes from a series of travel books published by the firm Louis Vuitton as an offshoot from their usual trade in designing high-end luggage. For each title an artist is invited to travel to a place unfamiliar to them and produce an illustrated book based on their experience. Primarily a figure painter, Liu prefers to work *en plein air* and is drawn to painting people on the fringes of society, especially those affected by displacement, environmental degradation and urban development. His practice also takes in film, photography and the written word, and in *South Africa* these interests come together when he combines the traditional art of painting with digital photography. By painting figures and wildlife in loose brushstrokes and layering them over brightly coloured digital photographs, Liu creates a tension between fact and fiction, movement and stillness, the traditional and the contemporary. [CG]

1.

2.

3.

The New Colonists

MONICA ALCAZAR-DUARTE

PUBLISHED BY BEMOJAKE IN COLLABORATION WITH
THE PHOTOGRAPHERS' GALLERY, LONDON, 2017

V&A 38041018020727

2.

3.

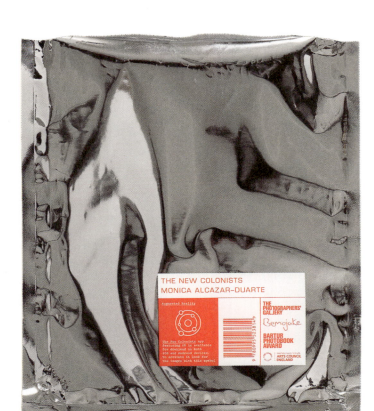
1.

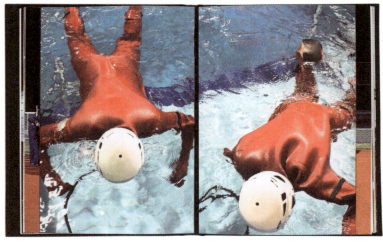
4.

This photobook by Monica Alcazar-Duarte is issued in a silver vacuum pack (1) and opens to reveal photographs of the small town of Mars in Pennsylvania, United States. The views, mainly taken at twilight, depict gas stations (3), football fields and fast-food restaurants – symbols of an all-American life. Interspersed and juxtaposed with these uncanny earthly images are five sequences of pictures from the European Space Agency's Mars colonization programme. They show views of artificial landscapes of rock and sand (2) and would-be astronauts being put through their paces in preparation for a future Mars mission (4). Alcazar-Duarte pushes the boundaries of illustration by making use of augmented reality. Through an app, readers can interact with 3D animations by Levan Tozashvili of spy satellites and space colonies, and listen to narration from experts including Dr Ian Crawford, Professor of Planetary Science and Astrobiology at Birkbeck, University of London, who speaks about the notions of 'space law' and 'space ethics'. The overall effect is a multi-layered reading experience combining audio and visual elements that extend beyond the printed page and encourage the reader to contemplate the enduring human fascination with exploration. [CG]

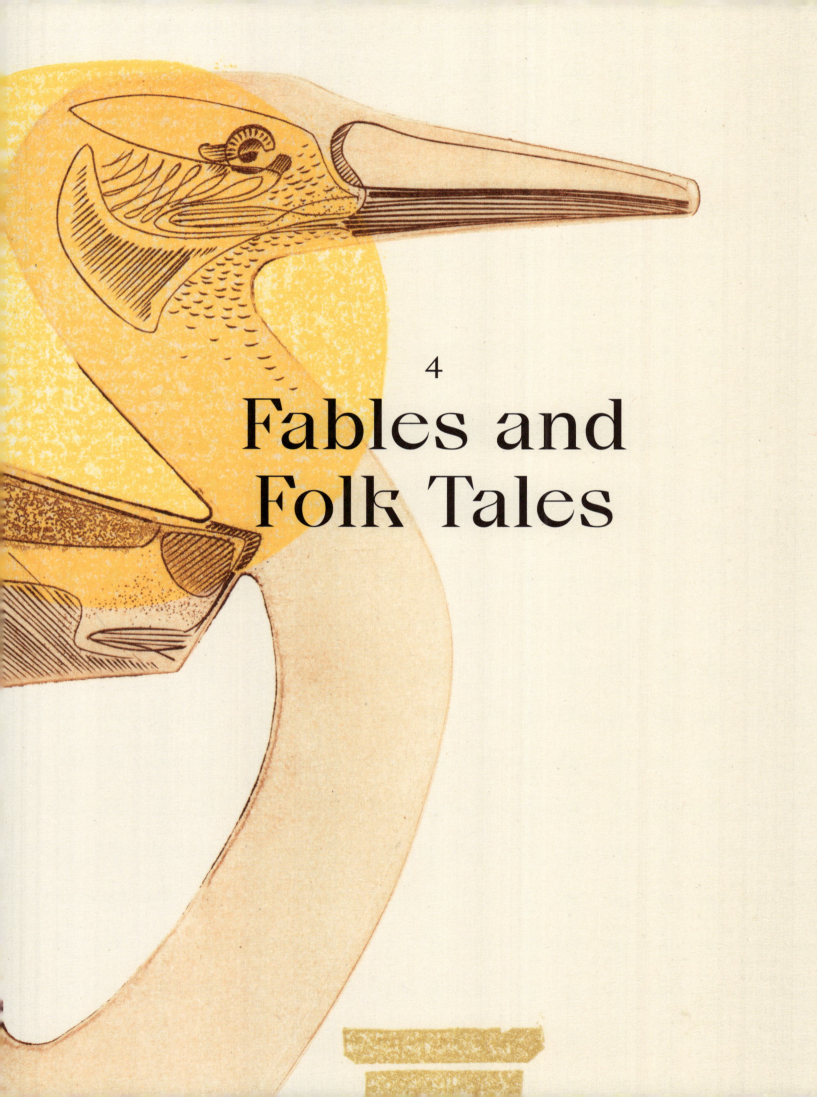

4
Fables and Folk Tales

Fables and Folk Tales

Juliet Ceresole

Before widespread literacy, the tradition of oral storytelling passed on cultural beliefs and wisdoms. Developed and expanded upon with each recounting, these folk tales cannot be attributed to one author; it is more accurate to ascribe them to the communities from which they come. Occasionally, such stories were collated and formalized in written collections, as in the twelfth-century *Reynard the Fox*, which brought together French, Dutch, German and English folk stories. They were not, however, consistently recorded until the nineteenth century. Then, the European Romantic movement, with its focus on primitivism and the 'common man', coupled with an anxiety over the loss of traditional life to industrialization, led to a renewed interest in folk tales. It was the work of the German brothers Jacob and Wilhelm Grimm, and their recording of German folk tales in *Kinder- und Hausmärchen* (Children's and household tales) between 1812 and 1815, that led to the development of the formal study and chronicling of folklore, which today extends across the globe.

It is from this oral folk tradition that fables developed as their own literary form. The protagonists are the cunning foxes and vain peacocks of folk tale, but these short stories are always based in the humble human realm, with an explicit moral for the reader to apply in their daily life. There are no magical interventions to save these characters and the ending is often unhappy. Warning us that pride comes before a fall and reminding us that slow and steady wins the race, they are woven into the fabric of our everyday lives. Perhaps, then, it is not surprising that the first dated, printed illustrated book in Europe was a collection of fables. Their enduring popularity means that the history of book illustration can be tracked through their publication, from that first collection to the present day.

The printed collections of fables that are most familiar to us today take their stories from two main sources. Several hundred are attributed to the Greek storyteller Aesop, who is said to have lived on the Greek island of Samos sometime between about 620 and 560 BCE. Collections of fables credited to him were transmitted across the centuries by a series of authors writing in Greek and Latin. Almost as widely repeated are the fables attributed to the Indian sage Bidpai, also known as Pilpay. His stories are believed to have been written for the first time in the *Panchatantra*, sometime between 100 BCE and 500 CE, and translations had made their way across Asia and into Europe by 1100 (right).

In medieval Europe, monasteries took a leading role in the dissemination of stories in manuscripts and in 1350 the Dominican monk Ulrich Boner collected 100 fables based on Aesop's in *Der Edelstein* (*The Gem Stone*, opposite top). The popular collection was widely copied and eventually reproduced in print in 1461 by Albrecht Pfister in Bamberg, Germany. Not only is Pfister's the first-known collection of fables in print but its 101 woodcuts, hand-stamped into blank spaces in the text, make it the first dated, printed illustrated book.

ABOVE
Anvar-i Suhayli, 'King Dabishlim with the sage Bidpai in his Cave', manuscript, paint and ink on paper, southern India, late 16th century
V&A IS.13:42/2-1962

Pfister's *Edelstein* was quickly followed by two editions of Aesop's fables printed separately in Germany and Italy. The most influential of these was produced in the German town of Ulm, where Johannes Zainer printed a life of Aesop and his fables in about 1476. Written by Heinrich Steinhöwel, it used illustrations that drew heavily on the 1461 *Edelstein* edition and is now commonly referred to as the 'Ulm Aesop'. The book met with popular success and the printing blocks were passed to Günther Zainer, an Augsburg printer, and were reused and reworked in editions published across Europe (below right). The popularity of the fable book, widely available and with attractive illustrations, took root. In the three decades before the year 1500, Aesop's fables were printed as frequently as the Bible and in over 123 different editions. In the following centuries the stories were adapted and interpreted by diverse authors from across the globe. Often adding extra elements from local traditional folk tales, writers including Jean de La Fontaine in France, John Gay in England and Ivan Krylov in Russia created their own original stories that were added to the fable canon.

The short form of fable texts equally made them attractive for teaching Greek and Latin grammar to young scholars, and in 1513 the humanist scholar and theologian Maarten van Dorp published the first edition specifically created for this purpose. Diverting illustrations and practical wisdom soon saw fables recommended for the general education of the young. A fable could teach a youth to read and write, while introducing a subtle moral education. Animal stories and traditional folk tales were already a nursery staple, and this encouraged publishers to create collections of fables specifically aimed at children. The Industrial Revolution made it possible to mass-produce books in colour and the nineteenth century ushered in a golden age of children's literature. Artists such as Walter Crane (p.91) and Arthur Rackham (p.92) were invited to illustrate fables, and detailed illustrations began to overshadow the texts. The animal imagery in traditional fable stories also inspired Beatrix Potter in the development of her books for children. She had studied fairy and folk tales from around the world before becoming a published author and practised her art by illustrating Aesop's fables. She later developed these early studies into her own characters and stories, with her drawings for Aesop's 'The Town Mouse and the Country Mouse' (bottom right) evolving into *The Tale of Johnny Town-Mouse*, which she dedicated to 'Aesop in the shadows'.

By the end of the 1900s folk literature was firmly classed as being for children and had otherwise fallen out of favour. One-dimensional characters and black-and-white morals no longer accurately reflected the multiple and nuanced perspectives of contemporary society. As Aesop would tell us, familiarity breeds contempt. However, In 1956 the American humorist James Thurber reinterpreted Aesop's 'The Fox and the Crow' by giving the tale of theft by flattery four separate endings, including one in which the crow 'outfoxes' his adversary into returning his stolen cheese. In his joke, Thurber highlighted the endless adaptability of the folk tale. Writers today are recasting traditional characters in contemporary stories for books, television series and films, to great global success. The enduring appeal of the familiar folk tale continues to evolve for authors, artists and readers alike.

TOP
'The Dancing Monkeys', woodcut, coloured by hand, from Ulrich Boner, *Der Edelstein* (*The Gem Stone*), Bamberg, 1461
Herzog August Library, Wolfenbüttel

MIDDLE
'The Fox and Grapes', woodcut after the 'Ulm Aesop' of 1476/7, from *Vita Æsopi fabulatoris clarissimi e greco latina ...* (The life of Aesop, and the most famous fables from the Latin and Greek ...), Augsburg, 1479
V&A 38041800152118

BOTTOM
Beatrix Potter, 'The Town Mouse and the Country Mouse', watercolour and pen and ink over pencil, *c*.1900
V&A LC 21/B/3

FABLES AND FOLK TALES   85

Vita et Æsopus moralisatus

(Life [after Rinucius] and moralized fables of Aesop)

FRANCESCO DEL TUPPO

PRINTED BY THE GERMANI FIDELISSIMI, NAPLES, 1485

44 WOODCUTS

V&A 38041800149239

While the 'Ulm Aesop' (p.85) was hugely influential across Europe, and cities such as Strasbourg, Cologne and Nuremberg dominated early printing, a rival tradition existed in the Italian city states. Francesco del Tuppo's *Æsopus moralisatus*, printed in Naples in 1485, was the main source for early Italian fable illustration, while the German tradition did not arrive for another 100 years. Del Tuppo's version followed an earlier edition translated and adapted by Accio Zucco and printed in Verona in 1479 by Giovanni and Alberto Alvise. The edition was created not for scholars, but to teach students to read and write, with the text in both Latin and Italian. The Italian editions were much more lavishly illustrated than the German. One image depicts a character who may be Aesop in a highly decorative architectural environment, framed by exaggerated ornamental borders (1), which, unlike the plainer illustrations of the 'Ulm Aesop', are integral to the image and make up a third of the print. The brick floors, marked by short, repeated dashes, are a typically Dutch technique, perhaps giving a clue to the nationality of the printers who created the images for del Tuppo. [LS]

1.

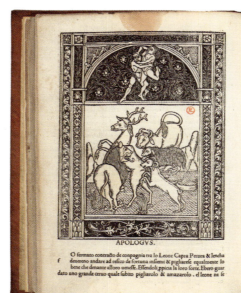

2.

3.

86 • FABLES AND FOLK TALES

Esbatement moral des animaux

(Moral entertainment of animals)

ANONYMOUS (PREFACE BY PEETER HEYNS)

PRINTED BY PHILIPPE GALLE, ANTWERP, 1578

ETCHINGS BY MARCUS GHEERAERTS THE ELDER

V&A 38041800152027

1.

Esbatement moral translates as 'moral entertainment', reflecting the fable's dual purpose to instruct and delight. Gheeraerts' beautiful, etched illustrations provide the entertainment, and biblical quotes underneath outline their Christian message.

Gheeraerts, a renowned draughtsman of animals and birds, drew from life to populate his scenes with realistic creatures. For the rendering of 'exotic' animals, such as the camel, he may have visited cabinets of curiosities or consulted books such as Conrad Gessner's *Historia animalium* (1551–8). He chose to use etching, a freer technique than woodcut or engraving that allows for fine details and flowing lines, capturing the feel of fur and feathers (2). His illustrations ground the fables in the villages and landscapes of the Low Countries, giving the impression that the stories take place in the real world while people go about their business in the background.

Gheeraerts' hugely influential illustrations were reused and reworked for different translations and editions of fable books. This French-language edition is printed from reworked plates originally created for the Dutch *De warachtighe fabulen der dieren* (The truthful fables of the animals) published in 1567. His compositions, such as the lion caught in a net (1), became archetypal and inspired artists for centuries to come, including Francis Barlow (pp.88–9). [SB]

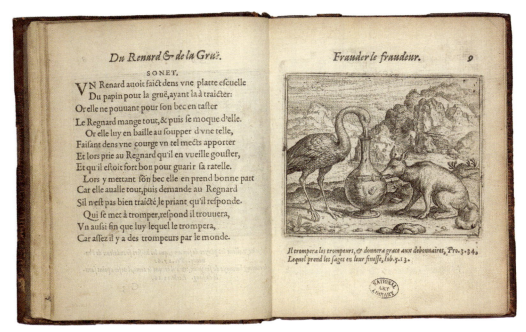

2.

FABLES AND FOLK TALES

Æsop's Fables, with His Life

In English, French and Latin

PRINTED BY HENRY HILLS JR FOR FRANCIS BARLOW, TO BE SOLD BY CHRISTOPHER WILKINSON, LONDON, 1687

ETCHINGS

V&A 38041800377632

Francis Barlow was Britain's first true wildlife artist and the first native-born illustrator of printed books. His edition of Aesop's fables was one of the most prestigious publications of its day. Much of the first edition, published in 1666, perished in the Great Fire of London. This 1687 version boasts 'One hundred and twelve Sculptures' illustrating the fables, and an additional 31 lavish full-page engravings, illustrating the life of Aesop (1).

While many of the illustrations follow traditional fable compositions (p.87), Barlow's detailed and naturalistic style brings a vivid realism to the plates, which he designed and engraved himself. The animals are not pantomiming human behaviours and are at home in the detailed landscapes they inhabit – sometimes disappearing entirely, as in his depiction of the 'Ant and the Grasshopper' (4).

The illustrations were very popular and copied onto all manner of domestic wares, including serving dishes, dinner services and decorative tiles. Barlow's illustration to the 'Fox and the Cat' (3) can even be found in eighteenth-century furniture manuals for carpenters to copy and render in three dimensions on table legs and mirror surrounds. [JC]

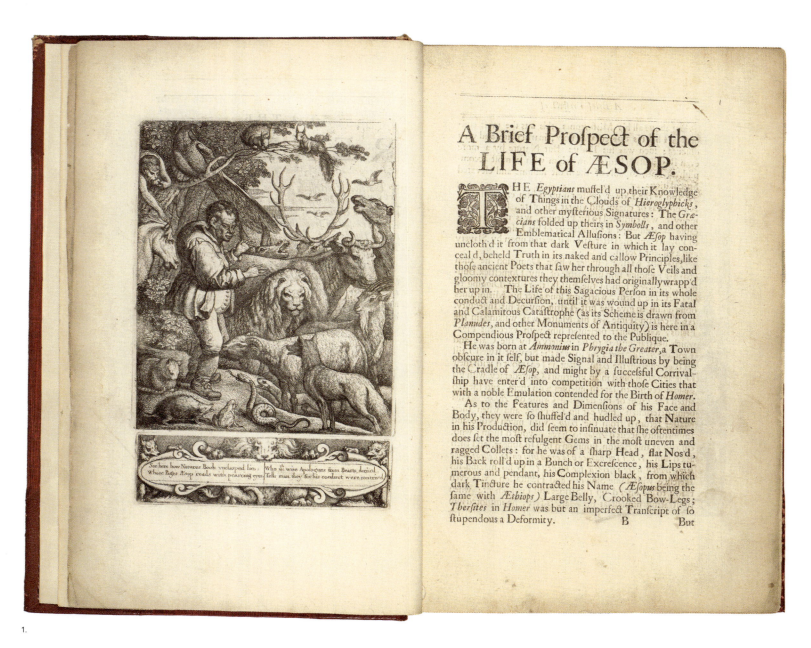

1.

2.

3.

4.

FABLES AND FOLK TALES ❧ 89

Fables nouvelles: dédiées au roy

(New fables: dedicated to the king)

ANTOINE HOUDAR DE LA MOTTE

PRINTED FOR GRÉGOIRE DUPUIS, PARIS, 1719

ENGRAVINGS BY CLAUDE GILLOT
AND OTHER ARTISTS

V&A 38041800377277

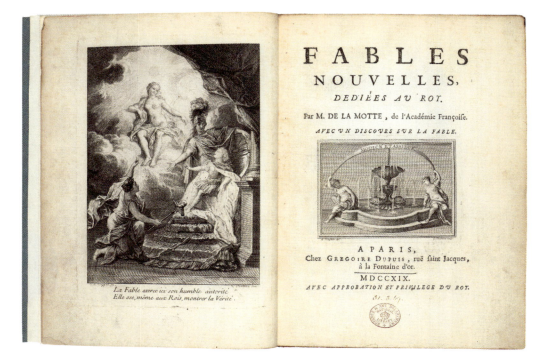

1.

2.

3.

The French poet Jean de La Fontaine is one of the world's most celebrated fabulists. His first collection of fables, published in 1668, expanded on traditional tales to create original stories that are still widely published today. In the introduction to his *Fables nouvelles*, the French author Antoine Houdar de La Motte recognized La Fontaine's talents, remarking that 'he has given the fables of the Ancients such delicate and agreeable turns'. Yet he then turns critical, accusing La Fontaine of exhausting 'his fine genius upon ornament and decoration which in reality are no more than accessory invention' and confidently declaring that his own writings 'have proposed nothing but truths, entirely new'. La Motte believed in the use of fables for instruction and dedicated his book to the young King of France, Louis XV, who was only nine years old at the time.

The book is illustrated with many beautifully detailed plates by the celebrated artist and theatrical designer Claude Gillot. Although Gillot did not train as a professional printmaker, he was a successful book illustrator and his designs for these fables were later independently published in albums. [JC]

Baby's Own Aesop

Being the fables condensed in rhyme with portable morals pictorially pointed

WALTER CRANE

PUBLISHED BY GEORGE ROUTLEDGE & SONS, LONDON AND NEW YORK, 1887

COLOUR WOOD ENGRAVING BY EDMUND EVANS

V&A 38041803046614

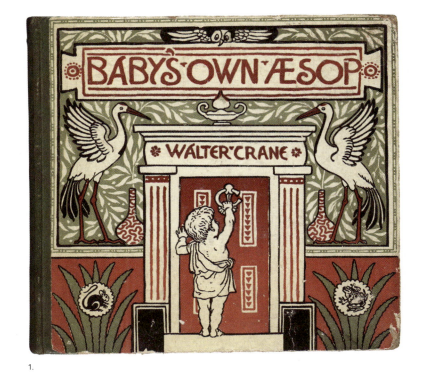

1.

2.

Baby's Own Aesop came out of the collaboration between the artist Walter Crane and the engraver, printer and publisher Edmund Evans, and was one of the first illustrated Aesop's fables to use photo-etching. It was one of the 'toy books' pioneered by the pair, which generally had eight pages printed in colour and sold for sixpence. For Crane, cheap did not mean poor quality, and he was keen to avoid what he saw as the 'generally careless and unimaginative woodcuts' that had come before. As printing technology evolved, Crane adapted his style to working in colour, simplifying the images and, inspired by Japanese printmaking, adding strong black outlines (1). Crane was also influenced by William Morris and the Arts and Crafts movement, and he believed that his decorative art could form a radical style for the international socialist movement. Aesop's fables are therefore a perfect fit for Crane's visually succinct images aiming to make socialism digestible to the youngest of minds, the moral of the 'King Log and King Stork' being simply: don't have kings (2). [LS]

Aesop's Fables

V.S. VERNON JONES, WITH AN INTRODUCTION BY G.K. CHESTERTON

PUBLISHED BY W. HEINEMANN, LONDON; DOUBLEDAY, PAGE & CO., NEW YORK, 1912

COLOUR AND BLACK-AND-WHITE ILLUSTRATIONS BY ARTHUR RACKHAM

V&A L.2589-1972

Arthur Rackham made his name illustrating children's books, and believed in the 'stimulating and educative power of imaginative, fantastic, and playful pictures and writing for children in their most impressionable years'. In this gift book, produced for Christmas 1912, Vernon Jones's elegant retellings of Aesop's fables are accompanied by Rackham's illustrations, drawing the reader into a fantastical world where humans, animals, trees and even inanimate objects interact.

The book is illustrated with black-and-white line drawings and 12 half-tone colour plates – an early form of colour photographic reproduction that had the subtlety to translate Rackham's sharp pen-and-ink lines and delicate watercolour palette. His anthropomorphic animals emphasize the fables' relevance to human behaviour. The creatures wear clothes and are made individual through gestures and expressions. In the tale of the hare and the tortoise, the animals whisper conspiratorially behind their disturbingly humanlike hands (1). Indeed, Rackham does not shy away from darker elements; his forests are populated by sinister trees, their faces twisted in grimaces, and in the tale of the gnat and the lion he focuses on the fly's ultimate comeuppance in the spider's web (2). [SB]

1.

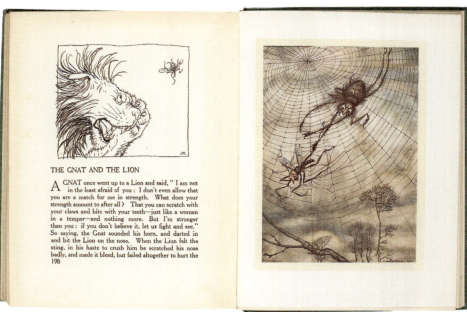

2.

Edmund Dulac's Fairy-Book: Fairy Tales of the Allied Nations

EDMUND DULAC

PUBLISHED BY HODDER & STOUGHTON, LONDON AND NEW YORK, 1916

COLOUR AND BLACK-AND-WHITE ILLUSTRATIONS

V&A 38041802176586

1.

2.

3.

Working in London in the opening years of the twentieth century, the French artist Edmund Dulac established a reputation as an exceptional illustrator. His first book illustrations, for the novels of the Brontë sisters, were published in 1905, and in 1907 he was invited by the Leicester Galleries in London to exhibit 50 watercolours for *Stories from The Arabian Nights*. These were licensed for publication by Hodder & Stoughton as a sumptuous 'gift book' and proved very popular. This initial success led to Dulac producing a new set of illustrations for the gallery and publishers each year, until the outbreak of the First World War in 1914. With nations ravaged by fighting and dwindling resources, these extravagant books no longer seemed appropriate and Dulac turned his attention to the war effort instead. His 1916 illustrated collection *Fairy Tales of the Allied Nations* brings together folk tales from Ireland, Belgium, France, Italy, Russia (1), Serbia and Japan (3), uniting them under the patriotic banner of the Allied fighting nations. The international scope of the stories allowed Dulac to indulge his interest in non-European art but the elephants in his illustration for 'The Serpent Prince' are somewhat incongruous to this Italian folk tale (2). [JC]

Fables

JEAN DE LA FONTAINE

PUBLISHED BY TÉRIADE ÉDITEUR, PARIS, 1952

2 VOLUMES, ILLUSTRATED BY MARC CHAGALL

V&A L.161:1 to 2-1984

When the publisher Ambroise Vollard (who died in 1939) originally commissioned Russian-Jewish artist Marc Chagall to illustrate the fables of La Fontaine, many critics saw him as an inappropriate choice for this 'most French of our poets'. However, Vollard believed Chagall would be the first artist to do justice to the magical realism of the tales, as can be seen, for instance, in the uncanny 'The Cat Transformed into a Woman' (1). Chagall's prints, created as his wife, Bella, read the tales aloud to him, combine influences of both Hasidic Jewish tradition and the French countryside. Chagall began his illustrations by creating a hundred 'dazzling' gouaches in colour, which ultimately proved too difficult to translate into engravings, so were then carefully reworked in black and white. He focused on many nuances of shadow and light: in the example shown here illumination from a light bulb catches a glinting wine bottle and sacks of grain in the thick darkness of the room (2). While best-known for working in vibrant colour, Chagall found a different kind of magic in this process, of which he wrote: 'while holding a lithographic stone or a copper plate, I thought I was holding a talisman.' [LS]

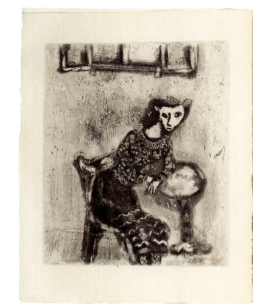

1.

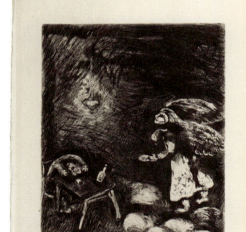

2.

3.

Fables

FENG XUEFENG, TRANSLATED BY GLADYS YANG

PUBLISHED BY FOREIGN LANGUAGES PRESS, BEIJING, 1953

WOODCUTS BY HUANG YONGYU

V&A 38041803198506

In the early part of the twentieth century many Communist scholars in China focused on traditional folk songs, fables and stories to celebrate a Chinese cultural identity that was from and for the people. After Mao Zedong declared the creation of the People's Republic of China in 1949, the Communist Party reinvented and reinterpreted many of these traditions for the political cause. Fables were particularly suited to this task, with morals emphasizing the virtue of the working commoner against the dangers of imperialism. This collection, published in 1953 by the Foreign Languages Press in Beijing (then Peking), includes a tale warning against the imperialist weasel (3) and makes an example of a cow who cannot escape servitude because of her insistence on clinging to the 'property' of her rope tether (4). In 1954, just one year after this collection was published, the author Feng Xuefeng fell foul of the ruling Communist Party himself. His outspoken views against the tight political control of literature and his refusal to reinterpret classical texts along strictly political lines saw him accused of 'bourgeois' and 'anti-party' beliefs. He was eventually sent to the countryside for 'reform through labour' in 1957. [JC]

1.

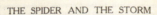

2.

3.

4.

XXIV Fables

JEAN DE LA FONTAINE

PUBLISHED BY ABRAM KROL, PARIS, 1959

COPPER AND WOOD ENGRAVINGS BY ABRAM KROL

V&A L.1663-1966

The illustrations to collections of fables have often held high, if not equal, stature to that of the text, and in the 400 years since *Der Edelstein* (p.85), fables have followed a symbolic visual language that is instantly familiar to readers. The image of a hare and a tortoise, for example, no longer needs accompanying text to be interpreted. The challenge of restyling traditional symbolism for a contemporary audience makes fables a rich source of inspiration for fine artists. In this collection, produced by Abram Krol in 1959, we can immediately identify Jean de La Fontaine's stories from Krol's striking wood-engraved illustrations. The images are now abstracted and no longer follow the archetypal compositions refined by artists such as Marcus Gheeraerts (p.87). Yet the image of the stork, fox, long-necked bottle and bowl is immediately identifiable as La Fontaine's interpretation of Aesop's 'Fox and the Stork' (3). The text has become superfluous; the image alone can now tell the story. A focus on illustration is now the main driver behind modern adult interpretations of fables, with new author interpretations confined to children's literature. [JC]

1.

2.

3.

4.

5.

FABLES AND FOLK TALES ❧ 97

A Fable of Bidpai

NICHOLAS SIEGL (TRANS.)

TRANSLATED FROM *BUCH DER WEISHEIT* (BOOK OF WISDOM), 1483

PUBLISHED BY JANUS PRESS, WEST BURKE, VERMONT, 1974

14 WOODBLOCK PRINTS BY HELEN SIEGL

V&A L.1827-1990

The *Panchatantra* or *Fables of Bidpai* are a collection of Indian folk tales that tell of a wiseman, Vishnu Sharma, who is entrusted by King Amarasakti to educate his three sons in statecraft. He does this by telling five animal fables that teach the princes about human nature. The tales were first written in Sanskrit sometime between 100 BCE and 500 CE; Arabic and Persian interpretations rapidly spread across Asia and translations appeared in Europe by the eleventh century. In 1678 Jean de La Fontaine acknowledged their influence in his second collection of fables, noting, 'I owe a great part to Pilpay [Bidpai], an Indian Sage'.

Despite their previous widespread popularity, these fables are now often overlooked in modern European and American collections. This 1974 artist's book uses a modern English translation of a German text from 1483. It is illustrated by the print artist Helen Siegl, who was known for her innovative techniques that combined etching with wood, lino and sometimes even plaster blocks, in one print. However, for this book, in keeping with the tradition of the original text, she created 14 beautifully detailed compositions in simple, single-colour woodcuts. [JC]

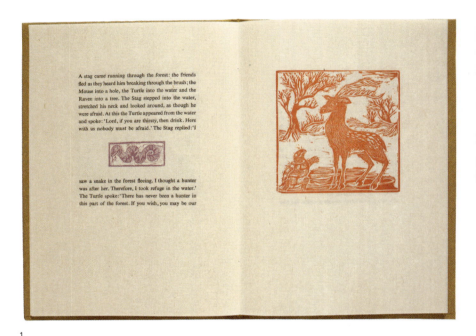

1.

2.

3.

Anansi Company

A collection of thirteen hand-made wire and card rod-puppets animated in colour and verse

PUBLISHED BY CIRCLE PRESS, LONDON, 1992

ARTIST'S BOOK BY RONALD KING, WITH ROY FISHER; SILK SCREEN-PRINTS

V&A 38041993103159

Anansi is one of the most important figures from West African folk tales. Also known as Ananse, Anancy and Kwaku Ananse, he is a mischief-maker who takes the form of a spider and uses his ingenuity to outwit stronger foes, even taking on the gods. His stories are probably the best-known African tales outside that continent, having travelled to the Caribbean and America with enslaved people, for whom these stories of triumph over adversity were a defiant link to home. Recounting the tales was a way of passing on their West African cultural heritage and the American stories of Br'er Rabbit can be traced back directly to the Anansi stories told by enslaved people. In this interpretation by the book artist Ronald King, the poet Roy Fisher bases his verse on the Jamaican tradition of Anansi tales, collected by Walter Jekyll in his book *Jamaican Song and Story* (1907). The traditional characters literally come off the page in a series of 13 colourful wire puppets, in the style of South-East Asian shadow puppets. Within the pages of the book, they become part of bold compositions that are a riot of silk-screened colour and collage of contemporary photographic images with found objects. [JC]

1.

2.

3.

FABLES AND FOLK TALES   99

5
Literature

Literature

RUTH HIBBARD

Literature comes in many genres, including poetry, drama, novels and epics. Although non-fiction, such as diaries and biography, can be classed as literature, the term is more commonly associated with imaginative fiction. These are the works more often illustrated and which are presented here. The National Art Library collects illustrated books of literature as important examples of the work of artists. This chapter showcases some intriguing approaches to illustrating literature and explores the myriad relationships possible between author and artist.

Literature can tell the most engaging stories, delve deep into the human condition and elucidate aspects of human culture. It captures the imagination across time and space, with a quality and longevity that are at once celebrated in its place of origin and also appreciated around the world. Unlike in non-fiction, where a depiction should be true to life, there is greater licence within fiction for an artist to draw on their imagination and perspective in responding to the text. Literature is naturally fertile ground for an illustrator, who can expand upon the author's creativity with their own. Imaginative and inspired illustrations can enrich and explain a work of literature. Images manifest the fictional and give an extra dimension to the narrative's characters, setting or mood. In some cases text and illustration are produced together, creating a harmonious coupling that draws the reader deeper into the story. But illustrations can also be surprising: an artist, sometimes separated from the original by many years and/or miles, can respond to the text with a different view, forming an additional layer for the reader to experience the episodes and ideas that the text presents.

Illustration is sometimes integral to a literary work, such as the Japanese *Genji monogatari emaki* (*Tale of Genji*). Arguably the world's first novel, it was written in the eleventh century by Murasaki Shikibu, a lady-in-waiting at the imperial court. Her elite audiences saw themselves reflected in the works' courtly protagonists and their preoccupations. The earliest surviving version, from the twelfth century, exists as an illustrated scroll, now split between the Tokugawa Art Museum, Nagoya, and the Gotoh Museum, Tokyo. A scene in the scroll depicts reading texts and images as a collaborative experience: Lady Ukifune sits looking at a page of illustrations, while a lady-in-waiting reads the text aloud from a different sheet (opposite bottom). The similarity of the characters' faces shows them to be idealized figures. Their emotions are betrayed by their stance and sometimes a subtle inflection of eyebrows. The scroll's illustrations are as celebrated as the story: reproductions appeared on twentieth-century stamps and banknotes.

From the time of its composition by the Persian poet Ferdowsi in the late 900s CE, the epic known as the *Shahnama* (*The Book of Kings*), was frequently produced as a luxury illustrated manuscript. The colourful pages, filled with delicate, jewel-like details of costume, architecture and landscape, were part of a decorative culture designed to entertain and delight a noble audience. The popular episodes were the most often illustrated, and enabled their survival as part of the canon of stories as the *Shahnama* evolved. By the fourteenth century, royal courts in Islamic kingdoms across Asia had bookmaking workshops (*kitabkhana*) devoted to luxury editions of stories and poems with lavish illustrations and calligraphy. These works demonstrate illustration as integral to the production, and enjoyment, of books. In the seventeenth century, the artist Riza Abbasi's superior ability to produce beautiful images of people and places is evident in his exquisite illustrations to the tale of *Khusraw u Shirin* (pp.106–7).

The addition of illustrations to a work of literature is often also a recognition of the importance of those works that are so well known and well loved that they are central to a nation's culture. A 1564 version of Dante's *Divine Comedy* (written between 1308 and 1320) features not only depictions of the protagonists' incredible journey through hell, purgatory and paradise but also a frontispiece featuring a portrait of the author (opposite top left). These illustrations support the canonization of both work and author as national treasures. François Boucher's illustrations to the plays of Molière (opposite top right), Ivan Bilibin's to the story of Ivan, the tsar's son, the fire-bird and the grey wolf (p.111), and Salvador Dalí's to *Don Quixote* (pp.112–13) are among many notable pairings of artists celebrating their native literature.

OPPOSITE TOP LEFT
Title page, with woodcut portrait of the author, to *Dante con l'espositione di Christoforo Landino, et di Alessandro Vellutello, sopra la sua comedia dell' inferno, del purgatorio, & del paradiso* (*Divine Comedy*), printed by Giovambattista, Marchiò Sessa & fratelli, Venice, 1564
V&A 38041800390924

OPPOSITE TOP RIGHT
Portrait by Charles Antoine Coypel, engraved by Nicolas Bernard Lépicié; plates by François Boucher, 'Le Cocu Imaginaire', engraving by Laurent Cars from Molière, *Œuvres de Molière*, printed by Pierre Prault, Paris, 1734
V&A L.804-1889

OPPOSITE BOTTOM
Murasaki Shikibu, *Genji monogatari emaki* (*Tale of Genji*), facsimile reproduction of the existing fragments of the scroll, Tokyo, 1971
V&A 38041800390726

In a truly integrated approach, there are notable examples of authors illustrating their own books, such as William Makepeace Thackeray, Edward Lear (below right) and Beatrix Potter (p.85). This method brings unity of perspective, the author retaining control over the visual presentation of their work, but the possibility of a depiction different to the author's vision is lost.

There are of course examples of an author's dislike of artists providing illustrations to their works. When Edward Moxon published Alfred Tennyson's *Poems* in 1857, he commissioned several artists for the volume. Tennyson thought it cheapened his work for an undeserving readership who wanted a pretty picture book and not a serious volume of poetry. Furthermore, the daringly passionate illustrations by Pre-Raphaelite artists, including Dante Gabriel Rossetti (right), John Everett Millais and William Holman Hunt, clashed with the more subdued landscape images of the more traditional artists included, such as William Mulready and Thomas Creswick. Tennyson may have felt vindicated as the book sales were initially disappointing, but the illustrations mark Pre-Raphaelitism's introduction to a public that soon became entranced with its sensuous style.

Often the most intriguing relationships between word and image can be when the artist is separated from their source material by time and distance; an artist can recreate a story for a new audience. Paula Rego (pp.118–19) found much in Jane Eyre's story that resonated with her own preoccupation with women's challenging lives, depicting Charlotte Brontë's cruel characters in her distinctively grotesque style. William Kentridge's illustrations to Gogol's *The Nose* (1836) do not even attempt to depict the characters or locations of the novel, but concentrate on the satirical message of the work that was of central importance to his own art (bottom).

Artists and readers both revel in the coupling of word and image. A combination of enchanting literature and imaginative illustrations can result in a work greater than both these elements alone. The marriage of literature and art can be harmonious or rocky, loyal or unfaithful, but the relationship always reveals a common passion for captivating storytelling.

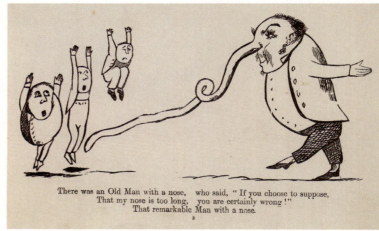

TOP
The Brothers Dalziel after Dante Gabriel Rossetti, illustration for 'The Palace of Art', wood engraving from Alfred Tennyson, *Poems*, London, 1857
V&A Dyce 9788

LEFT
William Kentridge, illustration for Nikolai Gogol, *The Nose*, translated by Stanislav Shvabrin, published by The Arion Press, San Francisco, 2021
V&A 38041021003090

ABOVE
Edward Lear, lithograph from *Book of Nonsense*, London, 1863
V&A 38041803015676

La Vita et Metamorfoseo d'Ovidio

(The life and *Metamorphoses* of Ovid)

GABRIELE SIMEONI (VERSE ADAPTATION)

PUBLISHED BY JEAN DE TOURNES, LYON, 1559

WOODCUTS BY BERNARD SALOMON

V&A L.2466-1905

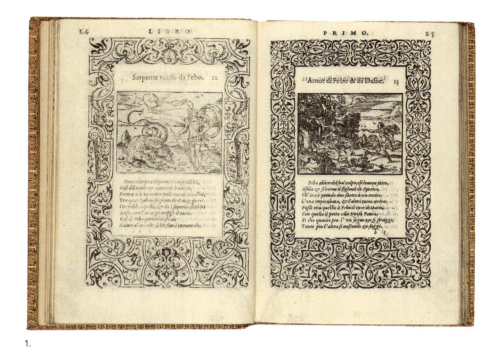

1.

2.

In the classical revival of the fifteenth and sixteenth centuries, Ovid's *Metamorphoses*, with its stories of transformation, love, violence and death, proved popular with readers throughout Europe. The first illustrated version was published in Bruges in 1484, and over the next century more than a hundred others followed. Here, Bernard Salomon's dramatic and skilful woodcut illustrations take centre stage, framed by elaborate borders decorated with grotesque figures and ornamental patterns. The book's impact is primarily visual, with Ovid's 12,000-line poem condensed into eight lines of verse below each illustration. Renaissance illustrations of Ovid were less allegorical and symbolic than those of the Middle Ages. Salomon represents Ovid's text literally and aims at historical accuracy in architecture and clothing. The rigid appearance that often characterizes woodcut images is replaced by flowing lines. Clothes and hair stream behind fleeing characters, and smoke billows from fires (1). Many of the illustrations show several phases of transformation within the same image, using perspective to distinguish between past and present. Here, for example, the nymph Dryope picks a lotus flower in the background, while, in the foreground, she is rooted to the earth as she transforms into a poplar tree (2). [SB]

LITERATURE 105

Khusraw u Shirin

(Khusraw and Shirin)

NIZAMI GANJAVI

MADE IN TABRIZ, ISFAHAN, 1680

19 PAINTINGS IN INK, GOLD AND COLOURS ON PAPER BY RIZA ABBASI

V&A MSL/1885/364

The Persian epic poem *Shahnama*, written down in the late 900s, provides the source material for Nizami Ganjavi's text. There is a strong tradition of illustration accompanying Persian literature, where brightly coloured, full-page paintings complement the text. These were produced for an elite audience who expected lavish images, richly inhabited by their favoured characters and episodes. This seventeenth-century version of the doomed romance between Prince Khusraw and Princess Shirin was illustrated by Riza Abbasi, a celebrated miniaturist. Perhaps he particularly relished the episode in which the painter Shapur produces a portrait of Khusraw to enchant Shirin, revealing the face of the man who hopes his love for her will be reciprocated (1). Renowned for his ability to portray beauty, Riza Abbasi used his talent to depict the lovers during their fluctuating courtship. The landscape and courts through which the star-crossed couple travel on their rocky romantic path have the characteristic flatness of Persian manuscript illumination. Ultimately the doomed lovers only enjoy transitory happiness with each other, but the exquisite illustrations that depict their eventful romance bring an audience back to relive their story again and again. [RH]

1.

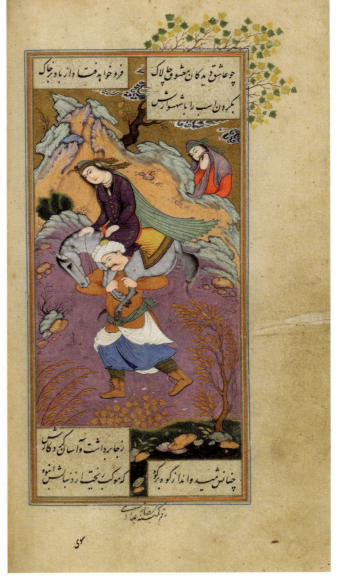

2.

3.

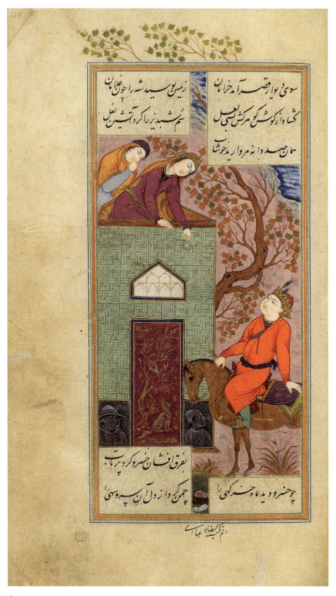

4.

5.

LITERATURE ⚜ 107

Evelina

Or, female life in London: being the history of a young lady's introduction to fashionable life

ANONYMOUS [FRANCES ('FANNY') BURNEY]

PUBLISHED BY JONES AND CO., LONDON, 1822

ENGRAVINGS, COLOURED BY HAND, AFTER ILLUSTRATIONS BY WILLIAM HEATH

V&A L.6273-1982

Fanny Burney published the satire *Evelina* anonymously, for fear of exacting the judgment of a Georgian society obsessed with propriety, respectability and reputation. The story describes Evelina's entrance into London society, where her disputed illegitimate status makes her progress uncertain. William Heath was no stranger to satire, specializing in the political prints that so engaged people of the day. His illustrations capture the whimsy of Burney's prose and the comic grotesqueness of some of her characters, such as the ludicrously affected grandmother Madame Duval, dancing with an extravagant headdress (2), and Evelina's many unsuitable admirers, including Mr Lovel (1). Heath's images also identify the social minefield of the dance floor that Evelina must negotiate, and the importance of shopping for the latest fashions to project the best image of yourself and attract a potential husband (3). Illustrations in works of literature were not often coloured at this time, but were perhaps included to entertain the growing number of female readers, who pored over novels to see aspects of their own lives reflected back to them in humorous and enthralling stories. [RH]

1.

2.

3.

Bleak House

CHARLES DICKENS

PUBLISHED BY BRADBURY & EVANS, LONDON, 1852–3

ILLUSTRATED BY HABLOT KNIGHT BROWNE ('PHIZ')

V&A L.1041-1988

Dickens's novels were originally published in instalments to make them affordable to a wide readership, and the accompanying illustrations increased their mass-market appeal. These pictures cemented the images of Dickens's characters in the popular imagination and have informed later adaptations of his work. Hablot Knight Browne illustrated 10 of Dickens's novels over 23 years and even took the nickname 'Phiz' to match the writer's 'Boz'. His illustrations were often produced at the same time as the text was being written, so there was close collaboration between author and illustrator. *Bleak House* contains two distinct styles of illustration. Phiz's typical style is satirical and rich with character, often with symbolic details added by the illustrator. In a lawyer's study, red tape litters the floor and a book is open at a picture of a maze, reflecting the law's labyrinthine nature. In the corner of the room, a spider web ready to catch its next victim is a worrying omen for the client (3). The book also includes 'dark plates', which favour atmosphere over incident, bringing to life the squalor of London slum Tom-all-Alone's (1), with its crumbling buildings, and spotlighting Lady Dedlock on a gloomy staircase (2). These illustrations reflect the mood of one of Dickens's darkest works. [SB]

1.

2.

3.

4.

Salome: A Tragedy in One Act

OSCAR WILDE

PUBLISHED BY ELKIN MATHEWS & JOHN LANE, LONDON, 1894

LINE BLOCK PRINTS BY AUBREY BEARDSLEY

V&A L.1880-1985

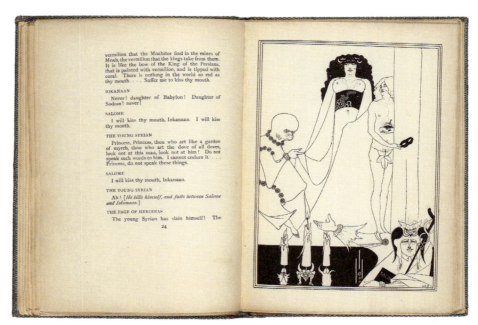

1.

Oscar Wilde's scandalous retelling of the biblical story of King Herod's stepdaughter requesting the head of John the Baptist as a reward for dancing led to his play being banned in England. When *Salome* was published in 1894 (three years after the original stage production), the remarkable illustrations by Aubrey Beardsley contributed to the play's infamy. Abandoning the biblical setting, Beardsley favoured elements from Japanese prints, *fin-de-siècle* decadence and mischievous eroticism. His sparse background and strongly delineated details and figures reference Japanese art; his characters' clothing, particularly the peacock skirt, is redolent of a kimono (2). The erotic scenes known from Japanese *shunga* prints bolstered this style's disrepute. This was combined with the equally tainted symbols of the Aesthetic Movement's love of demonstrative beauty: feathers and flowers. This style's effete reputation, suggestive of Wilde's homosexuality, is endorsed by the phallic-shaped candlesticks (1). Wilde himself appears as a joker figure holding a copy of 'Salome'. Beardsley's illustrations enjoyed a greater afterlife than Wilde's play. While 'Salome' is infrequently staged and not well known, Beardsley's bold images and refined draughtsmanship influenced the psychedelic art of the 1960s and remain a popular motif on cards and posters. [RH]

2.

Skazka ob Ivane-tsareviche: Zhar-ptitse i o serom volke

(The story of Ivan, the tsar's son, the fire-bird and the grey wolf)

IVAN BILIBIN

PUBLISHED BY IZDANIE EKSLEDITSII ZAGOTOVLENIA GOSUDARSTV. IUMAGZ, ST PETERSBURG, RUSSIA, 1901

COLOUR LITHOGRAPHS

V&A L.3162-1968

1.

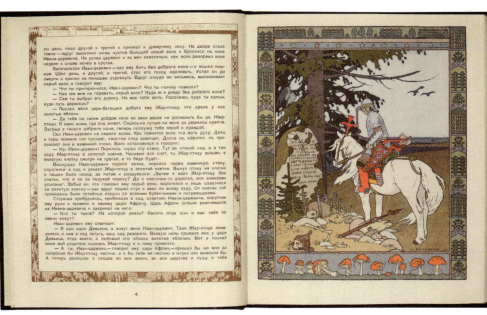

2.

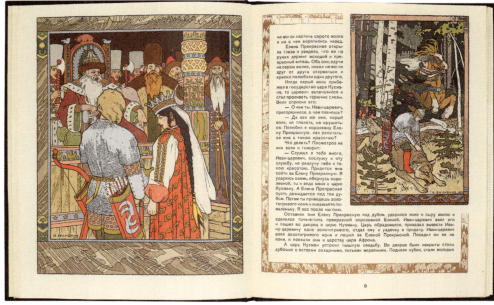

3.

From the reign of Tsar Peter the Great (1682–1725) to the beginning of the nineteenth century, most educated Russians looked to Europe, particularly France, for their art and literature. The French emperor Napoleon's invasion in 1812, however, prompted them to take a patriotic interest in their own culture. The artist Ivan Bilibin's illustrated tales encapsulate the peak of the renewed popularity of Russian tradition, art and history. His characters – including Ivan Tsarevich, the story's hero, who is helped in his adventures by the firebird and a wolf (1) – wear the tunics and robes of Russia before Peter's reign. Essential features of the Russian landscape are celebrated in depictions of mushrooms (2), the gathering of which is a traditional pursuit, and the silver birch forest. Each page has decorative borders populated with the bright colours, natural figures and geometric shapes also seen in traditional architecture and crafts. Once limited to the peasant village, these ornate shapes are here incorporated into decorative art for the wealthy. Previously dismissed by an elite audience as inconsequential, by the time Bilibin's traditionally illustrated tales were published, Russian art and literature were celebrated as the glory of the nation. [RH]

The First Part of the Life and Achievements of the Renowned Don Quixote de la Mancha

MIGUEL DE CERVANTES

PUBLISHED BY RANDOM HOUSE, NEW YORK, 1946

FACSIMILES OF ETCHINGS COLOURED BY HAND BY SALVADOR DALÍ

V&A L.2887-1947

A classic of Spanish literature, *Don Quixote* was written in the seventeenth century by Miguel de Cervantes. The novel follows the extraordinary adventures of the noble Don Quixote, who, fuelled by reading a surfeit of chivalric romances, decides to embark on his own misjudged quests. The Don charges at windmills (2) and sheep, thinking them enemies to vanquish; mistakes a barber's bowl for a magical helmet; and projects a fantasy of courtly love onto a local peasant woman (1). Salvador Dalí endowed this antiquated tale with his own modern understanding of the subconscious, using elements from Surrealism to interpret this eccentric and visionary tale.

The plains of La Mancha echo the stark deserts in Dalí's own works and are similarly populated with strange, unsettling scenes (3). Reality and the Don's delusions are both visible in Dalí's illustrations: fantasies are shown within a sectioned compartment inside the Don's head, seen via a cutaway, or appear as a vision in the air. A double-yoked egg, a favoured motif symbolizing two realities hidden in one, is also incorporated into the scene (4). Dalí's illustrations elevate the psychological elements of Cervantes's enigmatic novel, and present the Don's ridiculous escapades as a Surrealist exploration of the subconscious. [RH]

1.

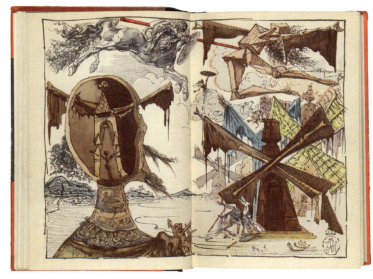

2.

3.

4.

LITERATURE 113

La Tempête

(*The Tempest*)

WILLIAM SHAKESPEARE

PRINTED IN PARIS, 1965

ILLUSTRATIONS BY LEONOR FINI

V&A 38041800179004

Many artists who have illustrated Shakespeare throughout the ages have also designed theatre costumes and sets. From Francis Hayman to Edward Gordon Craig, artists have recreated Shakespeare both on the stage and on the page. The Argentinian–Italian artist Leonor Fini designed the costumes for a 1954 film adaptation of *Romeo and Juliet*, among many other theatrical projects, before turning to *The Tempest*. Fini's characteristically hazy watercolours are as bedraggled as the characters who survive the shipwreck that opens the play. Shakespeare's curious late work, featuring the sorcerer Prospero and the spirit Ariel, was a fitting subject for Fini, whose art embraced both the magical and enigmatic aspects of Surrealism. In the play Prospero conjures up a vision of a masque to celebrate Miranda and Ferdinand's betrothal, performed by a trio of goddesses (3). Fini often featured powerful and sometimes erotic goddess figures in her own work, which subverted societal gender norms of passive femininity. Shakespeare's plays have been noted for his many strong female characters, even though these would have been played by boys on his stage. Fini herself used clothing, both male and female, to create characters for herself, declaring, 'I have always loved, and lived, my own theatre'. [RH]

1.

2.

3.

4.

Crow: From the Life and Songs of the Crow

TED HUGHES

PUBLISHED BY FABER AND FABER, LONDON, 1973

PRINTED FACSIMILES OF PEN-AND-INK
ILLUSTRATIONS BY LEONARD BASKIN

V&A L.7485-1979

1.

2.

3.

In the beginning was the word, and usually the images follow, as is seen in the other books in this chapter, but this is not the case for *Crow*, since the artist Leonard Baskin first approached the poet Ted Hughes for poems to complement his series of pen-and-ink drawings of crows. Hughes's earlier poetry had explored the rawness of nature, but Crow here is a more spiritual and elemental figure, stalking the pages of the book. A shape-shifter, he appears in the images as both a bird and a monstrous hybrid of creature and man (1 and 3), while in the poems he similarly displays intellect and brutality: 'He rested a dead vole in one hand / and grasped Relativity in the other.' Crow is a godlike figure who transverses time, bringing disorder to the Garden of Eden and travelling into space in a rocket. His essential darkness, corresponding to the ink of the text, reflects the void before creation and the finality of death (2). With a Christ-like duality, Crow also occupies the bodily world, viscerally experiencing a hunger and pain that is evident in his sometimes contorted, tortured posture. Hughes's poems bring a voice and mythology to the character, fully fleshing out Baskin's images. [RH]

(Compound Frame): Seven Poems by Emily Dickinson

PUBLISHED BY GEFN PRESS, LONDON, 1998

ARTIST'S BOOK BY SUSAN JOHANKNECHT, WITH ELIZABETH STEINER; WOODCUT AND LINOCUT PRINTS

V&A 38041998102065

Susan Johanknecht's artist's book *Compound Frame* attempts the seemingly impossible task of illustrating the infinite and the soul – recurring themes in the work of the American poet Emily Dickinson. This thoughtfully constructed book's experimentation with structure and surprising illustrative elements reflects the artfulness of Dickinson's poetic style and her playfulness with form. The poems that open and close the book express the infinite, beyond what is seen or conceived. This boundlessness is suggested by cut-outs showing the pages beyond; the transparent covers, bound by Steiner, imply an unfixed boundary to the book. The poems in the inner section pertain to the soul's containment within the body. The literal image of the ribcage seems inescapable, as thick ink makes it visible through the pages. Upon close examination the block print images contain scattered needles, and zips combined with nails. The book's title is drawn from the poem 'A Weight with Needles on the Pounds' (1862), in which the resistant soul is pierced. Nails and needles can both fix materials closely together but also pierce through them. The poems and illustrations both repay careful examination, as they explore how the enclosed soul can break out of its accustomed confines and experience the infinite. [RH]

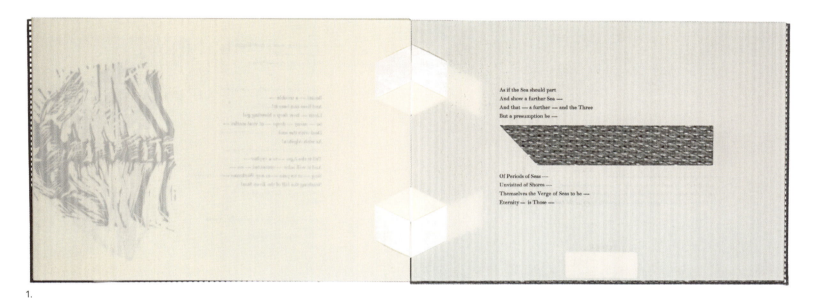

1.

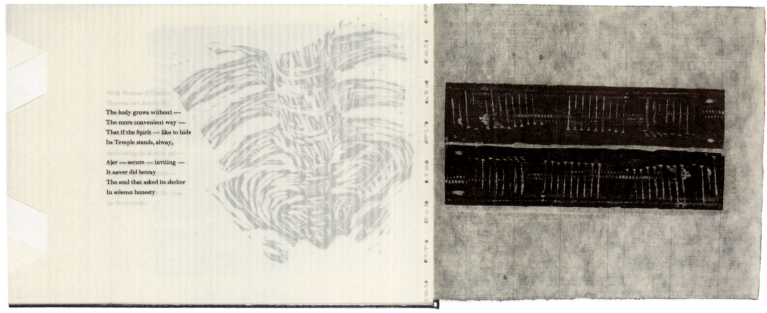

2.

Jane Eyre

CHARLOTTE BRONTË

PUBLISHED BY ENITHARMON EDITIONS,
LONDON, 2003

FACSIMILES OF LITHOGRAPHS AND PASTELS
BY PAULA REGO

V&A 38041003209350

Charlotte Brontë's novel *Jane Eyre* (1847) follows the eponymous heroine from girlhood to marriage with the enigmatic Mr Rochester (2). Jane's life is marked by struggles against a difficult upbringing, as she navigates the limited roles and behaviours allowed for women in nineteenth-century society. Jane does not allow this to dim her singular character, and her first-person narrative demonstrates a psychological complexity. The Portuguese-born artist Paula Rego's work explores similar themes, and her interest in the novel culminated in a series of lithographs and pastels accompanying selected episodes. Rego's dark, menacing style, often inhabited by grotesque figures, corresponds to the oppressive nature of the novel. Her unsettling illustrations capture Jane's experiences enduring a bullying family, harsh school life and the challenges of working as a governess (3). Rochester's first wife, Berthe, is sympathetically shown as a victim as much as a perpetrator of brutality (1). Imagination allows escape and Jane finds solace in Thomas Bewick's *History of British Birds*, admiring their freedom and natural habits (4). Rego's inventive and disconcerting illustration shows Jane literally consuming the book's content. Rego's illustrations respond to Brontë's exposure of women's endurance of the tyranny of social expectations, and how spark and imagination triumph over them. [RH]

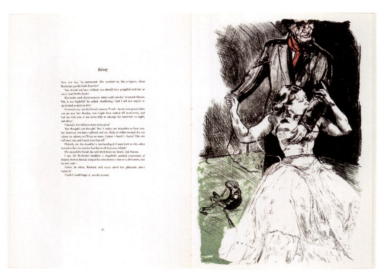

1.

2.

3.

4.

Ten Poems from Hafez

HAFEZ (XĀWJE SHAMS-OD-DĪN MOHAMMAD HĀFEZ-E SHĪRĀZĪ)

PUBLISHED BY SYLPH EDITIONS, LEWES, 2006

TRANSLATION AND ILLUSTRATIONS BY JILA PEACOCK

V&A 38041009021726

1.

Calligraphic shape poems are a traditional and celebrated art form in the Islamic world. Jila Peacock's *Ten Poems from Hafez* are truly 'pictures worth a thousand words'. She has formed the words of the esteemed fourteenth-century Persian Sufi poet into calligraphic representations of animals alluded to in the text. Hafez's love poems, or *ghazals*, contain a duality: he celebrates love and wine, while alluding to spirituality – the narrator yearns for both physical and spiritual sensations. Similarly, Peacock's images are simultaneously dynamic creatures and symbols of particular characteristics within the Sufi tradition, such as a lion's courage or a nightingale's yearning for god. Peacock uses a version of the *nast'aliq* script, a popular calligraphic style originally developed in fourteenth-century Persia. The fluidity of the line allowed her to create letter shapes that suggest a delicate fish's fin (1), an elegant deer's antlers (2) or the pattern of a butterfly's wing (3), while also allowing the text to remain legible. Peacock's dexterous shape poems ensure both word and image encourage readers to delight in the poetry of Hafez. [RH]

2.

3.

LITERATURE 119

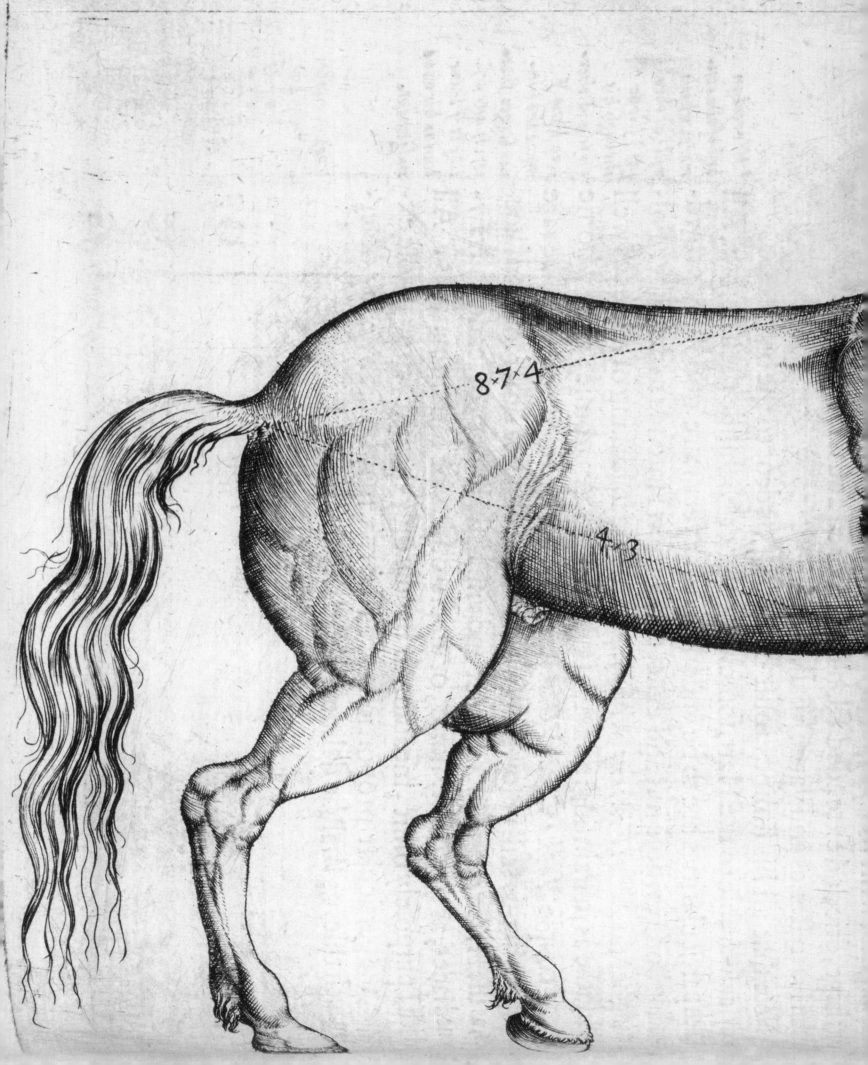

6
Art Making

Art Making

Emily Knight

Not all books about art making are illustrated. Publications detailing technical aspects of artistic production or theoretical perspectives do not necessarily require extensive visual information alongside their text. Nonetheless, illustrated books have played an essential role in the history of art and design practice. Whether as 'how-to' guides intended to inform practitioners (amateur or professional), documentary sources that record makers' processes and techniques, or theoretical justifications for different approaches, the combination of text and image allows the author to present an artistic concept to their target audience. Each book in this chapter sheds light on the motivations behind producing art-making books, whether to promote a particular style, secure the legacy of a specific artist, or capitalize on a popular technique or subject.

The instructive guide – describing the process of making a particular object type or employing a particular style – is the broadest and most significant category of illustrated books on art making. The publication of practical books demonstrates a motivation to share and circulate knowledge to a wide audience, but this concern has not always been paramount. Some historic manuals known in manuscript form were not published and were instead preserved by enthusiasts and collectors of a particular object type. Cipriano Piccolpasso's treatise *Li tre libri dell'arte del vasaio* is a unique and extraordinary survival that illustrates the process of making maiolica ware (a type of tin-glazed earthenware) in 16th-century Italy (below). Piccolpasso prepared his detailed description of the manufacture of maiolica at the request of Cardinal François de Touron (1489–1562), ambassador to the French King Henry II in

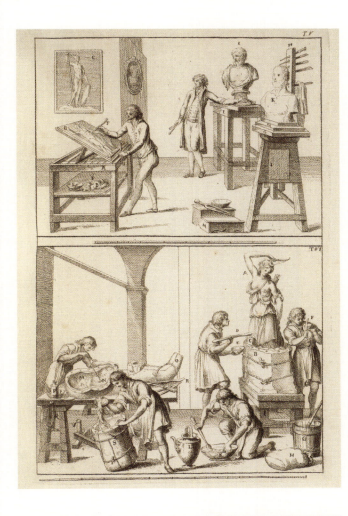

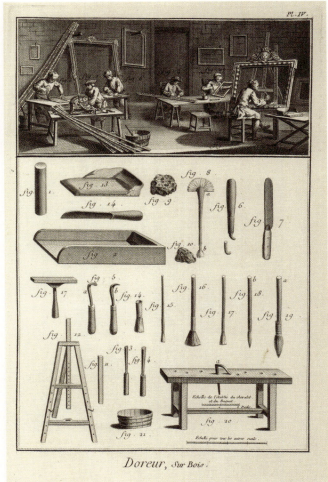

Italy. Originally, the intention was to publish the treatise but this was only achieved in the mid-19th century. Before then, the manuscript was passed between collectors until it made its way into the South Kensington Museum in 1860.

Throughout their history, instructive guides were variously intended to serve either an amateur or a professional market. Books in the former category were largely meant to encourage interest in an art or craft form, whereas those in the latter could often be used in the workshop or studio. The use of illustration was often crucial to the successful transmission of practical knowledge and skill. Francesco Carradori's *Istruzione elementare per gli studiosi della scultura* (1802) is a relatively rare and notable instance of a sculpture manual for art students. It includes detailed illustrations of the tools and techniques used by sculptors working in various media, as well as instructions for processes such as casting plaster or bronze (left). The additional benefit of these animated illustrations for the present-day reader is the window they offer into early nineteenth-century Italian sculpture workshops and the collaborative nature of this art form.

These kinds of monographic books about different materials, techniques and approaches were by no means the sole manner in which artistic instruction was disseminated. Dictionaries and encyclopedias such as Denis Diderot and Jean Le Rond d'Alembert's *Encyclopédie, ou Dictionnaire raisonné des sciences, des arts et des métiers* (1751–72) also provided illustrated descriptions of different arts and crafts. Initially envisaged as a straightforward translation of Ephraim Chambers' two-volume *Cyclopedia* (1728), its scope was expanded and the project became a mammoth undertaking with numerous contributing *encyclopédistes*. This was an Enlightenment attempt to define and categorize all human knowledge. For example, a detailed description of the work of a *doreur* (gilder) is accompanied by a depiction of a workshop

OPPOSITE
Manuscript pages from Cipriano Piccolpasso, *Li tre libri dell'arte del vasaio* (The three books of the potter's art), Castel Durante (now Urbania), *c.*1557
V&A MSL/1861/7446 (folios 15v–16r)

ABOVE LEFT
Etching from Francesco Carradori, *Istruzione elementare per gli studiosi della scultura* (Elementary education for students of sculpture), Florence, 1802
V&A 38041800426967

LEFT
'Doreur sur bois' (gilder on wood), engraving from Denis Diderot and Jean Le Rond d'Alembert (eds), *Encyclopédie, ou Dictionnaire raisonné des sciences, des arts et des métiers* (Encyclopedia, or Systematic dictionary of sciences, arts and crafts), vol. 3, Paris, 1763
V&A 38041800165870

ART MAKING 123

(p.123) in which several craftspeople carry out different stages of the water gilding process: coating a wooden frame with gesso (chalk mixed with glue), covering it with liquid clay, dampening the surface with water, applying gold leaf and, finally, burnishing the gold surface. This lively portrayal is accompanied by illustrations of the tools used at each stage.

Pattern books similarly hold an important position in the history of illustrated art-making books. These compilations of motifs or expressions of style often promote the work of an individual artist or designer, but, in many instances, they offer a more general sourcebook to be used by makers of various kinds (see Chapter 9). Martin Gerlach's *Die Pflanze in Kunst und Gewerbe* (1886), for example, presents the reader with a variety of stylistic approaches to the depiction of plants, for use in art and manufacturing (below). His aim for this richly illustrated publication was to encourage artists and designers to look back at styles of old to inspire their own work. In this way, Gerlach was following a long tradition of similar books that served an important function in workshops and studios around the world.

Illustrated art-making books could also serve a purpose beyond the concerns of the immediate artist, designer or maker. There is a smaller category of book that is primarily concerned with documenting different styles or techniques, rather than acting as a means of instruction or inspiration. Towards the end of the nineteenth century Nitya Gopal Mukerji, who worked for the Government of Bengal (part of the administration of the British Empire in India), was tasked with writing an in-depth study of the silk-weaving industry in Bengal. This was part of a long-standing scheme established in 1880 by the British colonial government to promote commerce in Indian goods and preserve various

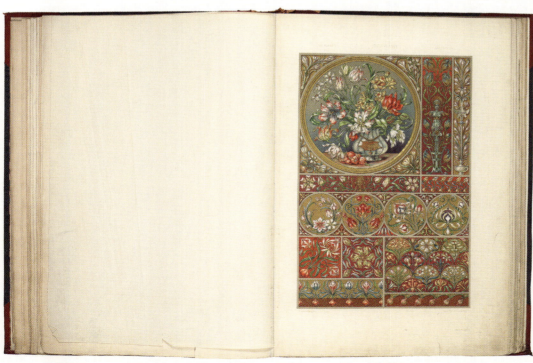

LEFT
Colour lithographs from Martin Gerlach, *Die Pflanze in Kunst und Gewerbe* (The plant in art and trade), vol. 1, Vienna, 1886
V&A 38041800367708

OPPOSITE TOP AND BOTTOM
Pages from Nitya Gopal Mukerji, *Monograph on the Silk Fabrics of Bengal*, Kolkata, 1903
V&A 246-1904

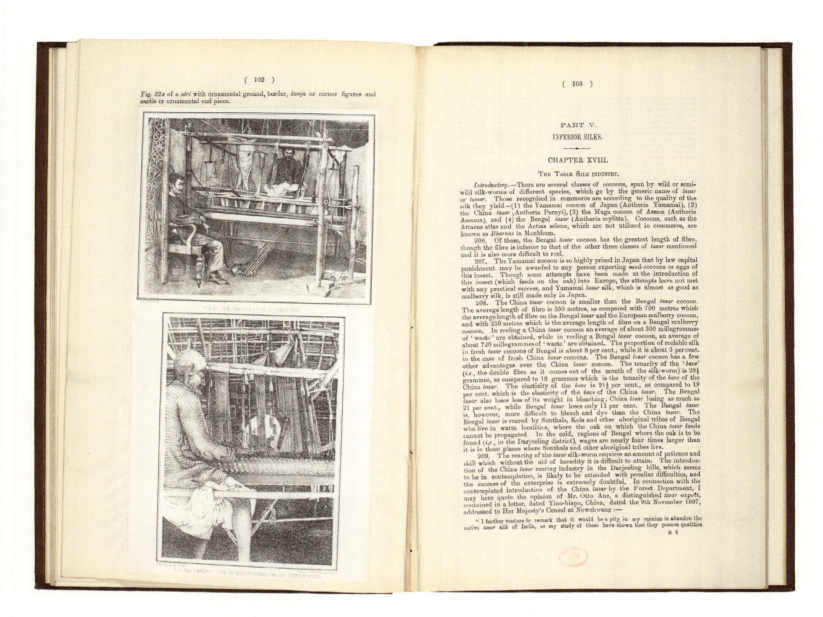

crafts. Mukerji's description of the production and trade of Bengali silk is accompanied by illustrations of equipment, documentary photographs of craftspeople at work and chromolithographic reproductions of colourful fabric designs (above and right).

In addition to books that deal with the transference of practical skills, numerous attempts have been made to elevate the status of the artist by providing theoretical justifications for a particular artistic approach. This was certainly the case in seventeenth-century France following the founding of the Académie Royale de Peinture et de Sculpture in 1648, which sought to distinguish itself from the established guild system. Charles Le Brun's lecture to the newly formed Académie on the expression of emotion in art was one such attempt (p.130). He aimed to underpin his thoughts on representation with theories about the physical location and manifestation of the 'passions'. Forging this association between art and philosophy enabled artists such as Le Brun to champion their profession and stake their claim as 'learned gentlemen' rather than mere artisans.

The inclusion of illustrations in books on art making illuminates working practices past and present, and expresses the concerns of artists and designers at particular moments in time. These illustrated books have made hugely significant contributions to the perpetuation and promotion of different styles, techniques, materials and approaches in countries across the globe and throughout history.

ART MAKING 125

Champ fleury

au quel est contenu lart et science de la deue et vraye proportion des lettres attiques, quon dit autrement lettres antiques et vulgairement lettres romaines, proportionnées selon le corps et visage humain

(Champ fleury, in which is contained the art and science of due and true proportion of Attic letters, which are otherwise called ancient letters and vulgarly Roman letters, proportioned according to the human body and face)

GEOFFROY TORY

PUBLISHED BY GEOFFROY TORY
AND GILES GOURMONT, PARIS, 1529

116 WOODCUTS

V&A 885-1895

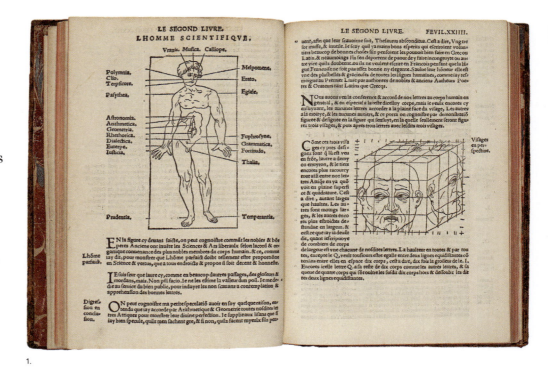

1.

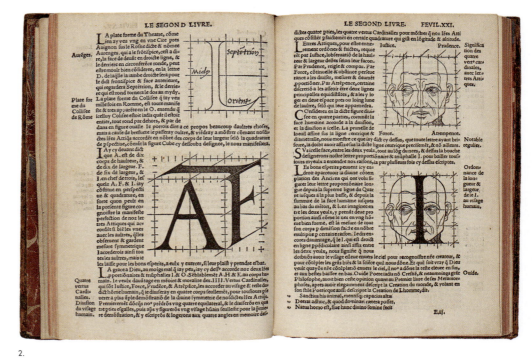

2.

This theoretical treatise on the design of Roman capital letters was produced by Geoffroy Tory, one of the main printers in Paris at the beginning of the sixteenth century. The book played a significant part in popularizing the Roman letter over the more prevalent Gothic. It was so successful that in 1531, François I honoured him with the title of Imprimeur du Roi (Printer to the King). In the text Tory proposes the use of accents, the apostrophe and the cedilla, as well as various punctuation marks. He also demonstrates how to draw letters with the help of geometrical aids and relates their proportions to those of the human body, interspersing the text with explanatory illustrations (1 and 2). While not unique in this regard – the German artist Albrecht Dürer, of whom Tory was critical, had similarly proposed this proportional analogy – Tory's book had a significant influence on typography. [EKn]

A Tracte Containing the Artes of Curious Paintinge Carvinge & Buildinge

GIOVANNI LOMAZZO
RICHARD HAYDOCK (TRANS.)

PRINTED FOR GIOVANNI LOMAZZO
BY JOSEPH BARNES, OXFORD, 1598

ENGRAVINGS

V&A 38041800158909

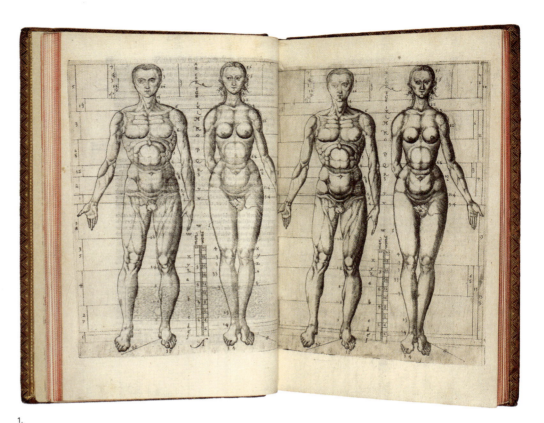

1.

2.

Richard Haydock's translation of the *trattato* (treatise) by the Italian painter Giovanni Lomazzo was one of the earliest texts of its kind to be published in English. Haydock included the first five books of the original publication only but listed the remaining two books in 'A Table of the Chapters of the whole volume'. The original Italian version was not published with illustrations but Haydock included engravings to enhance the text. Alongside biographies of contemporary artists, Lomazzo's treatise includes practical instruction on the making of art. Haydock's publication of the first book on proportion includes a number of illustrations including proportional measurements of the male and female forms (1), as well as those of a horse from both the side (2) and the back. [EKn]

ART MAKING

Chieh Tzu Yuan Hua Chuan

(*Manual of the Mustard Seed Garden*)

WANG GAI

PRINTED IN NANJING, 1701

COLOUR WOODBLOCK PRINTS AFTER LI LIUFANG

V&A E.4777 to 4780-1916

1.

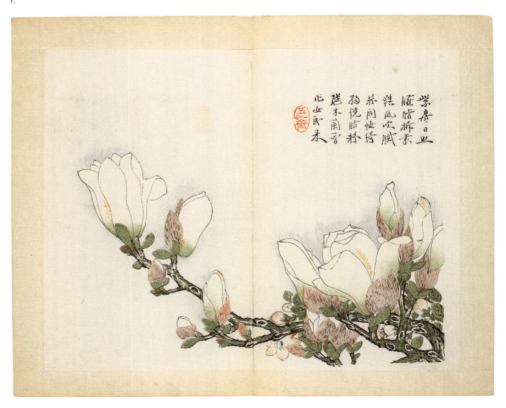

2.

This manual is a virtuoso performance of woodblock printing designed to provide technical knowledge and historical inspiration for aspiring painters. This three-part, multivolume publication took its name from Chieh Tzu Yuan, or the 'Mustard Seed Garden', the home of the playwright, novelist and publisher Li Yu. His son-in-law, Shen Xingyou, commissioned the painter Wang Gai to copy the teaching drawings of the late Ming dynasty painter Li Liufang and supplement them with further instruction in painting. The first album, which included a preface by Li Yu, focused on landscape painting and was so well received that two subsequent parts were produced. Part 2 concentrated on the 'four nobles': plum, orchid, bamboo and chrysanthemum. Part 3 (shown here) considered the depiction of flowers, birds and insects. As well as providing models for novice painters, each part also included brushwork techniques and examples of works by other famous painters. Many artists in China began their artistic training with this manual, and it also became hugely popular in Japan and Korea, being reprinted on numerous occasions. [EKn]

3.

4.

5.

Méthode pour apprendre à dessiner les passions, proposée dans une conférence sur l'expression générale, et particulière

(Method to learn how to draw the passions: proposed in a lecture on general and particular expressions)

CHARLES LE BRUN

PUBLISHED BY FRANÇOIS VAN DER PLAATS, AMSTERDAM, 1702

43 ENGRAVINGS

V&A 38041800890758

In 1668 Charles Le Brun delivered a lecture on the expression of emotion in art to the French Académie Royale de Peinture et de Sculpture. At the time he was the influential Master and Rector of the Académie, as well as the King's First Painter. This lecture was first published eight years after his death and includes numerous illustrations to help painters represent the passions of the soul through facial expressions, which include 'Hope' (1), 'Fright' and 'Extreme Despair' (2).

Le Brun argued that 'Expression ... marks the Motions of the Soul, and renders visible the Effects of Passion', an idea that was greatly indebted to the French philosopher René Descartes' *Les Passions de l'âme* (*Passions of the Soul*, 1649). During the seventeenth century a considerable amount of attention was devoted to the expression of emotion in art, but few could compete with Le Brun's systematic and extensive *méthode*, which proved particularly enduring. [EKn]

1.

2.

A New Book of Ornaments Consisting of Tables, Chimnies, Sconces, Spandels [sic], Clock Cases, Candle Stands, Chandeliers, Girondoles &c.

MATTHIAS LOCK AND HENRY COPLAND

PUBLISHED BY ROBERT SAYER, LONDON, 1768
(SECOND EDITION)

12 ENGRAVINGS INCLUDING TITLE PAGE

V&A E.5035 to 5046-1907

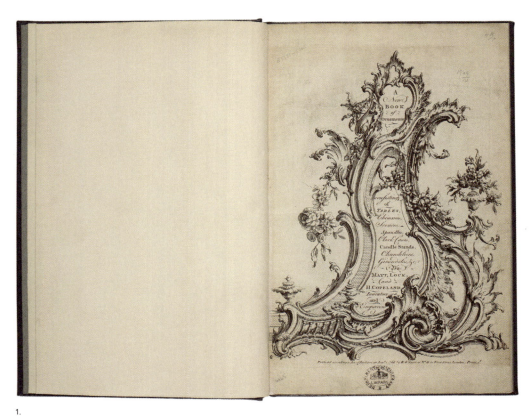

1.

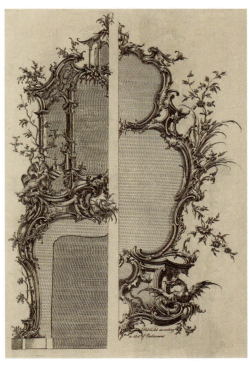

2.

3.

Matthias Lock and Henry Copland are credited with being the first Englishmen to publish Rococo ornament designs in Britain during the mid-eighteenth century. Individually and together, they produced several suites of engraved designs, including *A New Book of Ornaments* (first published in 1752 and again in 1768 with various alterations). This modest but important publication (1) preceded Thomas Chippendale's more ambitious compendium *The Gentleman and Cabinet-maker's Director* (1754, p.265), to which Lock contributed several furniture designs. In Lock and Copland's book, their whimsical and exuberant designs, replete with scrolling acanthus leaves and floral arrangements (2), also include Chinoiserie motifs, such as depictions of pagodas and musicians perched on C-shaped scrolls (3).

Unlike some of Lock's previous publications, which were often theoretical celebrations of the Rococo or 'French style', the designs in *A New Book of Ornaments* are for actual furniture forms, to be used by furniture designers and makers who served the new market for this imaginative style. [EKn]

Chōjū ryakugashiki

(Simplified drawings of birds and animals)

KUWAGATA KEISAI

PUBLISHED IN OSAKA, 1797

WOODBLOCK PRINTS IN SIX COLOURS

V&A E.14973-1886

1.

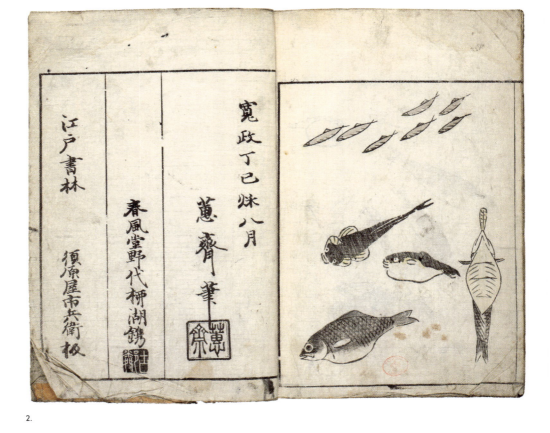

2.

3.

4.

Towards the end of the eighteenth century Kitao Masayoshi was official painter to the *daimyō* (feudal lord) of Tsuyama, Japan, working under the name Kuwagata Keisai. This was a high-status position and affected the kind of book illustration that Keisai could publish. In his newly elevated role he had to leave behind his practice of illustrating satirical books and instead produce instructional manuals such as this one. In this book he shows how to paint in the *ryakugashki* (abbreviated) style: specifically, the sparing use of simple lines to capture the various shapes of birds and animals. In this way, the corresponding stylistic section of the *Manual of the Mustard Seed Garden* (pp.128–9) was an important source for Keisai. [EKn]

Practical Perspective Exemplified on Landscapes

THOMAS NOBLE

PUBLISHED BY EDWARD ORME, LONDON, 1809
(SECOND EDITION, FIRST PUBLISHED 1805)

🫖

12 LEAVES OF AQUATINTS BY JOHN CLARK

V&A 38041800444689

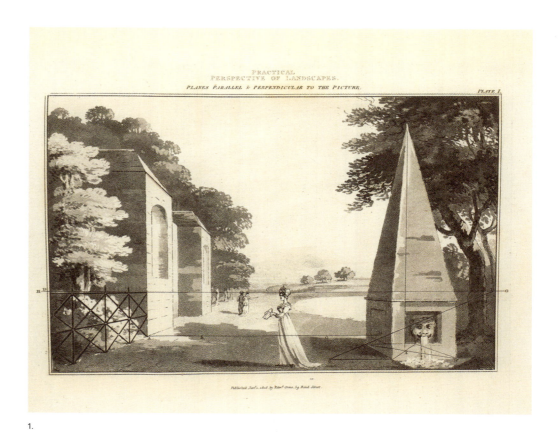

1.

Thomas Noble's richly illustrated manual follows a long tradition of didactic literature on the principles of perspective. Rather than unpicking the intricacies or lineage of this 'grammar' of art, Noble seeks to establish a set of fixed principles 'rendered simple and accessible'. Each principle is illustrated with an explanatory plate. These include 'Planes Parallel & Perpendicular to the Picture' (1) and 'Circular Objects Parallel to the Picture' (2). Noble was a teacher of perspective in Blackheath, London, where he offered lessons three times a week. This book would have been a suitable accompaniment to his teachings, as well as providing the interested amateur with the tools to develop their skill in depicting landscapes. The plates were produced by John Clark, after drawings probably made by Noble himself. The V&A holds seven of these preparatory drawings (E.1917 to 1923–19), which are surrounded by hand-written notes that were reproduced on separate pages in the book. [EKn]

2.

Erklärung der zu Goethe's Farbenlehre gehörigen Tafeln

(Theory of Colours)

JOHANN WOLFGANG VON GOETHE

PUBLISHED BY J.G. COTTA'SCHEN BUCHHANDLUNG, STUTTGART, 1810

V&A 38041800775405

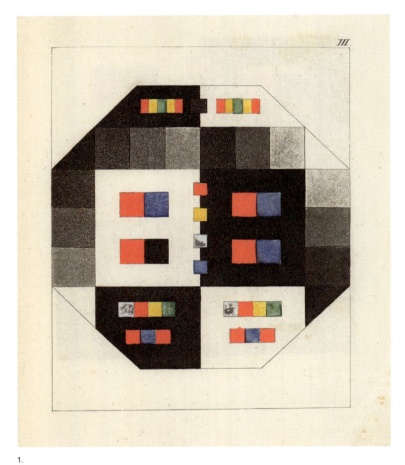

1.

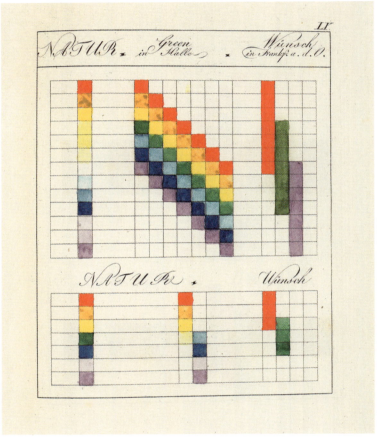

2.

In his *Theory of Colours*, Goethe attempted to record the way in which humans perceive colour. Unable to reconcile the observable qualities of light and colour with Sir Isaac Newton's theories, he proposed that colour was created through the interaction of light and dark. Goethe assigned specific qualities to colours which he categorized as either 'plus' or 'minus'. He proposed, for example, that orange was 'noble' and yellow 'good', while violet was 'unnecessary'. This provided artists with a system to convey a particular feeling or quality in a painting. In 1840, the book was translated into English by the painter Sir Charles Eastlake (later President of the Royal Academy and then Director of the National Gallery), who, while recognizing its flaws, found Goethe's observations on colour both useful and interesting. As a result, Goethe's text became highly influential within artistic communities in Britain and prompted artists such as J.M.W. Turner to experiment with colour in new ways. [EKn]

A Treatise on Landscape Painting and Effect in Water Colours

From the first rudiments to the finished picture: with examples in outline, effect, and colouring

DAVID COX

PRINTED BY J. TYLER, RATHBONE PLACE, FOR S. AND J. FULLER AT THE TEMPLE OF FANCY, RATHBONE PLACE, LONDON, 1814

52 ETCHINGS AND AQUATINTS BY RICHARD REEVE

V&A 677-1880

1.

2.

Following the publication of the artist William Gilpin's writings on 'that peculiar kind of beauty which is agreeable in a picture' and the landscape designer Uvedale Price's development of the term 'picturesque', professional and amateur artists alike developed a keen interest in capturing topographical views. The portability of watercolour paint, and its capacity to capture the delicate, subtle effects of the picturesque landscape, made it an ideal medium for touring artists. David Cox was both a successful watercolour artist and a key promoter and instructor in the technique. He became President of the Associated Artists in Water-Colour in 1810 and was elected Associate of the Society of Painters in Water-Colours in 1812. He began teaching in 1808 and went on to publish three books on artistic instruction, beginning with this treatise. Here, Cox describes the techniques used to fully exploit the effects of the medium. The text is accompanied by soft-ground etchings after his own drawings, as well as aquatints after his sepia studies and watercolours. The careful and clever use of these printmaking techniques to convey the effects of entirely different media speaks to the advances in reproductive printmaking during the late eighteenth and early nineteenth centuries. [EKn]

The Chemistry of Light and Photography, and their Application to Art, Science and Industry

HERMANN VOGEL

PUBLISHED BY H.S. KING & CO., LONDON, 1876

WOODCUT ILLUSTRATIONS AND PHOTOMECHANICAL PLATES

V&A L.2462-1986

Hermann Vogel was a highly influential photographer, scientist and professor at the Königliche Technische Hochschule (Royal Technical School) in Berlin. In 1873 he discovered dye sensitization, the technology behind colour photography, marking a major contribution to the history and development of the medium. As professor, he gave his students a firm grounding in the history and practical processes of photography, and kept them abreast of the latest scientific developments. This book similarly addresses these topics and includes a number of woodcut illustrations and specimen examples to explain the text. But as the title makes clear, Vogel was also concerned with the application of photography, including its relationship to art. In his chapter 'On the Correctness of Photographs' he encourages the reader to consider the aesthetic qualities of photography and makes a case for its use in disseminating reproductions of artworks. While Vogel makes a clear distinction between photography as a 'faithful picture of form' and art as 'a faithful picture of the character', he encourages his reader to seek the kind of truth achieved only in full by what he defines as art. [EKn]

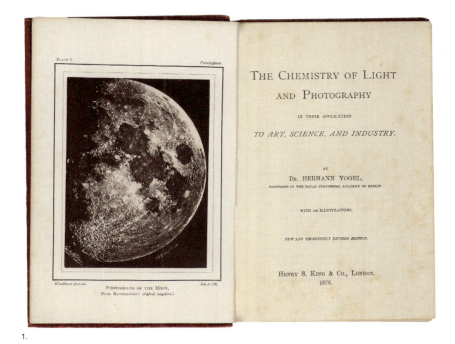

1.

2.

3.

ART MAKING 137

The Art and Craft of Lino Cutting and Printing

CLAUDE FLIGHT

PUBLISHED BY B.T. BATSFORD, LONDON, 1934

COLOUR ILLUSTRATIONS FROM LINOCUTS

V&A L.3650-1934

Claude Flight was an important advocate of linocutting in the early twentieth century. As well as organizing annual linocut exhibitions from 1929 to 1937, he published two books on the subject, the first in 1927 and the second, this book, in 1934. In 1926 he became a teacher of linocutting at the Grosvenor School of Modern Art in London and continued to champion the technique during his time as editor of the journal *Arts and Crafts Quarterly*. Flight believed that linocuts were ideally suited for capturing the dynamism of modern metropolitan life, the malleability of linoleum allowing for fluid cut lines and bold, simple forms. This is exemplified by the reproduction of his linocut *Speed* (*c*.1922) on the front cover of this book (1). Flight's depiction of vibrant red buses speeding along London's Regent Street, boldly delineated in vivid blue, exploit the simplicity of the medium. Flight considered linocut – requiring just a few inexpensive tools and materials – a truly democratic printmaking technique. [EKn]

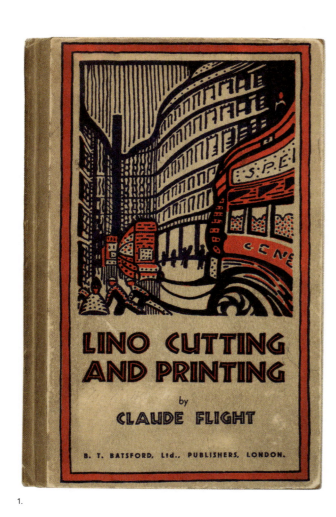

1.

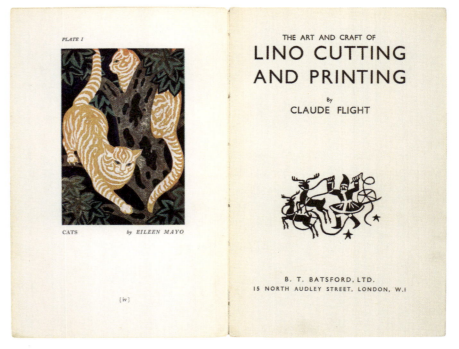

2.

3.

Process Compendium 2004–2010

CASEY REAS

PUBLISHED BY REAS STUDIO, LOS ANGELES, CALIFORNIA, 2010

V&A 38041011006061

The American artist Casey Reas created Processing, an open-source programming language and environment for the visual arts, with Ben Fry in 2001. This book is both a body of work and a record of its production, created entirely in Processing. Each work, or Process, in the series begins with a written text describing the interactions between forms such as 'circle', behaviours including 'move in a straight line', and elements, the combination of forms and behaviours. This is then translated into machine-readable code. The artwork produced by this process can be understood as the manifestation, or software interpretation, of the original written instructions. *Process Compendium 2004–2010* includes archive prints, images that capture alternative software interpretations, and stages in the development of forms. This is accompanied by a complete text description of each Process and an illustrated catalogue of all works created before publication in 2010. [EKn]

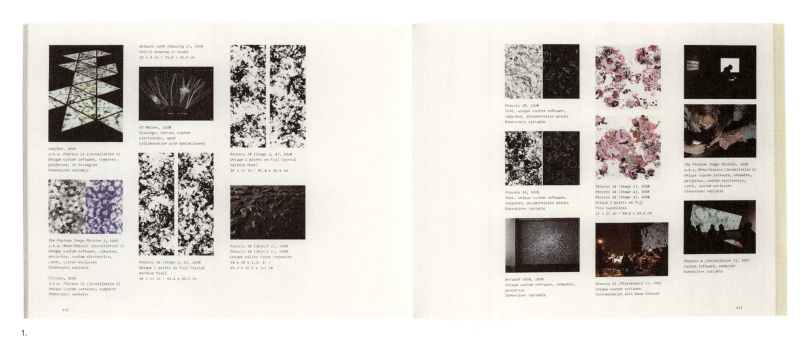

1.

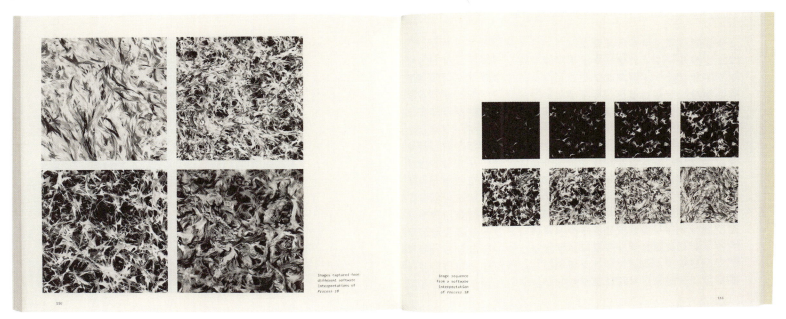

2.

ART MAKING 139

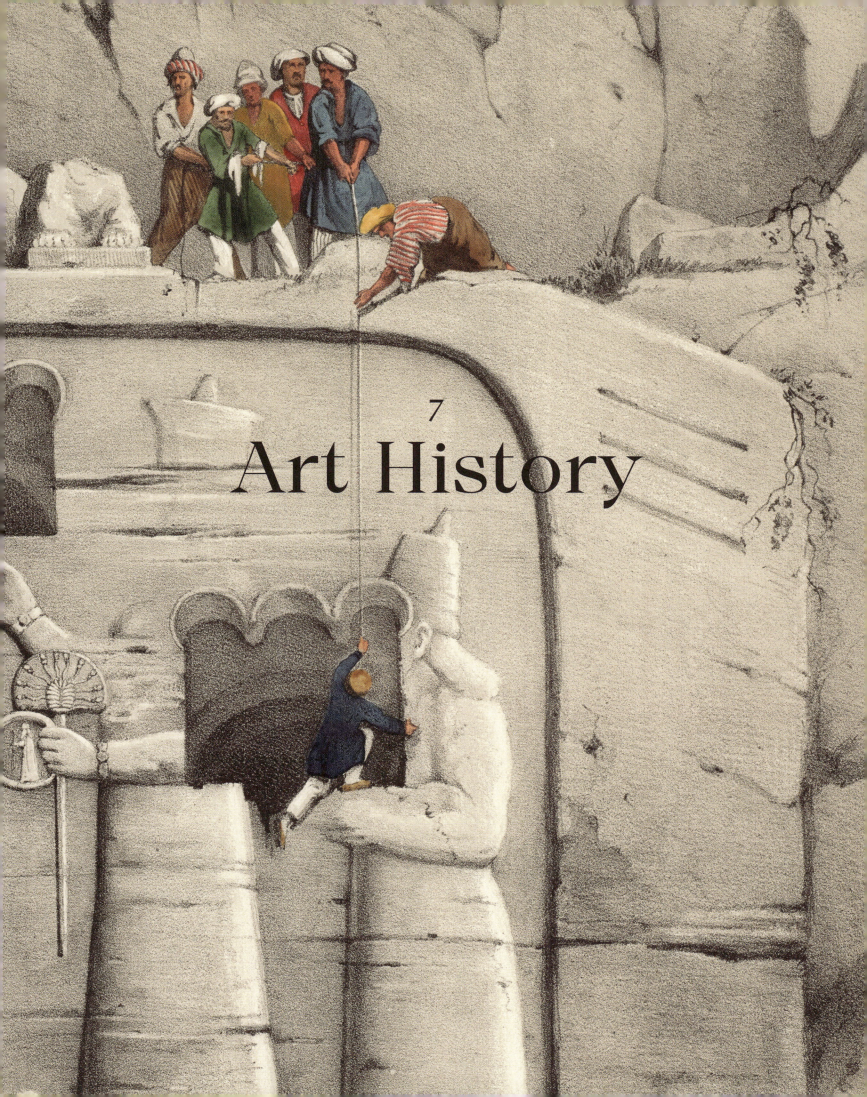

7
Art History

Art History

Elizabeth James

The main objects of art history are works of art, often themselves representational, and the challenge of art illustration is to render them with justice in another graphic medium. Good reproductions of artworks were always expensive to produce. There was a viable market for individual prints (such as, famously, Marcantonio Raimondi's after Raphael in the sixteenth century). Sometimes issued in groups, they might be bound in volumes with a title page, but were not really conceived as books. The early eighteenth-century project of Pierre Crozat and associates, to publish 'all the most beautiful paintings and drawings located in France' (p.147), has a claim to be the first art book in a modern sense, combining high-quality reproductions with a substantive historical text.

Contrary to the colourful impression given by the art shelves in any twenty-first-century bookshop, however, the relationship between text and outstanding illustration in art history books is not always self-evident. Many of the most important contributions to art history and theory in fact circulated with few or no reproductions, with artworks 'illustrated' instead through verbal description. The classical source to which all Western art history refers is Pliny's *Natural History* (first century CE). Pliny related the arts to their use of natural materials, but also discussed Greek and Roman artists and artworks in the framework of human history. His text survived unillustrated until the Renaissance, when its treasured status is evidenced by superbly illuminated manuscript copies (right). Giorgio Vasari's classic sixteenth-century survey of Renaissance art (p.146) instigated a biographical approach to art history that was frequently emulated. It was furnished with a remarkable series of artist portraits but no images of artworks.

In the eighteenth century Johann Joachim Winckelmann's *Geschichte der Kunst des Alterthums* (*History of the Art of Antiquity*) set out a new, systematic approach that would support all subsequent studies; his subjective and lyrical descriptions of artworks were also influential. Winckelmann selected key objects of personal significance to decorate his chapters' start and end, such as a vase (bearing a comic scene from a play) owned by a close friend, and an engraved gem that had been lost since it was depicted (opposite top). By contrast, lavish illustration was employed in the spectacular volumes presenting the British diplomat and antiquarian Sir William Hamilton's collection of classical painted vases (pp.148–9). The expense of the work turned out greater than Hamilton had anticipated: even selling the collection to the British Museum in London barely covered his costs.

A little later, Jean Baptiste Séroux d'Agincourt put resources into comprehensive rather than luxurious illustration, his survey of medieval art providing thousands of images, valuable both for academic and more general readers (p.150). The potential for attracting a popular audience is one of the strongest drivers for illustrated publishing, and the nineteenth century saw such a readership grow greatly in Europe and the anglophone

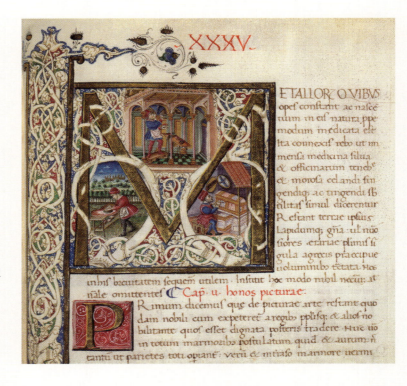

ABOVE
Historiated initial M showing painters at work, ink, bodycolour and gold on parchment, from Pliny the Elder, *Historia Naturalis* (*Natural History*), Rome, 1460s
V&A MSL/1896/1504

RIGHT
Johann Joachim Winckelmann, *Geschichte der Kunst des Alterthums* (*History of the Art of Antiquity*), engravings, Vienna, 1776 (first published Dresden, 1764)
V&A L.1652-1980

BELOW RIGHT
C. Drury E. Fortnum, *Maiolica* (South Kensington Museum Art Handbooks), wood engravings, London, 1876
V&A L.589-1880

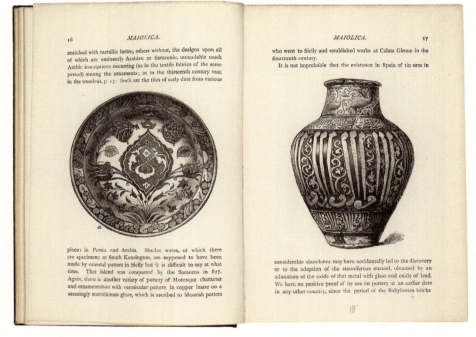

world. Furthermore, entrepreneurs and employees working in the burgeoning 'industrial arts' needed relevant education. From the 1840s chromolithography was employed, often to stunning effect, especially for decorative art objects, as exemplified in Jules Labarte's *Histoire des arts industriels* ... (pp.152–3). But traditionally skilled engravers in wood or metal could also render the qualities of such objects remarkably well, and with greater economy, in black and white (above). Publishing partnerships, such as that of Chapman and Hall with the South Kensington Museum (now the V&A), gave publishers access to images and authorial expertise: the resultant 'art handbooks' in turn fulfilled the new museum's educational mission.

As specialized discourse in art developed, images were sometimes required to convey data or support an argument rather than fully to represent an object. Makers' marks, for example, are fundamental to ceramics and silver experts. The connoisseurship that attributes authorship of paintings on the basis of stylistic quirks, championed by the assertive Giovanni Morelli, is served by small outline details (p.144, top). Heinrich Wölfflin employed comparative images to illustrate his influential theory of style: binaries such as linear, painterly; plane, recession; open, closed etc. underlay the epochs of art such as Classic, Renaissance and Baroque (p.144, bottom). He still preferred to illustrate some paintings with engravings rather than photographs, writing that 'the ordinary stock of reproductions is insufficient ... Everything looks blurred'.

In the nineteenth century photographic technologies served to improve existing reproductive media; in the twentieth the photographic image came to dominate. The impact of book illustration now depended on authors, editors and designers rather than artists and craftspeople. (Individual photographers emerged only occasionally as credited contributors.) The art of illustration became one of selecting, cropping and sequencing. In the 1930s European émigré art publishers brought

ART HISTORY

expertise in both production and design of photographic illustration, black-and-white and colour, to the anglophone world. Their powerful deployment of images, seen, for example, in Ludwig Goldscheider's *Michelangelo* (p.156), was widely influential, as in *The Voices of Silence* by the French writer André Malraux, with more than 600 captivating images and telling details (opposite top). Malraux famously declared the potential of art books, in this new age of reproduction, as a 'museum without walls', accessible to all.

The compact but comprehensive art history such as Malraux's, including some coverage beyond the Western world, proved a successful genre for publishers, combining popular appeal with textbook utility. *The Story of Art* by Ernst Gombrich (p.155) has been an enduring bestseller, as have the American *Art Through the Ages* by Helen Gardner (1926) and H.W. Janson's *History of Art* (1962), both long outliving their original authors. The same market of students and general readers was targeted, and successfully expanded by Thames & Hudson's World of Art monograph series (p.158).

From the 1960s art history was increasingly related to contemporary art criticism. Beyond academic and art world institutions new scholarship and interpretation revealed artists past and present overlooked through cultural prejudice, especially women and artists of colour in diaspora. New, and especially contentious, approaches typically lack resources for publications, but the well-illustrated catalogue for a 1989 London exhibition, *The Other Story: Afro-Asian Artists in Post-War Britain*, was a notable breakthrough (opposite bottom). With a titular allusion to Gombrich, the artist-curator Rasheed Araeen contested the stereotypes that limited these artists to being seen as 'native', 'exotic' or 'primitive'.

Exhibitions drew art publishing to a high point in the 1980s, with catalogues from well-funded institutions (among others, New York's Museum of Modern Art) combining new research and interpretation with excellent illustrations, of both objects and contextual material (p.157). Those standards became increasingly attainable, at affordable prices, thanks to factors including digital technologies and competitive colour printing in Asia. Conversely, fees for reproducing in-copyright works rose significantly: this can favour contemporary art, as living artists often waive such fees if they welcome the coverage. Art history is opening up in many ways, and visual fashions are changing, but the unimagined scale of pictures and words online has not yet abolished art books as a channel of choice for historians, curators, practitioners – and readers.

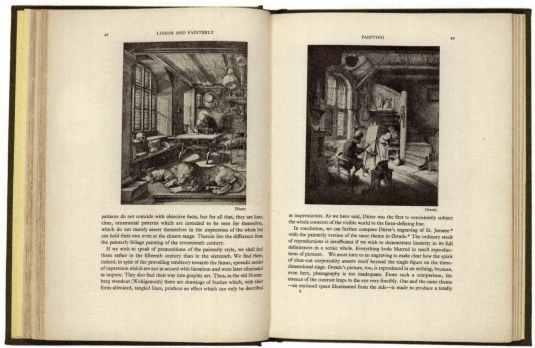

ABOVE
Giovanni Morelli, trans. Louise Richter, *Italian Masters in German Galleries*, London, 1883 (first published in German, Leipzig, 1880)
V&A 1090-1883

LEFT
Heinrich Wölfflin, trans. M.D. Hottinger, *Principles of Art History: the problem of the development of style in later art*, London, 1932 (first published in German, Munich, 1915)
V&A L.458-1932

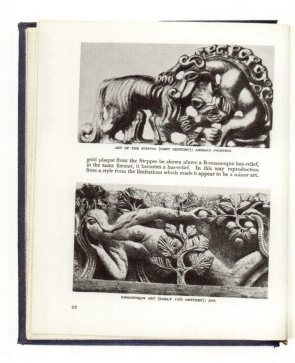

LEFT
André Malraux, trans. Stuart Gilbert, *The Voices of Silence*, Secker & Warburg, London, 1954 (first published in French, Paris, 1951)
V&A L.582-1954

BELOW
Lubaina Himid, 'The Carrot Piece', 1985, from Rasheed Araeen, *The Other Story: Afro-Asian Artists in Post-War Britain*, Hayward Gallery Publishing, London, 1989
V&A L.624-1990

Confronting the System

---

bring the work of Black women artists before the public, it will also provide a forum where artists can come together and discuss their work and share ideas, and point to their full potential as artists.'²⁵

Himid's oeuvre can be divided into three areas: it satirizes white society; it pokes fun at society's heroes (white/male artists); and it celebrates what she calls 'Black creativity'. The first two attempt both to expose the contradiction of the dominant culture in terms of its racism and patriarchy, and to confront the oppressiveness and inhumanity of the system through metaphors which are sometimes quite hilarious, while the latter seems to be an essential strategy for survival and celebration of life in a hostile environment.

One of the psychological effects of racism is to make its victim powerless. Himid is aware that a strategy is necessary that confronts the problem without accusing the other party of deliberate mischief: 'If I just decide in my head something that I know, and everybody knows, that white people are racist when it comes to making decisions about sharing things, what do you do — you could

Lubaina Himid
The Carrot Piece
1985

ART HISTORY 145

Le vite de' più eccellenti pittori, scultori et architetti

(Lives of the Most Eminent Painters, Sculptors and Architects)

GIORGIO VASARI

PUBLISHED BY I GIUNTI, FLORENCE, 1568
(SECOND EDITION)

3 VOLUMES, WOODCUTS BY 'MASTER CRISTOFANO'
AFTER VASARI'S DRAWINGS

V&A L.1304 to 1306-1903

1.

2.

3.

4.

Giorgio Vasari was a productive Italian Renaissance artist and architect, many of whose works survive (1). He is most widely known, though, for this book, *Le vite de' più eccellenti pittori, scultori et architetti*, a series of artists' biographies from Cimabue in the thirteenth century to Vasari's own time. Its format of collected lives, familiar from earlier classical, religious and other examples, became established as the traditional approach to art history.

Vasari's overarching narrative of progress, first published unillustrated in 1550, culminated in Michelangelo, then still living. Further contemporaries were added to this second edition, in which the artists' portraits also first appeared. Set in ornamental borders with appropriate allegorical figures, these extended the book's appeal and enhanced the artists' celebrity. It was a major achievement to source 144 images, from paintings or prints in different locations. Not all may be authentic, but only a handful eluded Vasari completely. His drawings, sometimes with subtle details added to emphasize personality or status, such as the rich brocade of Michelangelo's garment (2), were skilfully translated by an engraver whose (incomplete) name is recorded among several reproductive artists honoured in the biography of Marcantonio Raimondi (3). Vasari praises women artists, in the chapter on the sculptor Properzia de'Rossi (4). [EJ]

Recueil d'estampes d'après les plus beaux tableaux et d'après les plus beaux desseins qui sont en France, ...

... dans le cabinet du roy, dans celuy de Monseigneur le duc d'Orléans, & dans d'autres cabinets ...

(Collection of prints after the most beautiful paintings and drawings in France, in the cabinets of the king, the duc d'Orléans, and others ...)

PIERRE CROZAT AND PIERRE-JEAN MARIETTE

PRINTED [FOR PIERRE CROZAT] AT THE IMPRIMERIE ROYALE, PARIS, 1729 AND 1742

2 VOLUMES, ENGRAVINGS BY NICOLAS LE SUEUR, LOUIS DESPLACES, 'M. LE C[OMTE] DE C[AYLUS]' AND MANY OTHERS

V&A 38041800386211 and 38041800386229

1.

2.

Though titled as a collection of prints, and emerging from a culture of print collecting among elite connoisseurs, this is really the first fully illustrated art catalogue ever published. The men responsible were Pierre Crozat, a wealthy banker, Pierre-Jean Mariette, an upwardly mobile art dealer, and the comte de Caylus, also a competent engraver. They aimed at a full history of painting from the Renaissance, organized by regional traditions (or 'schools'), illustrated from French collections. Costly and ambitious, the project concluded after two volumes. Mariette's text discusses both the artworks reproduced and the virtuoso art of engraving employed. More than 30 engravers were engaged, copying often directly from the originals. They used a mixed technique: engraving to render form, with etching for free drawing and tone. Engraving was seen to have an affinity with the north Italian style of artists such as Girolamo Muziano, as in his painting *Christ Washing the Feet of the Apostles* (1), and etching with Venetian colourists like Titian. Drawings, by contrast, like Giuseppe Cesari's dramatic *Fall of Phaeton* (2), were rendered in near-facsimile, with a tone and highlights printed from woodblocks over etched outlines and shading. [EJ]

ART HISTORY 147

Collection of Etruscan, Greek and Roman Antiquities from the Cabinet of the Honble Wm Hamilton ...

PIERRE D'HANCARVILLE

PUBLISHED IN NAPLES, 1767–76, SECOND EDITION, FLORENCE, 1801–8

4 VOLUMES, ENGRAVINGS BY ANTOINE A. CARDON, CARMINE PIGNATARI AND OTHERS AFTER DRAWINGS BY GIUSEPPE BRACCI, EDMONDO BEAULIEU AND OTHERS, SOME COLOURED BY HAND

V&A 38041800495491 (1767–76, v2); 38041800386351, 38041800386369, 38041800386377 and 38041800386385 (1801–8, v1–4)

Alongside serving as a British diplomat in Naples, William Hamilton studied nature and collected art, mixing with artists and antiquarians. Several illustrated books resulted. The motives for publishing his Greek vases likely blended altruism, vanity and potential marketing: this collection was later purchased for the British Museum. Explicitly, he intended to provide design inspiration to British manufacturers. Different types of visual representation thus convey complete information about the vessels. Fine engravings portray the objects in the round (1); measured elevations detail their forms and proportions. The admired pictorial designs on the vases are shown flattened and hand-coloured: here, scenes from a boar hunt (2). Some are embellished with invented borders (4). Superbly designed and printed, the hefty four-volume catalogue is no mere pattern book. Produced for Hamilton by Pierre d'Hancarville, an adventurer and art historian, its lengthy texts vied with experts such as Winckelmann (with whom both men were acquainted) in describing the ancient development of 'those arts which embellish Society and render life more agreeable' and explaining their basic principles. Additional illustrations suggest the archaeological context; vignettes and decorative initials with learned visual allusions are 'explicated' as seriously as the putative subjects of the vase paintings (3). [EJ]

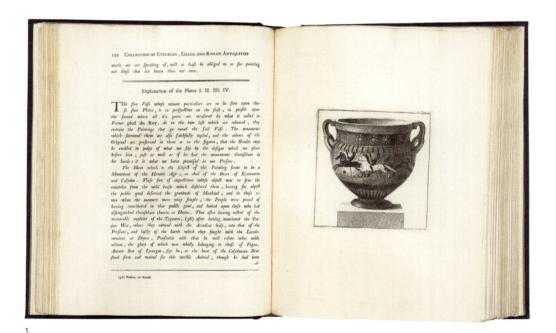

1.

2.

3.

4.

Histoire de l'art par les monumens, depuis sa décadence au IVe siècle jusqu'à son renouvellement au XVIe

(*History of Art by its Monuments, from its Decline in the Fourth Century to its Restoration in the Sixteenth*)

J.B.L.G. SÉROUX D'AGINCOURT

PUBLISHED BY TREUTTEL ET WÜRTZ, PARIS, 1810–23

6 VOLUMES, ENGRAVINGS BY GIACOMO MACCHIAVELLI, TOMMASO PIROLI AND OTHERS, AFTER DRAWINGS MOSTLY BY MACCHIAVELLI

V&A 38041800386278, 38041800386286, 38041800386294, 38041800386302, 38041800386310 and 38041800898215

Séroux d'Agincourt's work was original in the unprecedented scale and comprehensiveness of its visual reference, and its focus on the medieval period, then regarded as an era of 'decline'. He aimed to link Winckelmann's account of classical art (p.143) with the Renaissance. Chronological and national groupings of 'monuments' are combined with artistic schools, by then canonical classifications. More than 1,400 separately captioned architectural and art objects, miniaturized but legible, are illustrated in 325 plates; a two-volume essay weaves together the entire sequence. The work became a standard resource, especially on the decorative arts, throughout the nineteenth century.

The subjects were often copied from cited secondary sources. A conspectus of twelfth- to sixteenth-century 'Ultramontaine' (northern European) art draws on paintings – among them Hans Holbein's *Henry VIII* – prints, drawings, stained glass, manuscripts and the Bayeux Tapestry (3). The graphic style suits visual narratives and multi-scene artworks, and is sometimes enlivened by enlarged details, as in the fifteenth-century fresco *Marriage of the Virgin* by Lorenzo da Viterbo (2). Sixty-one plates devoted to manuscript illumination include early copies of Dante's *Divine Comedy* (1): the poet's descriptions of nature are praised as 'real pictures', and his influence on the visual arts is emphasized. [EJ]

1.

2.

3.

A Second Series of the Monuments of Nineveh

Including bas-reliefs from the palace of Sennacherib and bronzes from the ruins of Nimroud, from drawings made on the spot, during a second expedition to Assyria

AUSTEN HENRY LAYARD

PUBLISHED BY JOHN MURRAY, LONDON, 1853

71 LEAVES OF PLATES, CHROMOLITHOGRAPHS, DRAWN ON THE STONE BY LUDWIG GRUNER AFTER ORIGINALS BY THE AUTHOR AND OTHERS

V&A Forster 5196

1.

2.

3.

New art history is created when new objects are discovered. This large-format volume is a series of annotated plates supplementing A.H. Layard's *Discoveries in the Ruins of Nineveh and Babylon ...* (1853), which combined discoveries from his excavations with a travel and adventure memoir. The search for biblical sites in Assyria (in present-day Iraq) was started in the 1840s by French archaeologists. When Layard got involved, through diplomatic patronage, he saw high aesthetic merit and technical achievement in the hieratic figures (2), looming lamassu (winged bulls with human faces) and narrative relief friezes of Assyrian sculpture. Efficiently mobilizing local labour, he removed and transported many objects to the British Museum, London, where they proved highly popular with visitors. Yet some of the museum authorities, invested in the supremacy of Greek sculpture, called them merely 'curious' and 'bad art'. They funded Layard's 'second expedition', but meagrely, and declined to publish his illustrations, hence the trade publisher John Murray, which had issued his first title, *Nineveh and its Remains* (1849), a bestseller, took them on. The *Second Series* too was highly successful, selling 12,000 copies in the first year. The magnificent rock sculptures are aptly rendered by stone lithography (3). The volume is prefaced with a pictorial 'restoration' of the Nimroud palaces (1), and also includes site views and colourful artefacts.[EJ]

Histoire des arts industriels au moyen âge et à l'époque de la renaissance: album

(History of industrial arts in the Middle Ages and the Renaissance era: album)

JULES LABARTE

PUBLISHED BY A. MOREL ET CIE, PARIS, 1864

2 VOLUMES, 150 PLATES, CHROMOLITHOGRAPHS; PLATES PRINTED BY IMPRIMERIE LITHOGRAPHIQUE DE LEMERCIER

V&A 38041800386245 and 38041800386252

1.

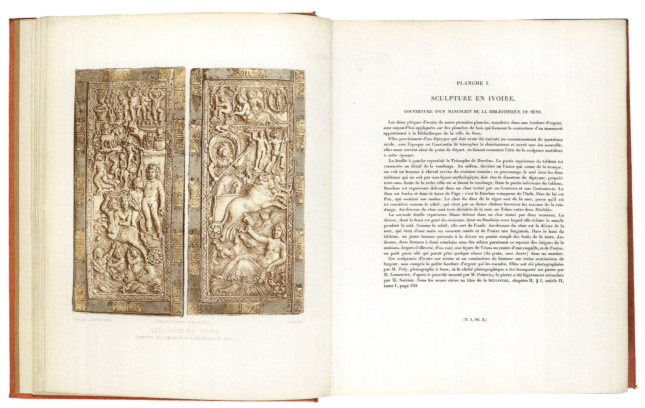

2.

Jules Labarte's history of the industrial, or decorative, arts was a landmark in art-historical publishing, for information and illustrations. Labarte's thorough scholarship was acquired while cataloguing his wealthy father-in-law's art collection. His four-volume main text was illustrated sparsely, on Winckelmann's model (p.143), with woodcuts at the beginning and end of each chapter, intended mainly, wrote Labarte self-deprecatingly, to diminish his text's 'aridity'. But he had means to supplement this with two large 'albums' of superbly printed chromolithographs. Their extra significance in illustration history lies in Labarte's use of photographic processes, intended to maximize the accuracy of images he regarded as 'evidence to support our story'.

The captions explain the image production as well as the object depicted, naming individuals who provided photographs, verified colours, or made drawings, from originals or reproductions, as well as the printer. The 'Poitevin process' was a photographic technique, for transferring images directly to the lithographic stone.

Labarte met a keen readership: in an age when manufacturers looked to aesthetics to help sell their products (see Chapter 11), historic decorative objects were of wider than antiquarian interest. His books remained key references in a burgeoning field of decorative arts publications. [EJ]

ART HISTORY 153

Popular Art in Britain

Cover title: *Popular English Art*

NOEL CARRINGTON AND CLARKE HUTTON

PUBLISHED BY PENGUIN BOOKS, LONDON AND NEW YORK, 1945

PRINTED BY R. & R. CLARK LTD, EDINBURGH (TEXT); 32 PLATES MADE AND PRINTED BY W.S. COWELL LTD, IPSWICH

V&A 38041800997876

1.

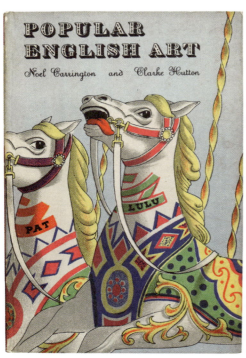

2.

3.

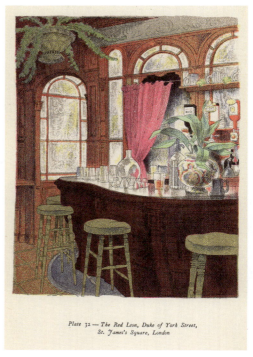

4.

The identity and success of Penguin Books were based on unillustrated paperbacks, yet within a decade of its foundation (and despite the Second World War) several colour initiatives were launched, including monographs on modern painters, and the King Penguin series (p.18). Mainly non-fiction, these were either edited selections from historic British illustrated books or newly commissioned titles, as attractive as children's picture books but with erudite texts (1).

At a shilling each they were immediately popular.

The war stimulated public interest in Britain's heritage and traditions, and several writers of the period were investigating popular and traditional arts and crafts. Carrington attributes their decline, since 'the Middle Ages, when all was popular', to the increasing academicism of art patronage, and implicitly to social stratification. Rather than a cathedral or a stately home, the palace of culture invoked in the final image is the egalitarian London pub, where everyone is welcome (4).

Noel Carrington and the illustrator Clarke Hutton had previously collaborated on creating the Puffin Picture imprint for Penguin (p.61). The objects are fittingly illustrated by Hutton's drawings, rather than photographs: Carrington refers to him as 'something of a genuine popular artist himself'. [EJ]

The Story of Art

E.H. GOMBRICH

PUBLISHED BY PHAIDON PRESS, LONDON, 1950

370 ILLUSTRATIONS; PRINTED BY GEO. GIBBONS LTD, LEICESTER; COLOUR PLATES PRINTED BY HUNT BARNARD AND CO., LEICESTER

V&A L.3150-1949

Its publisher claims that *The Story of Art* is 'the most famous and popular book on art ever published'. A bestseller for 70 years, its title is frequently referenced in those of other art books and reflects the fact that Gombrich, a learned academic, was aiming at a young audience (he had previously written a children's history of the world). The resulting infinitely knowledgeable, yet empathetic and accessible tone is one secret of the book's success, the approach to illustrations another. *The Story of Art* largely eschews the poetic deployment of images found in its near-contemporary, Malraux's *The Voices of Silence* (p.145) but illustrations are indispensable to its scheme. Gombrich omitted discussion of any work he could not show, and worked closely with the publisher to optimize the images' placement in relation to text. This was harder to achieve for colour illustrations, the placement of which was constrained by the processes involved when, as here, they were integral with the text block, not inserts or pasted in. In post-war austerity circumstances, just 21 were selected and given to a separate, specialist colour printer, providing moments of visual luxury. Successive editions became ever more colourful. [EJ]

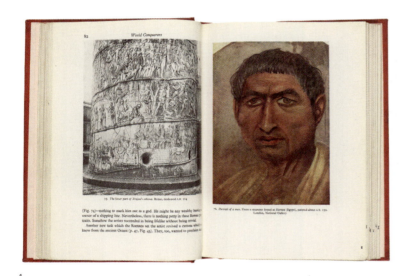

1.

2.

3.

4.

ART HISTORY 155

Michelangelo: Paintings, Sculptures, Architecture

LUDWIG GOLDSCHEIDER

PUBLISHED BY PHAIDON PRESS, LONDON, 1953

'DESIGNED BY THE AUTHOR'; TEXT AND COLOUR PLATES PRINTED BY HUNT BARNARD AND CO., LEICESTER; MONOCHROME PLATES BY CLARKE AND SHERWELL LTD, NORTHAMPTON

V&A L.2033-1953

1.

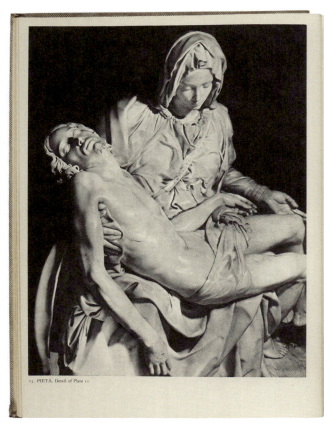
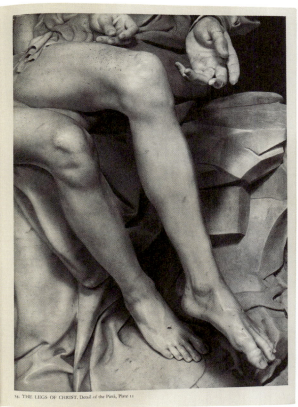

2.

Ludwig Goldscheider co-founded and directed the Phaidon Press, relocating from Vienna to London in 1938. He was a knowledgeable connoisseur and art historian who wrote numerous books, but his greatest satisfaction, reportedly, was in book design. His previous publications, including two large-scale volumes on Michelangelo, featured breathtaking sequences of photogravure reproductions. This catalogue raisonné of Michelangelo's complete works similarly deploys superb photographs, many newly commissioned. They convey visual information with detail and clarity, and Goldscheider's illustrative genius is in the way they are placed and juxtaposed on and across the pages, infused with drama and pathos (2). High-quality illustration, including colour, was a Phaidon hallmark. Here, fine colour reproductions of paintings were separately printed and tipped in (even though the same firm printed the text), allowing maximum quality control (1).

Goldscheider's text, though steeped in scholarship, is not lengthy, primarily (and usefully) detailing the bibliography: the images rule. In 1938 he had gone so far as to declare that 'the history of art has no connection with artistic experience': his *Art Without Epoch* was a pure photo-book, sequencing heterogenous objects to elicit an aesthetic and emotional experience equivalent to that of an art gallery visit, yet truly native to the book form. [EJ]

"Primitivism" in 20th Century Art

Affinity of the tribal and the modern

WILLIAM RUBIN (ED.)

PUBLISHED BY THE MUSEUM OF MODERN ART, NEW YORK, 1984

2 VOLUMES, 1087 ILLUSTRATIONS; PRINTED AND BOUND BY ARNOLDO MONDADORI, VERONA

V&A L.5339a to b-1985

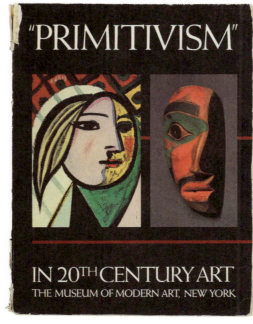
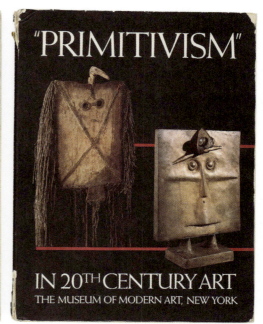

1.

2.

The Museum of Modern Art (MoMA) in New York is renowned for distinguished and well-designed publications. It also has a tradition of exhibiting objects from non-Western, prehistoric and folk cultures, in relation to modern art. While Pablo Picasso's use of African masks was well known, the curators and authors of *"Primitivism"* explained the ways in which many avant-garde European and American artists encountered tribal arts and cultures of Africa, Oceania and the Indigenous people in America. Their influences are shown to pervade key art movements, from Surrealism to Land Art. The value of the 'affinities' is strongly affirmed, and differentiated from the dangerous 'primitivism' within some unpleasant Western ideologies. Both text and image render the subject compelling. The themes are conveyed in numerous illustrations, efficiently placed with relevant text. Archive photographs reveal artists among their personal collections (2).

Self-aware scare-quotes around the term 'primitivism' did not protect the show from criticism for subordinating tribal objects to canonical modern art. The catalogue lacked adequate discussion of them; no index aided comparison of items from the same origin. Some were illustrated but not discussed: mere 'window dressing', said one reviewer. Yet their powerful aesthetic presence in these pages fostered respect.

Black Art and Culture in the 20th Century

RICHARD J. POWELL

PUBLISHED BY THAMES & HUDSON,
LONDON AND NEW YORK, 1997

❦

176 ILLUSTRATIONS, 31 IN COLOUR; PRINTED
AND BOUND BY C.S. GRAPHICS, SINGAPORE

V&A 38041997049010

The Viennese founders of Thames & Hudson, Walter and Eva Neurath, had experience and talent in design and production of illustrated books. Citing André Malraux's 'museum without walls', their business plan was to democratize art, and to operate internationally. The World of Art series, its strong visual brand combined with varied subject matter, grew highly successful from the 1960s as art education expanded and mass media promoted cultural pursuits. Its reach was wider than that of other respected but more academic series, such as the Pelican History of Art.

Titles are often highly topical and based on original research. At its first appearance this book, by an African-American art historian (and trained artist), was cutting-edge in its cultural-history approach. Focusing on works rather than individuals, it surveyed 'the changing visual representations of black culture', predominantly by Black artists in diaspora, particularly in America. It also considered media not yet then generally associated with Black creativity, such as video, digital and performance art.

Illustrations are numerous, finely printed and generally placed close to the relevant text. The relatively few colour images are large and well deployed. This successful book has had two later editions, each with expanded text and more pictures. [EJ]

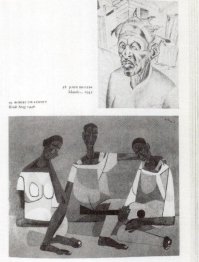

1.

3.

2.

Cuba Talks: Interviews with 28 Contemporary Artists

JÉRÔME SANS AND LAURA SALAS REDONDO (EDS)

PUBLISHED BY RIZZOLI INTERNATIONAL, NEW YORK, 2019

V&A 38041021007216

Where does art history end and the present begin? *Cuba Talks* is an arresting example of the vast field of books documenting contemporary art, and of the welcome emergence of voices from the Global South. The interviewees reflect on negotiations around artistic careers considering Cuba's difficult history and future uncertainties, and comment on their relation to art history and the global scene. Osvaldo Gonzalez, known for large-scale installations made with sticky tape, cites Giorgio Morandi, Paul Cézanne and David Hockney among his influences, while the young performance artist Carlos Martiel finds Cuba's art scene 'very first-world-centric, for a context that is anything but'. The interview format and visual style derive from magazine design. The book is printed in colour throughout (and even adds an extravagant cerise border to plain text pages). The illustrations do full justice to impressive artworks, from Elizabeth Cervino's installations, pile-carpeting a gallery with coconut fibres or whitewashing an entire street (1), to a looming but fragmentary head of the Cuban leader Fidel Castro constructed from found door hinges by Yoan Capote (2), or the celebrated Kcho's monumental assemblages (3). But the portraits are in charismatic black and white: we are still in Vasari's world of artists (4). [EJ]

1.

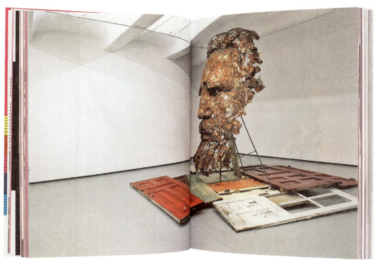

2.

3.

4.

8
Architecture

Architecture

Olivia Horsfall Turner

Buildings are stationary; books are not. The illustrated architecture book, therefore, transforms its subject from a static to a mobile one. Existing and imagined buildings spread their influence by projecting their image into different contexts through woodcuts, engravings, chromolithographs and photographs. As well as defying geography, illustrated architecture books confound practical limitations of size, compressing not just individual buildings and monuments but whole sites and masterplans into a small compass. Furthermore, illustrated architecture books transcend the limits of linear time by conjuring up as-yet-unbuilt edifices, recreating buildings that are no longer extant, or recording for posterity the ephemeral forms of triumphal arches and other fleeting scenography.

The National Art Library (NAL) might not immediately spring to mind as a repository of architecture books, in comparison to the well-known collections of the Royal Institute of British Architects or the Canadian Centre for Architecture, for example. However, its shelves contain an impressive range, from the classical canon of Renaissance treatises to the staples of the eighteenth-century country-house library, and rare volumes on planning and interior decoration, as well as contemporary architectural publications.

Perhaps predictably, the historical collection focuses on books from the Western European tradition. In part, this arises from the fact that the flourishing of the illustrated architecture book was driven by the development of mechanical moveable type by Johann Gutenberg in about 1450 and the rediscovery during the fifteenth century of the ancient past through its remaining fabric in Rome. Most architectural treatises, therefore, originated in Italy before the form was taken up across the rest of Western Europe. It was also an Italian architect, Andrea Palladio, who in the sixteenth century produced the highly influential *I quattro libri dell'architettura* (1570; right) in which he devised a way of presenting plans, sections and elevations within the same image – it went through 50 editions in the century following its initial publication.

Early architecture books in the Eastern tradition – for example, the oldest extant Chinese technical manual on building, the *Yingzao fashi* (*Treatise on Architectural Methods or State Building Standards*), published in 1103, or the *buke hinagata* (manuals of military architecture) and *yashiki hinagata* (manuals of domestic architecture), published over many centuries in Japan – do not feature in the NAL's holdings. Contemporary architecture books, however, are collected from around the globe, such as *S, M, L, XL* (1995) by the Dutch architect Rem Koolhaas and the Canadian designer Bruce Mau (opposite top), and *Made in Tokyo: Guide Book* (2001) by the Tokyo-based architects Atelier Bow-Wow.

Illustrated architecture books have been created for and used by a wide spectrum of readers, from artisans to travellers, historians and patrons, in an assortment of places, including the scholar's study, the

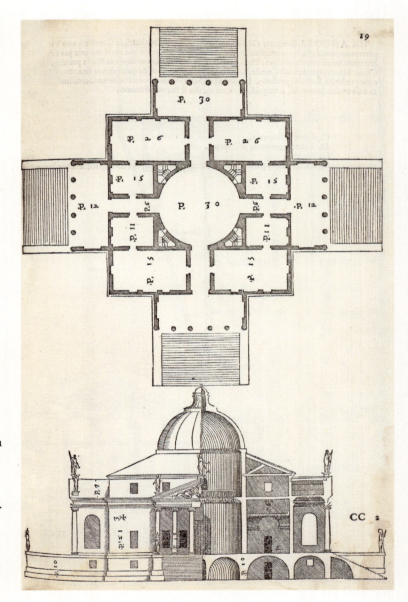

ABOVE
Andrea Palladio, Villa Almerico Capra (La Rotonda), from
I quattro libri dell'architettura
(*The Four Books of Architecture*),
Venice, 1570
V&A 38041800122202

architect's office, the builder's workshop, the gentleman's library and the designer's studio. Architecture books were often produced to provide practical advice: how to design, construct or ornament a building, or decorate an interior. Alternatively, they might document architecture from a particular period in history, from a specific place or by a certain architect. Often architects have produced them as self-promotional tools. The NAL is rich in all the major types of architectural book: treatises, archaeological accounts, monographs and pattern books, as well as others that defy neat categorization, such as Johann Steingruber's *Architectonisches Alphabet* (1773, below), which presents designs for buildings in the shapes of letters of the alphabet, or *Balbus* (1944), a children's rainbow-coloured picture book of architectural styles (p.164). Architecture's allied fields of perspective, geometry, surveying, fortifications, gardening, topography and antiquarianism also feature in the NAL's holdings but fall beyond the scope of this chapter.

ABOVE
OMA (Office for Metropolitan Architecture), model for La Défense Masterplan, Paris, from Rem Koolhaas and Bruce Mau, *S, M, L, XL*, Monacelli Press, New York, 1998 (second edition)
V&A 38041001084631

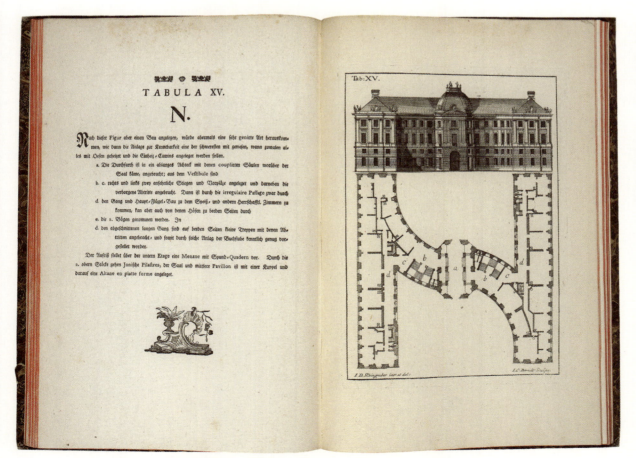

LEFT
Johann Steingruber, design for a building in the shape of the letter N, engraving by J.C. Berndt from *Architectonisches Alphabet* (Architectural alphabet), Schwabach, 1773
V&A 38041800393050

The purpose of illustrations within architecture books is often to make complex ideas comprehensible. Questions of geometry, construction, planning and style are given greater clarity through visual depiction. Images allow for more detail and technical specificity than a reader can digest in written form. The specific challenge of architectural books is to convey in two dimensions something that, in reality, is experienced in three dimensions. Architectural representation has evolved to offer conventions through which even the most complex building can be shown on paper: the plan (the building's footprint), the elevation (the vertical surfaces, either exterior or interior) and the section (a vertical slice through the structure). Architectural images are shown either in orthogonal view, that is, straight on, at 90 degrees to the vertical, or in perspective, which also represents depth. Orthogonal views produced by architects or their drawing assistants often show the building excised from its context to focus on the architecture's essential qualities. Such images are not only capable of conveying detailed information but also create a visual rhetoric of accuracy, leading the viewer to believe in the images as objective, even if they depart from reality or represent an unrealized building. Perspectives, created by artists as much as by architects, often include the setting of the building and conjure up the atmosphere of a place. The possibilities of architectural representation expanded rapidly in the twentieth century and traditional modes of hand-drawing have now been joined and enriched by photography and computer-aided digital design.

Though primarily intended to instruct or inform, illustrated books have performed a role in architectural culture beyond simply circulating information. Many publication projects have been driven by the desire not only to share knowledge but also to control it. The printed treatises of the late fifteenth and sixteenth centuries helped establish architecture as a liberal art distinct from the applied craft of building, thereby elevating its status and that of its practitioners. Architecture books contributed to the professionalization of the architect: rather than learning how to build solely through a practical apprenticeship, the architect acquired skill equally through book learning. Therefore, the decline of the medieval system of masons' lodges, where expertise was handed down through oral tradition and manuscript lodge books, and the rise of the illustrated architecture book are closely related. Given that the majority of proposed architectural projects remain unrealized, publication has always offered an important way for an architect to present their designs to a public audience. Despite the radical changes in the practice of architecture since Vitruvius's day (opposite), this continues to be the case.

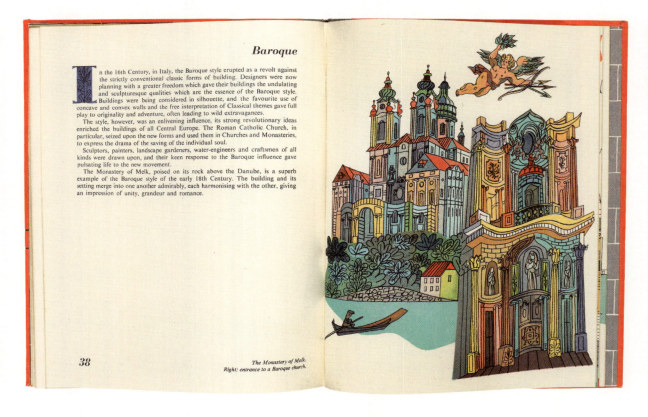

LEFT
Hans Tisdall, 'The monastery of Melk and the entrance to a Baroque church', from Oliver Hill and Hans Tisdall, *Balbus*, Pleiades Books Ltd, London, 1944
V&A 38041800393738

M. Vitruvius per locundum solito castigatior factus cum figuris et tabula ut iam legi et intelligi posit

(Giocondo's version of Vitruvius made more comprehensible than usual with the addition of figures and tables to aid reading and understanding)

MARCUS VITRUVIUS POLLIO, EDITED BY FRA GIOVANNI GIOCONDO DA VERONA

PUBLISHED BY GIOVANNI TACCUINO, VENICE, 1511

WOODCUTS BY FRA GIOVANNI GIOCONDO DA VERONA

V&A 38041800392987

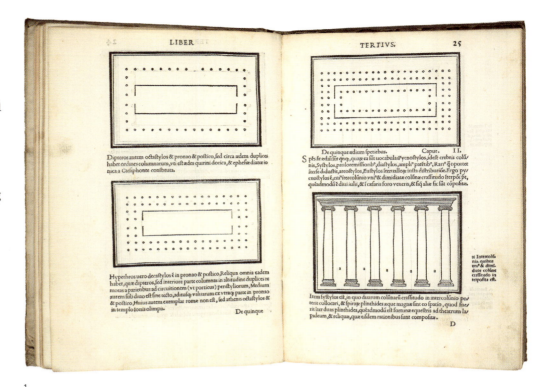

1.

2.

De architectura libri decem (*The Ten Books on Architecture*) by Marcus Vitruvius Pollio is the only major architectural treatise known to survive from antiquity. As a touchstone for the practice of classical architecture, it framed the discussion of architectural theory from the Renaissance to the nineteenth century. The fact that Vitruvius referred to illustrations in the text but that no copy containing them survived challenged Renaissance architects and printers to produce an illustrated version. The first was this Latin edition by the architect Fra Giovanni Giocondo da Verona (1). Many of the woodcuts are diagrammatic, such as the specifications for capitals (2); others present information within a realistic setting, such as the scenes showing agricultural machinery. The images do not necessarily correspond to the text alongside them, but they help to elucidate some of Vitruvius's more obscure descriptions. More ambitious and successful illustrated versions of Vitruvius followed, notably the Italian translation published by Cesare Cesariano in 1521, which matched woodcuts to the relevant text, but Fra Giocondo's reintroduction of images to Vitruvius marks a significant early moment in the history of the illustrated architecture book. [OHT]

Tutte l'opere d'architettura et prospetiva

(All the works of architecture and perspective)

SEBASTIANO SERLIO

PUBLISHED BY FRANCESCO DE' FRANCESCHI, VENICE, 1584

WOODCUTS

V&A 38041800384430

As the first fully illustrated handbook of architecture, this treatise by Sebastiano Serlio was designed to be practical and accessible. The seven 'books', first published together in 1584, progress from the first principles of geometry and perspective to complex architectural designs. Written in Italian rather than Latin, and comprehensively illustrated, the treatise was easy to use, popular and, therefore, influential. Serlio's early career as an artist producing paintings and woodcuts perhaps sharpened his awareness of the potential of illustrated text, still a relatively new print technology at the time. Book Four, first published individually in 1537, is notable for being the first publication in which the five architectural orders are illustrated and discussed systematically (1). Book Three uses the then recently adopted technique of orthographic projection (showing a three-dimensional object in plan and elevation without perspective) to depict ruins of ancient Rome, Greece and even Egypt. Another innovation was the interspersing of the images with texts in the style of contemporary scientific publications (3). The level of detail in Serlio's woodcuts made them suitable for adaptation by craftspeople in not only sixteenth-century Italy but also subsequent centuries and other countries who wanted to create interiors with a classical pedigree (2). [OHT]

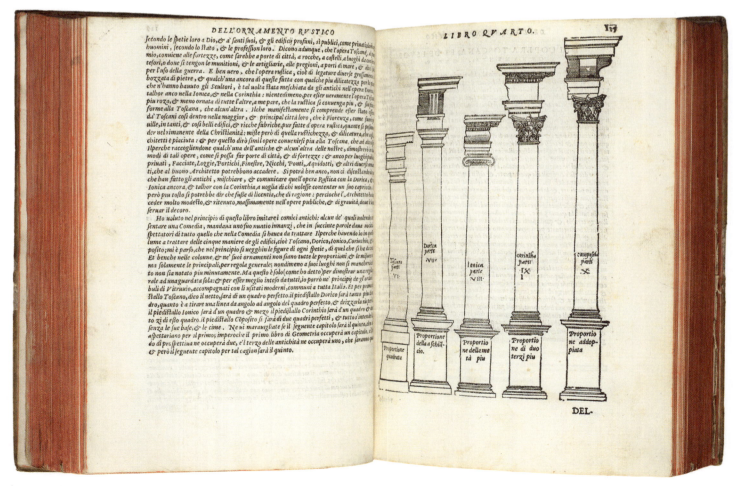

1.

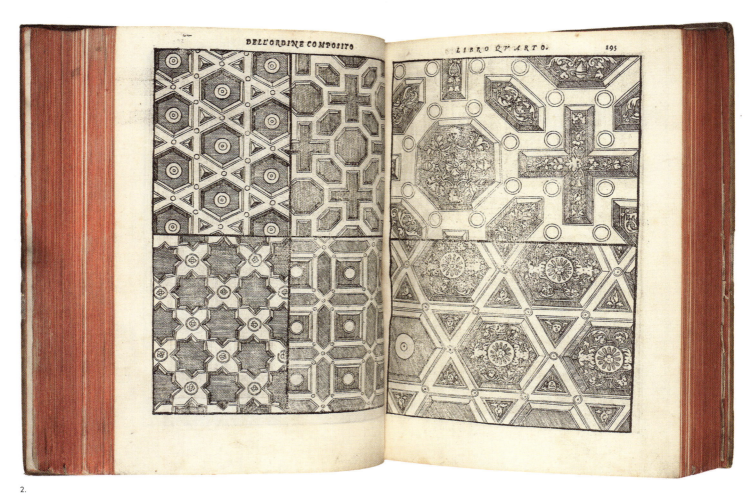

2.

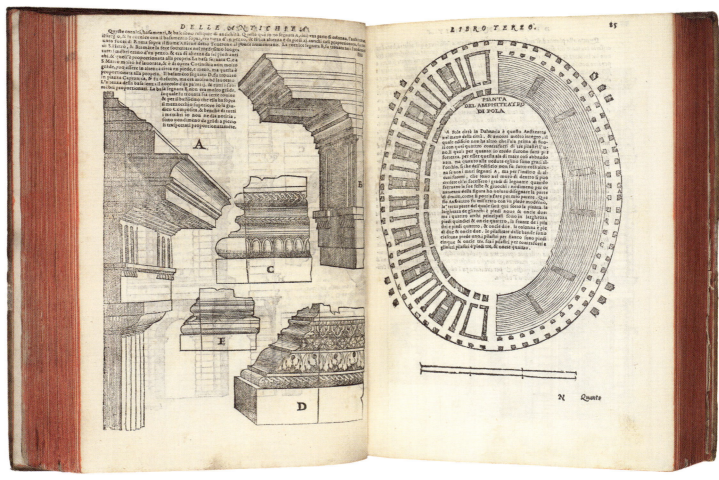

3.

Architectura von Außtheilung, Symmetria und Proportion der fünff Seulen

und aller darauss volgender Kunst Arbeit von Fenstern, Caminen, Thürgerichten, Portalen, Bronnen und Epitaphien

(Architecture of the arrangement, symmetry and proportion of the five orders: and all the resulting artwork of windows, chimneys, stone door jambs, portals, wells and gravestone inscriptions)

WENDEL DIETTERLIN

PUBLISHED BY BALTHASAR CAYMOCX, NUREMBERG, 1598

ENGRAVINGS

V&A 38041800392995

1.

2.

3.

The genre of the book of the architectural orders was given a new twist by Wendel Dietterlin. Such publications traditionally emphasized proportion, but Dietterlin was a painter and engraver rather than an architect, and his forte was inventive decoration. Taking each order as a starting point, he produced a series of full-page engravings that present fantastically embellished columns, windows, portals and fountains (1). His designs were inspired by the classical theory that emerged in Italy and travelled to northern Europe through editions of Vitruvius and Serlio. He was also influenced by the interpretation of Renaissance forms by northern European architects such as Hans Blum and Hans Vredeman de Vries. Dietterlin eclectically combined Renaissance elements with existing Germanic traditions, including medieval motifs and elaborate strapwork resembling cut and moulded leather (2). With minimal text, this is essentially a picture book: the concept of the five orders is just a starting point for expressive designs that, in their drama and sublimity, foreshadow the work of Giovanni Battista Piranesi. Sometimes uncanny, they even incorporate narrative – what has passed between those faceless figures at the fountain (3)? Proving highly popular with architects, masons and carpenters, the designs were crucial for disseminating Renaissance decoration in Germany. [OHT]

Rural Architecture in the Chinese Taste

Being designs entirely new for the decoration of gardens, parks, forrests, insides of houses, &c., on sixty copper plates, with full instructions for workmen; also a near estimate of the charge, and hints where proper to be erected

WILLIAM HALFPENNY AND JOHN HALFPENNY

PRINTED FOR ROBERT SAYER, LONDON, 1755 (THIRD EDITION)

COPPERPLATE ENGRAVINGS BY WILLIAM HALFPENNY

V&A L.213-1984

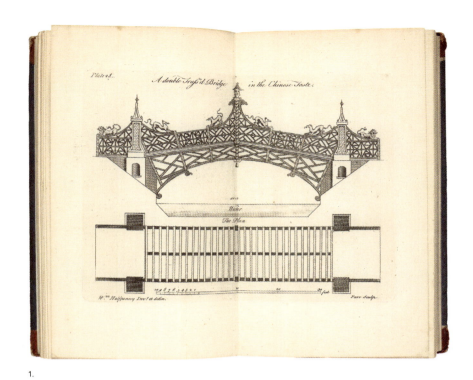

1.

William Halfpenny first trained as a carpenter and later practised as an architect of minor works, but it is as the prolific author of practical handbooks and pattern books that he is best remembered. His guides for builders and artisans outlined the basics of drawing and construction, while his design sourcebooks offered increasingly whimsical ideas largely for rural buildings: farmhouses, parsonages, inns and garden structures. Halfpenny used copper engravings to create fine but affordable books that were portable, allowing craftspeople to show fashionable designs to their clients. His son John collaborated with him on his later titles, including *Rural Architecture in the Chinese Taste*. Originally issued in parts between 1750 and 1752, it was the first publication to present architectural designs in the Chinese style as initiated by Frederick, Prince of Wales, in his commission of the 'House of Confucius', Kew (1749), from William Chambers. The plates feature wooden palisades, bridges (1), banqueting houses and gazebos (2), all ornamented with bells, fretwork, serpents and dragons. The plates were accompanied by a separate text (for the use of the builder, rather than the patron) describing the purpose of the design, the materials in which it should be executed and, significantly, the approximate cost. [OHT]

2.

Della magnificenza ed architettura de' Romani

(On the grandeur and the architecture of the Romans)

GIOVANNI BATTISTA PIRANESI

PRINTED IN ROME, 1761

ENGRAVING, ETCHING AND DRYPOINT

V&A 38041800393001

1.

Piranesi's large-format publications were intended for the gentleman's library rather than the artisan's bench. Drawing on the tradition of antiquarian topographical illustration that had flourished in Rome since the sixteenth century, Piranesi used his virtuosity as an artist and printmaker to represent ancient Rome's architecture and urbanism with originality. *Della magnificenza* contributed to the debate as to whether ancient Greek or Roman architecture was superior. Piranesi argued for the latter by presenting examples and reconstructions of ancient Roman buildings. As with his topographical and design publications, the power of this theoretical treatise derives from the spectacularly rich plates, heavily worked using etching, engraving and drypoint. Piranesi's unrealized aspiration to become a stage designer underpins the theatricality of his images. He not only conveys archaeological and architectural information but also conjures excitement and awe at the monumentality of Rome's past, accentuated through dramatic viewpoints and diminutive figures. As in his other work, the presentation of each image is sophisticated, filling every part of the plate and employing devices such as fictive pieces of paper pinned to the image to enrich its visual and intellectual content. The plates of *Della magnificenza* do not so much illustrate Piranesi's argument as make it themselves. [OHT]

2.

3.

The Works in Architecture of Robert and James Adam

ROBERT ADAM AND JAMES ADAM

PRINTED FOR THE AUTHORS, LONDON, 1778–86

3 VOLUMES, ENGRAVINGS BY VARIOUS ARTISTS

V&A 38041800989097, 38041800392151 and 38041800392169

1.

Robert and James Adam had an astute appreciation of illustrated publication as a means of self-promotion. *The Works* began as a scheme to avert the threat of bankruptcy, but out of crisis came an original, elegant book on a scale unprecedented in British publishing. The five-part collection of the Adams' *Works* comprised high-quality, large-format illustrations by various artists and engravers. It was not a pattern book but a record of the Adams' commissions for specific clients, aimed at 'persons of taste' rather than at practising craftspeople, for whom the cost was prohibitive. Robert Adam was torn between keeping his designs out of print to preserve their exclusivity and publishing them to avoid plagiarism: as he said, 'if you do not publish them yourself some other will which is worse'. The plates show interiors (1) and furniture (3), as well as architecture (2 and 4), to demonstrate the brothers' facility in all aspects of design. Alongside their archaeological publications, such as the *Ruins of the Palace of the Emperor Diocletian at Spalatro in Dalmatia* (1764), these volumes show how the Adams translated their meticulous first-hand study of antiquities into innovative designs in an 'antique' manner for eighteenth-century Britain. [OHT]

2.

3.

4.

ARCHITECTURE 173

Darstellung und Geschichte des Geschmacks der vorzüglichsten Völker in Beziehung auf die innere Auszierung der Zimmer und auf die Baukunst

(Presentation and history of the taste of the leading nations in relation to the interior decoration of rooms and to architecture)

JOSEPH FRIEDRICH ZU RACKNITZ

PUBLISHED BY G.J. GÖSCHEN, LEIPZIG, 1796–9

2 VOLUMES, ENGRAVINGS AFTER DESIGNS BY CHRISTIAN FRIEDRICH SCHURICHT, FINISHED BY HAND WITH WATERCOLOURS

V&A 38041800393795 and 38041800393019

1.

2.

3.

Drawing on travel accounts and literary descriptions, as well as architectural sources, Joseph Friedrich zu Racknitz published an analysis of 24 styles for architecture and interior decoration. From the fifteenth to the early eighteenth centuries, styles in western Europe and North America were largely inspired by ancient Rome and Greece. In these specially commissioned hand-coloured engravings, however, Racknitz presented a variety of historical and contemporary tastes, including Egyptian, Etruscan, Chinese, 'Old German', 'Old French', Persian (1), Turkish (2), Russian, Mexican (3) and Tahitian (4). Racknitz emphasized that it was a visual sourcebook rather than a comprehensive history; it aimed to provide 'practical assistance to artists and … amusement to lovers of art'. It was an eccentric project, and the text is uneven in quality, but Racknitz was unique and precocious in presenting a global analysis of 'taste' some 60 years earlier than Owen Jones's compendium of global design in *The Grammar of Ornament* (1856; pp.190–91). Coloured plates of interior design were an international novelty in 1796, and their quality in this publication was particularly high. The advertisement publicizing the volumes even suggested that they could be used to furnish a room, as an attractive and educational alternative to expensive and intellectually vacuous wallpaper. [OHT]

4.

Observations on the Theory and Practice of Landscape Gardening

Including some remarks on Grecian and Gothic architecture, collected from various manuscripts, in the possession of the different noblemen and gentlemen, for whose use they were originally written; the whole tending to establish fixed principles in the respective arts

HUMPHRY REPTON

PRINTED BY T. BENSLEY FOR J. TAYLOR, LONDON, 1803

WOOD ENGRAVINGS, AQUATINTS, AND AQUATINTS COLOURED BY HAND IN WATERCOLOUR

V&A 516-1888

1.

2.

A lavish combination of engravings and aquatints illustrates *Observations on the Theory and Practice of Landscape Gardening* by Humphry Repton. Nevertheless, the author insisted that he was 'less ambitious of publishing a book of beautiful prints, than a book of precepts'. He declared the plates were 'necessary rather than ornamental' and existed 'to illustrate the arguments rather than to attract the attention'. The most notable of the illustrations are undoubtedly the hand-coloured aquatints with moveable flaps (2). These plates were facsimiles of pages from Repton's famous 'Red Books' – bespoke presentation volumes for his patrons, in which he painted 'before' and 'after' scenes in watercolour with overlays to demonstrate the transformation that his intervention would have upon their property. Hand-coloured aquatint was the best way to approximate the softness and colour of Repton's original watercolours, though the artists who produced the plates remain anonymous, and, somewhat unsettlingly to our modern sensibility, Repton notes that the colouring of the plates 'in imitation of drawings' was carried out by children. It is because these images offer the viewer an immediate, visual way to understand the proposed works – appealing to the eye as well as the mind – that they are particularly satisfying. [OHT]

The Terra-cotta Architecture of North Italy (XIIth–XVth Centuries)

Pourtrayed as examples for imitation in other countries; from careful drawings and restorations

LUDWIG GRUNER (ED.)

PUBLISHED BY JOHN MURRAY, LONDON, 1867

WOODCUTS, CHROMOLITHOGRAPHS BY FRIEDRICH LOSE AND ONE ALBUMEN PRINT

V&A 38041800393035

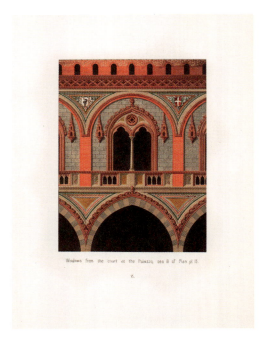

1.

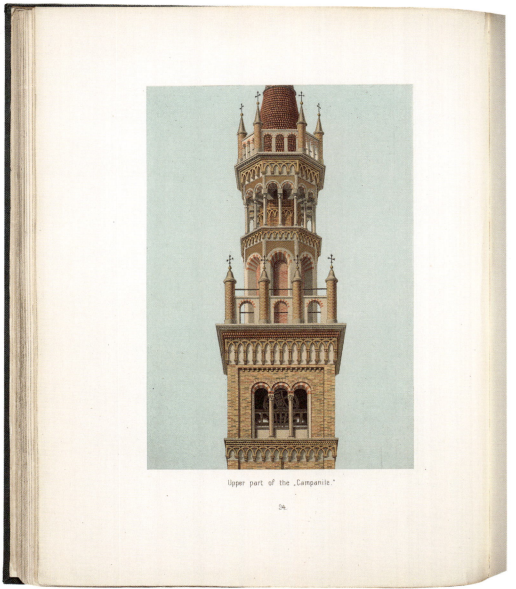

2.

The development of chromolithography in the early nineteenth century opened up a multicoloured world of printing possibilities. In this volume Ludwig Gruner, chief artistic advisor to Prince Albert, presented a compendium of terracotta architectural ornament to promote the revival of that art form in Europe. It consequently focuses on colour, texture and decoration, rather than structure or planning. Chromolithographic printing was pioneered by Owen Jones in his *Plans, Elevations, Sections, and Details of the Alhambra* (1842–5), which set a new standard for publishing architecture in colour. Gruner was quick to embrace its potential in the numerous books that he authored and edited. Terracotta architecture relied on polychromy for its effect and required representation in full colour, otherwise only achievable by costly hand-tinting. In *The Terra-cotta Architecture of North Italy* medium and subject matter were therefore well matched. Even the disadvantages of chromolithography were assets in this instance: its slightly flattening effect, caused by the even application of colour, produced clear images ideally suited to a practical sourcebook. The illustrations are based on drawings by the German artist Friedrich Lose, which, together with the original artwork for many of Gruner's other publications, are also held by the V&A. [OHT]

Vers une architecture

(*Towards an Architecture*)

LE CORBUSIER
(CHARLES-ÉDOUARD JEANNERET)

PUBLISHED BY G. CRÈS ET CIE, PARIS, 1924
(SECOND EDITION, FIRST PUBLISHED 1923)

V&A L.3264-1990

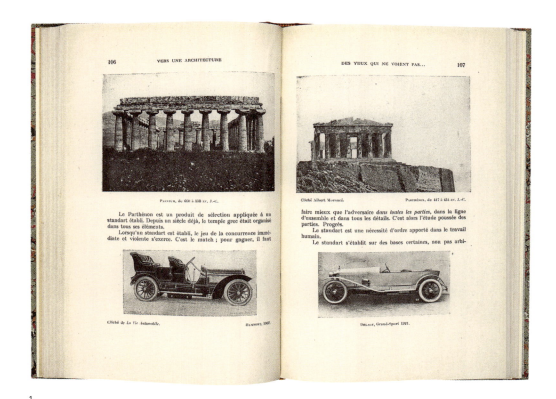

1.

2.

Unlike that of most architectural writers, Le Corbusier's theory preceded the bulk of his practice. Written when Le Corbusier was only in his mid-30s, *Vers une architecture* was a conscious manifesto. The images, in the form of photographs (1) and reproductions of Le Corbusier's hand-drawn diagrams and collages, are key to conveying both the content and spirit of his ideas. Very few of the photographs are obviously connected to architecture: cars, aeroplanes, cruise liners, ventilators and turbines feature more frequently than buildings do. This expresses Le Corbusier's belief in economy and function, as found in these engineered objects, as the necessary qualities of architecture. The illustrations, therefore, demonstrate his dictum, repeated throughout the text, that architecture is nothing to do with 'style'. The photographs' character, as well as their subject matter, makes his point: focusing on light and shade and offering details out of context he presents the products of engineering not just as functional forms but also as aesthetic possibilities. It was also here that Le Corbusier put forward for the first time the idea of a tower-block city, shown in diagrammatic plan and elevation (2). Together with those of his eight-volume *Œuvre complète* (1952–7), these illustrations continue to inspire modern architects. [OHT]

ARCHITECTURE 177

Learning from Las Vegas

ROBERT VENTURI AND DENISE SCOTT BROWN

PUBLISHED BY MIT PRESS, CAMBRIDGE, MASSACHUSETTS, 1972

V&A L.3451-1973

1.

Through an examination of the American vernacular as encountered on Route 91 in Las Vegas, Venturi and Scott Brown argued against the functionalism demanded by the Modernist architect Ludwig Mies van der Rohe in favour of a return to the symbolic nature of architecture and the use of ornament. The book has three parts: an analysis of the commercial strip as a new, valid type of urban form; a theorization of symbolism in architecture; and a description of their firm's work as applied examples of that theory. Each section has a different visual tone: rich double-page spreads of photographs and diagrams characterize the first (1), followed by more detailed diagrams in the second (2) and, in the third, the inclusion of design material (3). Venturi and Scott Brown noted they had 'a particular interest in finding graphic means ... to describe "urban sprawl" urbanism and particularly the commercial strip'. Their aspiration is particularly evident in Part I, which not only includes plans and diagrams analysing the relationship between building and moving viewer, but, influenced by the visual techniques of Pop Art, also presents photo spreads to convey the sensation of travelling along the strip and the cumulative effect on the viewer of neon signage. [OHT]

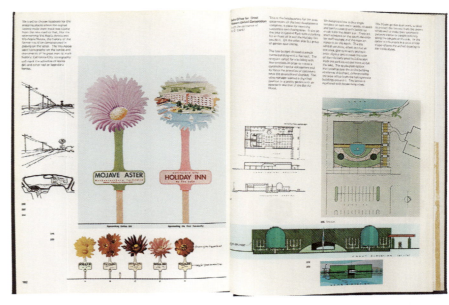

2.

3.

178 ARCHITECTURE

Zaha Hadid: Complete Works

PATRIK SCHUMACHER AND GORDANA FONTANA GIUSTI (EDS)

PUBLISHED BY THAMES & HUDSON, LONDON AND NEW YORK, 2004

🐌

V&A 38041005132279, 38041005132170, 38041005132220 and 38041005132261

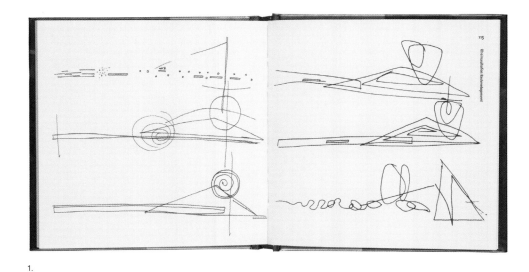

1.

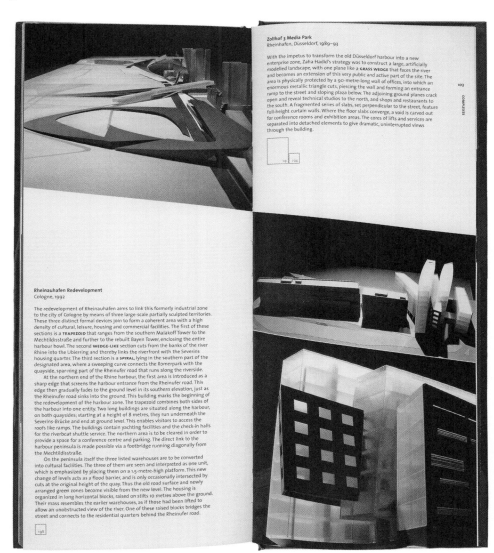

2.

These four volumes continue the long-standing tradition of representing an architect's complete works. Presented within a multi-apertured, red Lucite slipcase, they document the work of the Iraqi-born British, international prize-winning architect Dame Zaha Hadid. The books, three of which are illustrated, detail the different manifestations of her *oeuvre*. *Process: Sketches and Drawings* shows pages from Hadid's sketchbooks without any accompanying commentary (1), its hand-held size creating an intimate encounter with the early stages of her design process. *Projects Documentation* introduces design material such as models, drawings and digital renderings to highlight specific projects (2), while *Major and Recent Works* presents double-page spreads of the architect's paintings, drawings and computer-aided drawings as well as photographs of the buildings themselves. Hadid's most significant contribution to architectural representation was in her paintings, which she began to produce when a student and continued to create throughout her career as a means of architectural exploration. Her choice of medium was unusual for an architect but was heavily influenced by the art of Russian Constructivism. She found abstraction allowed her to avoid preconceived architectural ideas and generate new plans and forms. As testified by the illustrations in these volumes, representation was as important a part of her practice as her built works. [OHT]

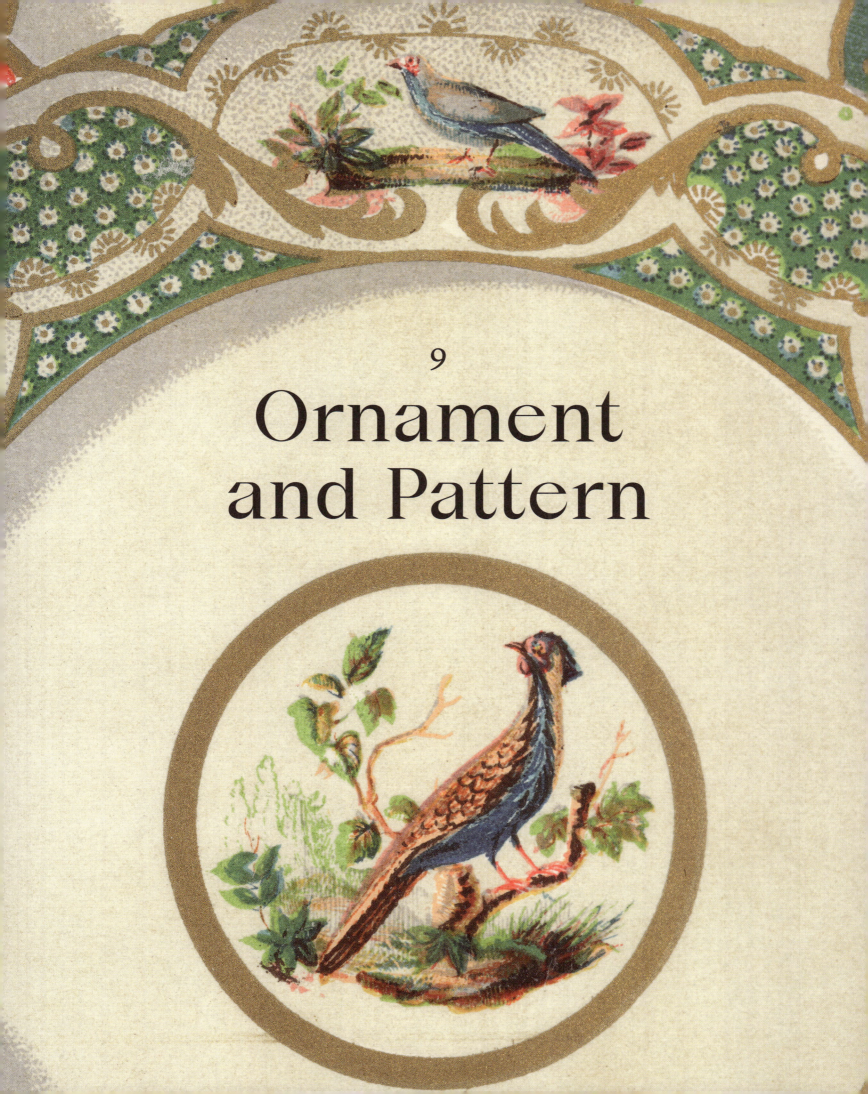

9
Ornament and Pattern

Ornament and Pattern

Sarah Grant

Ornament and pattern bring objects to life, lending visual interest, beauty, symbolism and meaning to physical form. Artists and craftspeople have always looked to a wide range of sources in the world around them for inspiration, but books devoted to ornament and pattern began to be produced in the late fifteenth century. These enabled a designer's work to be known more widely and facilitated the spread of designs and styles across borders. As a result, they are an indispensable guide to the waxing and waning of fashions, providing an overview of their origins and duration. We can admire the sheer breadth of creativity illustrated in their pages, but are also made aware of the cyclical nature of design. 'It is unlikely that anyone', observed Peter Thornton, a pioneering curator of interior design, 'has ever invented an entirely new design [...]. Innovation invariably builds on what has gone before.'

The production of these books, and the field later devoted to their study, was largely a Western tradition centred in Europe, which the examples in this chapter reflect. Like ornament itself, they were fluid, with no prescribed format. Some might provide templates and directions, some a comprehensive repertoire of motifs and repeating patterns, while others were intended to serve as a source for general ideas. The earliest examples were illustrated with woodcuts; their graphic nature was undeniably effective for conveying a range of monotone geometric patterns, but offered limited potential for realizing complex designs. The adoption of engraving towards the end of the sixteenth century led to more sophisticated plates and, consequently, to a high number of pattern books containing designs for embroidery, lacemaking and metalwork, whose fine detail was particularly well served by this technique (right). At that time most pattern 'books' were, in fact, small sets of single-sheet prints, loosely stitched together, which could be stored in a portfolio, bound together or mounted in an album.

Ornament and pattern books firmly established themselves during the sixteenth century, and over the next 200 years their popularity and the scale of their production grew exponentially. Some knowledge of ornament was considered central to any artist's training, and all artists would have had access to ornament prints and books. An array of great artists tried their hand at it, including Donatello (stained glass), Albrecht Dürer (textiles), Raphael and Peter Paul Rubens (architecture), Hans Holbein (jewellery), and François Boucher (motifs, textiles and fans). Dürer's six woodcut designs – known popularly as 'The Six Knots' (opposite) after their interlaced patterns, parts of which resemble the curling tendrils of grapevines – were originally based on designs by Leonardo da Vinci. Probably intended for use in textiles, the prints inspired a range of strapwork ornament on a variety of objects, including maiolica, demonstrating the wide application of such patterns.

The eighteenth century is now regarded as the golden age for pattern books. The period's constantly evolving styles led to a continuous demand for novel and ever more fantastical designs. Such was the global

ABOVE
Design for embroidery, copperplate engraving, from Margaretha Helm, *Kunst- und Fleiss-übende Nadel-Ergötzungen; oder neu-erfundenes Neh- und Stick-Buch* (The delights of the art and industry of the practising needle or the newly invented sewing and embroidery book), Nuremberg, *c.*1725
V&A E.3412-1932

OPPOSITE
Albrecht Dürer, woodcut from 'The Six Knots', 1505–7
V&A E.188-1885

ORNAMENT AND PATTERN · 183

appeal of the Rococo and the portable nature of pattern books and prints that modern scholars have traced designs from European pattern books as far as Latin America. The beauty and sheer ingenuity of these designs broadened their appeal to attract affluent collectors, and they began to be produced on a larger and more lavish scale. Thus, subscribers to George Richardson's elegant Georgian ceiling designs (p.187), a supreme example of high Neoclassicism, ranged from prominent architects and artists to aristocratic patrons. Similarly, the Chinoiserie productions of the prolific designer Jean Pillement were marketed for use by the emerging wave of upper- and middle-class women amateurs, as the title *The Ladies Amusement; or, Whole Art of Japanning Made Easy* makes plain (above). One of the most significant pattern books in the history of ornament was produced during this fertile period: Giovanni Volpato's *Loggie di Rafaele nel Vaticano* published in Rome between 1772 and 1777 (opposite left). Volpato's prints recorded on a spectacularly large scale, and for the first time in luminous colour, arguably the world's most influential patterns: Raphael's painted grotesques in the Vatican Palace loggia. Their publication caused a sensation and viewers were entranced by the extraordinary detail of the scrolling *rinceaux*, strings of pearls, gems, flowers and tumbling little animals.

If the eighteenth century produced the most inventive and whimsical pattern books, then the nineteenth century brought this movement to its zenith, with the introduction of glorious colour illustrations made possible by the invention of chromolithography. This highly skilled technique would eclipse the more laborious method of hand-colouring (opposite right). This period also saw the birth of the serious study of ornament, a natural expression of the Victorians' enthusiasm for both classification and historicism. In their desire to categorize and analyse the different styles and periods of ornament across the globe, we can also discern their imperial ambitions and sensibilities.

And so, together, the flourishing of colour book illustration and the establishment of the field of ornament study gave rise to a wave of high-end, multicoloured surveys, the most famous of which is Owen Jones's sweeping *Grammar of Ornament* (pp.190–91); its pages, thickly packed with colourful plates, showcase the crowded aesthetic beloved of Victorians. Jones, a great visionary, was closely involved with the Great Exhibition of 1851 and the South Kensington Museum (later the V&A), which acquired pattern and ornament books and prints in large numbers from its first days, as part of its crusade to instil the principles of 'good' design in its public. Jones's survey spawned many imitators seeking to capitalize on the newly omnivorous taste for ornament and pattern, the most successful of which was undeniably Auguste Racinet's majestic *L'Ornement polychrome* (p.192).

The fascination with ornament explored through sumptuously illustrated books continued across the century, encompassing specific vogues, such as Gothic Revival (p.188) and 'orientalism', and the patterns they disseminated continued to play a pivotal role in the decorative arts. A final flowering occurred in the 1920s, but the format was snuffed out conclusively by the widespread adoption of photographic illustrations together with the rise of Modernism, a movement that famously rejected ornament. And yet in recent times there has been a new wave of mass-produced publications on ornament and pattern, and the subject has again crept into the mainstream. The classification and interpretation of the patterns and motifs that make up our decorative world will always hold our attention because of their ability to stir our imagination. They are at once a portal to the past, capturing the spirit of a specific age and place, and provide fertile inspiration for the future.

OPPOSITE
Etching from Jean Pillement, *The Ladies Amusement; or, Whole Art of Japanning Made Easy*, London, 1762
V&A 38041800148983

LEFT
Giovanni Ottaviani after Pietro Camporesi and G. Savorelli, etched and hand-coloured detail from Giovanni Volpato, *Loggie di Rafaele nel Vaticano* (The Raphael Loggia at the Vatican), Rome, 1772–7
V&A E.335-1887

ABOVE
'An Egyptian Chimney-Front', etching and aquatint coloured by hand, from Rudolph Ackermann, *A Series, Containing Forty-four Engravings in Colours, of Fashionable Furniture ...*, London, 1823
V&A 38041800377608

ORNAMENT AND PATTERN 185

A Book of Sundry Draughtes

Principaly serving for glasiers: and not impertinent for plasters and gardiners: beside sundry other professions. Whereunto is annexed the manner how to anniel in glas: and also the true forme of the fornace, and the secretes thereof

WALTER GEDDE

PRINTED 'IN SHOOLANE, AT THE SIGNE OF THE FAULCON' BY WALTER DIGHT, LONDON, 1615

WOODCUTS

V&A 38041800377384

1.

2.

This pattern book was intended mainly for glaziers making a window from smaller panes of glass in a geometrical pattern (1), as was fashionable in the early seventeenth century. Although the technical instructions are specific to glazing, the author or the publisher sought to broaden the market for this book by suggesting the potential usefulness of these patterns to plasterers patterning walls or ceilings, or gardeners laying out flower beds. The empty area on the left page is filled with a so-called printer's ornament (2). These were introduced to fill up space and add visual appeal to a book's layout, and could be reused by the printer regardless of the subject matter of a particular book. Here, a satyr's mask, winged putti, a basket and festoons of fruit, and knotted drapery are set against a background of Renaissance strapwork, which looks like curling leather with holes cut into it. [EM]

A Collection of Ceilings

Decorated in the style of the antique grotesque; containing designs fit for adorning halls, parlours, antichambers, libraries, dining rooms, drawing rooms, and other principal apartments

GEORGE RICHARDSON

PRINTED FOR THE AUTHOR, NO. 105, GREAT TITCHFIELD-STREET; AND SOLD BY GEORGE NICOL, BOOKSELLER TO HIS MAJESTY, NO. 58, PALL-MALL, LONDON, 1793 (SECOND EDITION, FIRST PUBLISHED 1776)

ETCHINGS, COLOURED BY HAND
V&A 38041800377368

First issued in eight parts throughout 1776, this exquisite book of 48 ceiling designs was composed and etched by George Richardson, a Scottish architectural draughtsman who devoted his career to designing, etching and publishing books of decorative designs. Both editions of the book were widely disseminated across Europe and subscribers included leading artists, architects, craftspeople and builders. The book was dedicated to Sir Nathaniel Curzon, 1st Baron Scarsdale, who employed Richardson to produce the ceiling designs for the Grecian Hall at his country seat of Kedleston Hall, Derbyshire. Richardson was highly influenced by his mentors, the pioneering Neoclassical architects Robert and James Adam (pp.172–3). He accompanied James Adam on his Grand Tour of Europe from 1760 to 1763, and the eclectic designs in this book were directly inspired by the ceilings, bas-reliefs and fragments that Richardson saw and studied in Italy, particularly in Naples and Rome. Richardson hoped that those studying his book would be encouraged to 'blend parts of the ornament with others' and thus produce their own ceiling designs. All the plates are delicately hand-tinted in the refined Neoclassical palette of Dutch pink, sky blue and lemon. [HL]

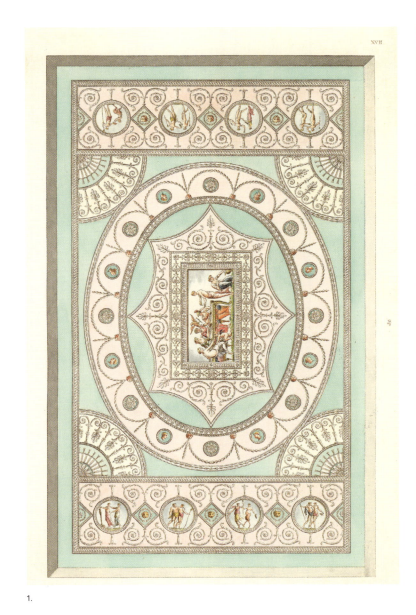

1.

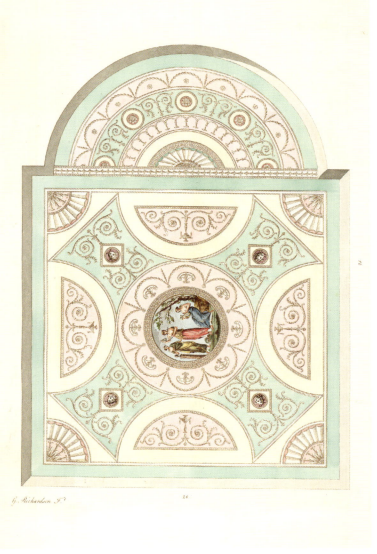

2.

ORNAMENT AND PATTERN 187

Glossary of Ecclesiastical Ornament and Costume

AUGUSTUS WELBY NORTHMORE PUGIN

PUBLISHED BY H.G. BOHN, LONDON, 1844

CHROMOLITHOGRAPHS WITH GOLD INK

V&A Forster 7211

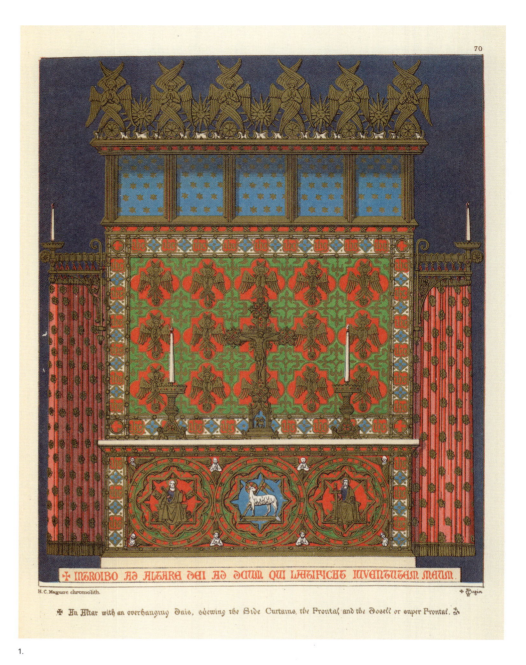

1.

A.W.N. Pugin was one of the nineteenth century's key architects and designers, best known for the Houses of Parliament. In addition to his involvement with most of the design movements of his time (a contribution curtailed only by his premature death at the age of 40), Pugin was both a pioneer of the Gothic Revival style and a prolific author of architectural and ornament treatises. These two elements are neatly encapsulated by this *Glossary*, which categorizes, illustrates and explains an array of sacred vestments, ornament and decoration. The exhaustive contents illustrate everything from richly embroidered mitres (2) to pomegranate-patterned diapering (3). Reflecting the precious metals of the treasures they sought to illustrate, the plates employ copious amounts of gold ink (1), and capture the gleam these objects would have cast in a church interior's low light. Pugin hoped these would provide models for other artists to follow, just as he himself had drawn on medieval sources. Equally as important was his object to awaken the desire to protect and restore existing works at a time when the significance and symbolism of ecclesiastical ornament had begun to fade from popular knowledge and many churches and their collections had fallen into neglect and disrepair. [SG]

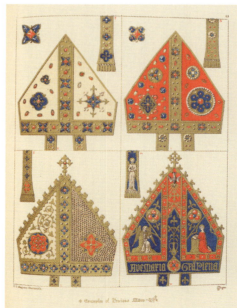

2.

3.

188 ORNAMENT AND PATTERN

Fresco Decorations and Stuccoes of Churches & Palaces in Italy

During the fifteenth and sixteenth centuries with descriptions by Ludwig Gruner, and a comparison between the ancient arabesques and those of the sixteenth century by A. Hittorff

LUDWIG GRUNER

PUBLISHED BY JOHN MURRAY, LONDON, 1844

CHROMOLITHOGRAPHS

V&A 1673–1899

1.

2.

Fresco Decorations and Stuccoes of Churches & Palaces in Italy was the first of a number of art books produced by the German engraver Ludwig Gruner (see also p.176) and dedicated to his patron Prince Albert. It was intended as a sourcebook for painters, and the colour illustrations vary from entire decorative schemes to extracted examples of ornament. One plate depicts the floors of the Papal Palace in Rome, in which the overall design is overlaid with individually printed colour tiles. In another, more than 20 frescoed designs by Giulio Romano from the Ducal Palace in Mantua are presented as discrete examples to be replicated (1). Despite being an engraver himself, Gruner was responsible only for a handful of the 46 plates that illustrate the text. Part I, on Roman palaces, was almost entirely based on Joseph Thürmer and Johann Gottfried Gutensohn's *Collection of Monuments and Decorations of Architecture in Rome* (1826). Recycling images was not uncommon, and while Gruner credited the architects for their work, he also critiqued the lack of 'variety and completeness' of the illustrations. Gruner felt his own publication, rich with visual examples, better served the tastes of his day. [EK]

ORNAMENT AND PATTERN

The Grammar of Ornament

OWEN JONES

PUBLISHED BY DAY AND SON, LONDON, 1856

3 VOLUMES, 100 CHROMOLITHOGRAPHS

V&A 38041800498990, 38041800499048 and 38041800499097

1.

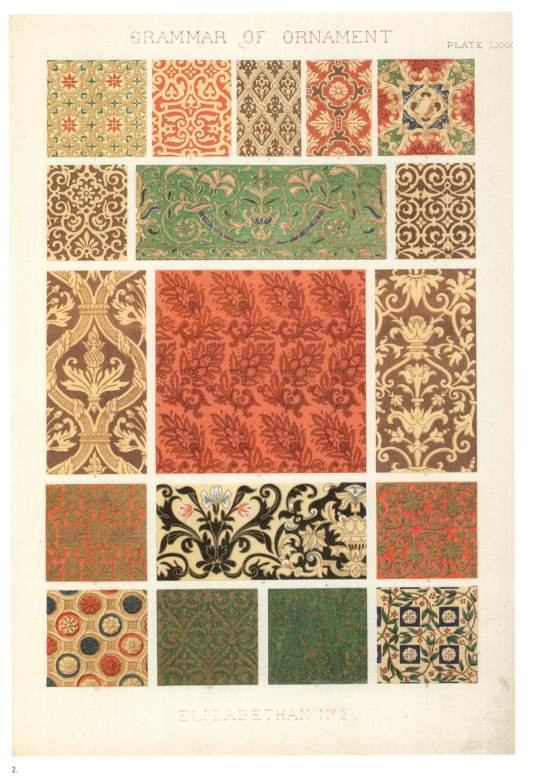

2.

This seminal book is a meticulous summary of the key design theories of Owen Jones, an influential English designer and architect who was responsible for the interior decoration of the Crystal Palace in 1851 and again when it was rebuilt in 1854. Jones's principal desire for this publication was that it would 'awaken the ambition' of students. He encouraged them to look back to the underlying theories – or 'grammar' – of the past for good design and colouring. The manual immediately became a set text for British schools of design and was reissued throughout the nineteenth and twentieth centuries. That the book is still in print is a testament to its continued relevance. Jones worked with the lithographer Francis Bedford and the publisher Day and Son to create the book's 100 folio-sized colour illustrations. These were all produced in the new technique of chromolithography, an elaborate and expensive method of printing requiring each layer of colour to be printed with a different lithographic stone. The resulting prints were innovative and lavish, juxtaposing art and architectural motifs and patterns from across the globe. Henry Cole, the first Director of the V&A, helped Jones to publish the book, and today the museum holds many of Jones's original drawings. [HL]

L'Ornement polychrome

(*The World of Ornament*)

AUGUSTE RACINET

PUBLISHED BY FIRMIN DIDOT, PARIS, 1869–87

2 VOLUMES, CHROMOLITHOGRAPHS WITH GOLD AND SILVER INK

V&A 134:1 and 2-1883

The French equivalent to *The Grammar of Ornament*, Racinet's *L'Ornement polychrome* enjoyed a phenomenal and enduring success; indeed, it is still in print, in the English-language facsimile, *The World of Ornament*. Like its forerunner, *L'Ornement polychrome* was sweeping in scope – covering global styles of decorative arts from antiquity to the eighteenth century – with lavish and detailed chromolithographed plates, embellished with gold and silver ink. These were a tour de force of execution: the plate illustrating Boulle marquetry (1), for example, evokes the glint of gilt-bronze mounts and transparency of tortoiseshell. The book dispensed, however, with the lengthy introductory text and analysis of Jones's model (Racinet was no design theorist), opting instead for a brief and highly readable description of each plate. About 2,000 motifs and objects are illustrated across 100 plates, providing a summary of each style in a range of 'masterpieces'. These were drawn from objects and sources then in French museums and private collections, or reproduced from existing illustrations in authoritative contemporary texts. Thus, the eighteenth century is represented by Gobelins tapestries and Sèvres porcelain (2), while the Chinese section includes motifs drawn from lost vases that had once been in the 'imperial museum of Peking'. [SG]

1.

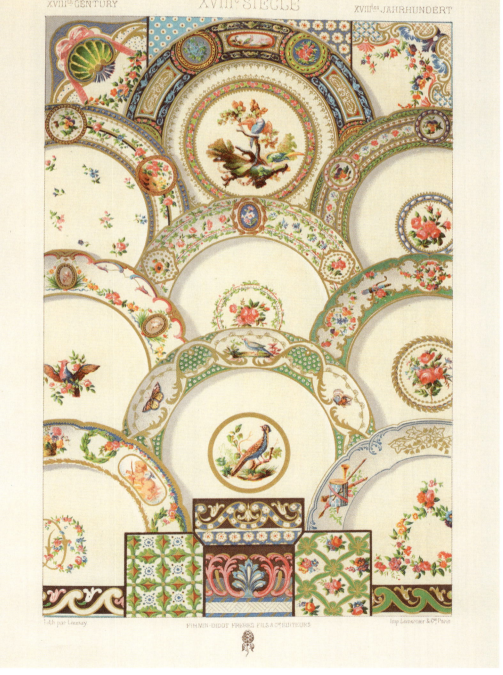

2.

Polychromatic Decoration as Applied to Buildings in the Mediæval Styles

Thirty-six plates in colours and gold with introductory and descriptive text

WILLIAM JAMES AUDSLEY AND GEORGE ASHDOWN AUDSLEY

PUBLISHED BY HENRY SOTHERAN & CO., LONDON, 1882

CHROMOLITHOGRAPHS, SOME FINISHED BY HAND WITH GOLD INK

V&A 1020-1900

1.

Written and designed by the Scottish architects and designers William James Audsley and George Ashdown Audsley, this exquisite book was published in London in 1882, before the brothers took their architectural practice to New York. The book is a visual and practical manual of decorative designs in the hugely popular Gothic Revival style, which looked back to the late medieval period for inspiration. It also contains a suggested colour palette comprising the dark, earthy tones associated with the Gothic (1). The publication was widely sought after by professional architects and artists, as well as amateur decorators, who used it as a sourcebook for their domestic designs. The 36 opulent illustrations were made in the innovative chromolithographic technique, used to print in multicolour. Many of the plates (2) were hand-finished with a gold ground (such as in the brocade patterns in plate 10), giving them the striking appearance of medieval illumination. Several copies of *Polychromatic Decoration* surviving in public collections show signs of their practical use. The plates in the V&A have paint stains, perhaps signalling that the book could have been used in a studio or workshop. (Although the curious fact that the NAL once allowed copyists to bring their paints into the library might also account for this.)
[HL]

2.

The Holy Carpet of the Mosque at Ardebil

EDWARD STEBBING

PRINTED BY ROBSON & SONS, LONDON, 1893

PHOTOLITHOGRAPHS, COLOURED BY HAND

V&A 708-1893

The subject of this outsize, deluxe volume is one of the largest and finest Islamic carpets in existence, woven for the mosque at Ardabil in Iran between 1539 and 1540. The text is from a paper on Persian carpets read by Edward Stebbing at a meeting of the Art Workers' Guild in 1891. Stebbing was also the managing director of the art importers Vincent Robinson and Company, which sold the carpet to the V&A in the year the book was published. The illustrations are a mixture of manual and photographic processes designed to produce the best possible results for a limited edition of 50 copies available only by subscription. To capture all the details and proportions, tracings were first taken of the carpet by a Mr Davies, who worked for Vincent Robinson and Company. These were turned into photolithographs, and for each copy of the book, six of them were hand-coloured by Henry and Rose Enid Stebbing (presumably relations of the author). Hand-colouring using watercolours could produce much finer and more accurate results in terms of colour matching with the carpet than was possible with any form of colour printing available in the 1890s. [EM]

1.

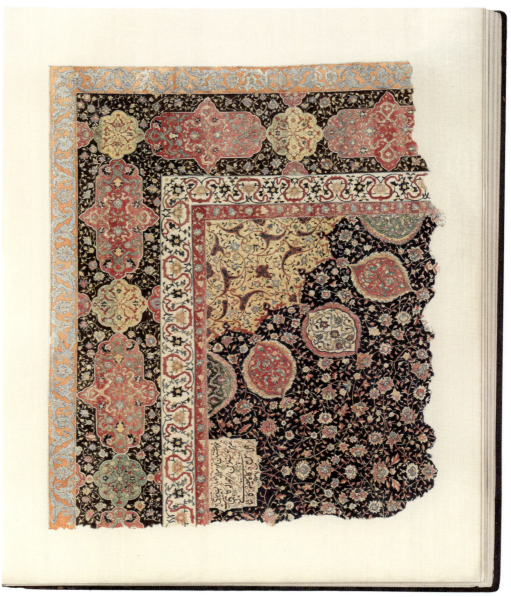

2.

Kaléidoscope, ornements abstraits; quatre-vingt sept motifs en vingt planches

(Kaleidoscope, abstract ornaments; 87 patterns in 20 plates)

AD. (ADÉLAÏDE PILLARD) AND M.P. VERNEUIL (MAURICE PILLARD)

PUBLISHED BY ÉDITIONS ALBERT LÉVY, PARIS, 1923–6

POCHOIR PRINTS BY JEAN SAUDÉ

V&A L.5005-1972

The very essence of Art Deco pattern is embodied in the bold abstract motifs of Adélaïde and Maurice Pillard's 87 textile designs for *Kaléidoscope*, all realized in punchy pochoir (colour stencil) by Jean Saudé, a master of the technique. This was one of a handful of key French pattern books that Saudé collaborated on that proved instrumental in popularizing the Art Deco style. Its visual appeal is clear: the vibrant, almost electrically bright palette of primary colours, rendered with crisp precision, is further heightened by the use of bronze and silver ink and contrasting black and grey, resulting in the designs leaping from the page. Saudé was a key player in the revival and refining of pochoir and published a separate treatise breaking down his process step by step. Colour was layered skilfully using hand-stencilling, and the technique was therefore reserved solely for high-end book and journal illustration, becoming synonymous with the luxurious Art Deco aesthetic. For today's reader, these illustrations vividly evoke all the exuberance and cosmopolitan elegance of the roaring twenties. [SG]

1.

2.

ORNAMENT AND PATTERN 195

Urformen der Kunst

(*Art Forms in Nature*)

KARL BLOSSFELDT

PUBLISHED BY ERNST WASMUTH, BERLIN, 1928

120 BLACK-AND-WHITE PLATES

V&A 38041002024651

Urformen der Kunst displays an array of magnified plant forms – leaves, stems, flowers and seeds – the stark photography generating an impression of solid manufactured design pieces. Karl Blossfeldt began his career as an apprentice at a German ironworks and produced the first of these photographic images in 1900. Never formally trained as a photographer, Blossfeldt improvised cameras, creating equipment that would magnify an image up to 30 times. He used the images while teaching design in Berlin, where he also established a plant photography archive. The aim of his thousands of images was to demonstrate how every small element from nature can be appreciated for its artistic form. The Berlin collector and gallerist Karl Nierendorf discovered Blossfeldt's archive and brought his work to public attention. Nierendorf exhibited a selection of the photographs and arranged the publication of 120 plates in a book that continues to enjoy popularity in various languages and editions. Though pedagogical in origin, the photographs influenced the Surrealists and are acknowledged as pivotal in the development of *Neue Sachlichkeit* (New Objectivity) and the typological approach in German photography during the 1920s. Nature in its minutiae provides a bridge between photography as a scientific and an artistic medium. [FW]

 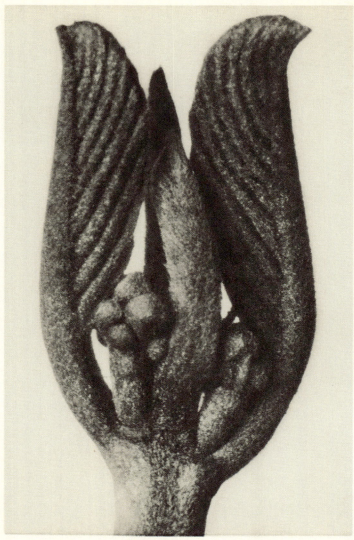 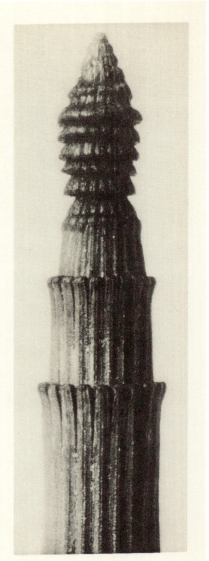

1.

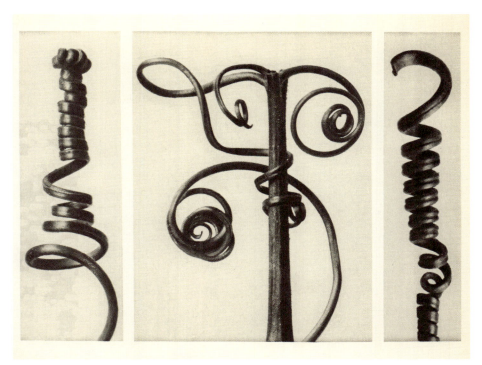

2.

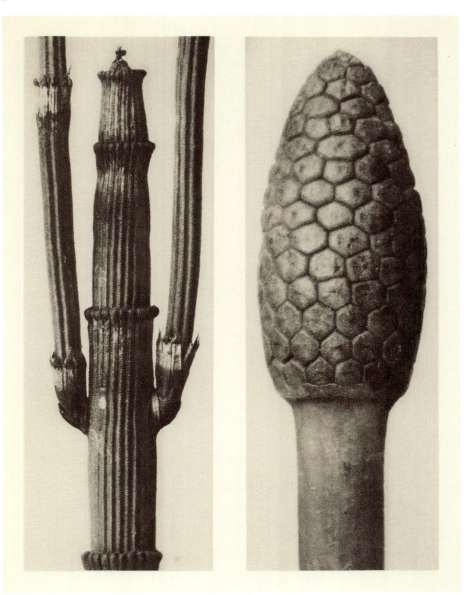

3.

ORNAMENT AND PATTERN   197

Melanesian Design
A study of style in wood and tortoiseshell carving

GLADYS A. REICHARD

PUBLISHED BY COLUMBIA UNIVERSITY PRESS, NEW YORK, 1933

2 VOLUMES, ILLUSTRATIONS FROM BLACK-AND-WHITE PHOTOGRAPHS AND DRAWINGS

V&A 38041800377509 and 38041800377616

This book on Melanesian carving, one of the first such studies, is still a key text for the study of Oceanic design. Striking illustrations record patterns of wooden bowls and turtleshell bracelets and armlets. Particularly distinctive is the 'Tami style', which hails from the Tami Islands, off the coast of Papua New Guinea. Illustrations of the armlets record narrow horizontal bands of geometric ornament, composed of ribbons, mouth designs, rectangles, chevrons and toothed borders. The carved areas would have been filled with white pigment to throw them into greater relief. Patterns from other parts of Melanesia include animals, such as turtles and lizards, and eyelike ellipsoids. The examples were chosen, the author readily admitted, because they were 'beautiful from my own point of view'. Reichard is best known today as a pioneer in the first wave of feminist anthropologists. When her book was published, Melanesia was virtually unknown to American and British audiences, though this changed rapidly with the onset of conflict in the Pacific during the Second World War. Reichard's text is highly analytical but the book is an apt example of the part played by anthropological literature in the study of ornament from cultures outside Europe. [SG]

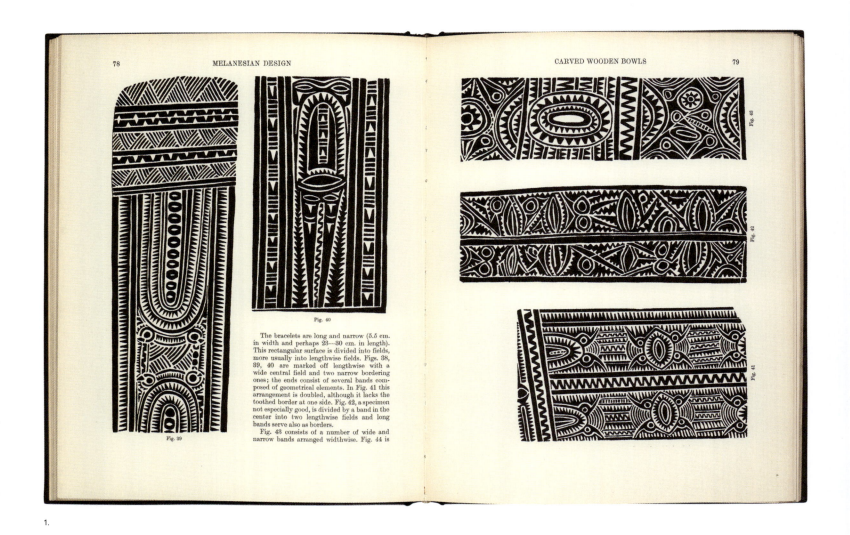

1.

Dunhuang Tang dai tu an xuan

(A selection of Tang dynasty designs)

SHUHONG CHANG

PUBLISHED BY REN MIN MEI SHU CHU BAN SHE, BEIJING, 1959

OFFSET LITHOGRAPHY

V&A L.3259-1959

This book presents a collection of ornamented patterns drawn from the ancient wall paintings decorating the Mogao cave in Dunhuang, in the middle of the west China deserts. Having been sealed in the eleventh century, the cave and the famous Dunhuang manuscripts within it were rediscovered in 1900. While the manuscripts are now kept in different institutions outside China, the wall paintings, which date from the Tang dynasty (618–906 CE), remain *in situ*. There was no electricity supply in the cave area until the 1980s, and the Chinese artists copying these paintings for illustration had to work with oil lamps and live in the most rudimentary conditions. Among the exquisite designs contained within the book, the three hares motif is uniquely fascinating (1). It shows a never-ending circle of three such animals chasing one another, representing peace and tranquillity. Remarkably, the motif is found on objects from ceramics and metalwork to textiles produced across the Middle East and Europe. In Britain it appeared on church roof bosses and illuminated manuscripts from as early as the thirteenth century. This motif is a potent reminder of the transcultural communications and connections that existed long before modern globalization. [XX]

1.

2.

3.

Festivals

Festivals

PATRICK PERRATT

On 4 July 1999 the England footballer David Beckham married the pop star Victoria Adams at Luttrellstown Castle in Ireland in the celebrity wedding of the year. Media access to the event was closely controlled: an exclusive deal had been made with the British magazine *OK!* Whether or not the couple craved a private ceremony, their celebrity status demanded that it be shared with the public. The full story appeared with official photographs by Brian Aris in a special issue of the magazine and a commemorative book.

In 1475 Costanzo Sforza, Lord of Pesaro, married Camilla of Aragon, a member of an important Neapolitan family with links to the King of Naples. The ceremony was surrounded by four days of processions, pageants, fireworks, jousts and other entertainments. The wedding represented an alliance between two great families, and the extravagance of the celebrations reflected the significance of that alliance. Five hundred years ago, just as now, it was important to be in control of your image. The printed record of this event details the lavish entertainments, noting the nobility and ambassadors who attended and the gifts received. It is the earliest identified example of a genre that has come to be known as the festival book: an official published description of a public spectacle.

Festivals of many types (ceremonies, processions, entertainments) were an important part of court and city life in early modern Europe. Beyond any meaning inherent in a ceremony, festivals were a means by which the court, civic authorities or church could present themselves to the public or one another. A public spectacle could convey messages of power, wealth, culture or learning. An official description of the event could contribute to this message, reaching a wider audience beyond the limited number of people who had attended and recording it for posterity.

By no means are all festival books illustrated (the description of the Sforza wedding was not), but, when present, illustrations can serve several purposes. Images might add to the luxury of an object intended as a gift, draw attention to the artistic aspects of the festival, or function as aids to understanding the often-obscure symbolism seen in festival pageantry. During the Renaissance, medieval festival traditions were supplemented by classical imagery, which could be found in the newly available editions of classical authors (such as descriptions of triumphal processions in Plutarch's biographies of the Roman emperors) or prints depicting Roman monuments. Humanist literature and scholarship provided another rich source, with illustrated books themselves influencing festival designs. For example, a recurring motif in sixteenth-century festivals is the elephant supporting an obelisk, first found in Francesco Colonna's *Hypnerotomachia Poliphili* (opposite top), an esoteric romantic allegory published in 1499. The narrative of this work

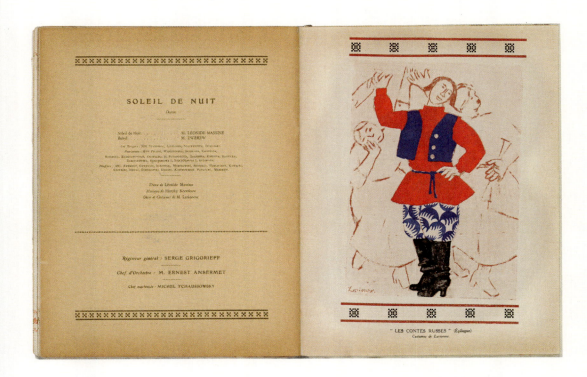

LEFT
Mikhail Larionov, costume design for souvenir programme from *Les Ballets russes à Paris: représentations exceptionnelles, Théâtre du Châtelet, mai 1917*, published by Maurice de Brunhoff, Paris, 1917
THM/DIS/2016/BR/1

deua ad intrare nella Elephantina machina exuiscerata.

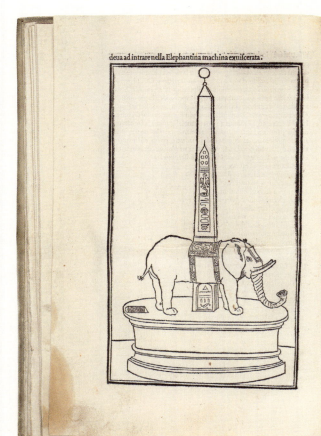

Per laqle cosa di curiosa auiditate grādemēte scitato, itrogresso mōtai Oue cauo tutto & uacuo il maximo & prodigioso monstro, & cauernato il trouai. Excepto, che il medesimo sodo era relicto ancora itestino, q̄le ex timo staua subiecto. Et haueua tanta itione, & uerso il capo, & uerso la parte postrema, quanto che l'homo naturale facea transito. Et quiui nel conuexo del dorso suspensa, cū laquei erei ardea una lampada iextinguibile, cum illuminatione carceraria. Per laqle iqsta posterga parte, mirai uno antiquario sepulchro cōcesso alla propria petra, cū una psecta imagine uirile & nuda, quāto il naturale cōmune, in coronata, dil Saxo, nigerrima. Cum gli denti, ochii, & ungue di lucente argento intecti. Soprastante al sepulchrale coperto in arcuato, & disquammea operatura inuestito, & di altri exquisiti liniamenti. Monstraua cum uno inaurato sceptro di ramo extenso il bracio, la parte anteriore. Et nella sinistra teniua uno carinato scuto, exacta la forma da losso capitale equino, inscripto di tri idiomi, cū picole notule. Hebræo, Attico, & Latino, di tale sentētia.

Per laquale inusitata cosa istetti non mediocremente stupido, cum alquanto horrore. Dique nō troppo differendo conuerso ad lo ritorno, ui di il simigliante ardere & lucere un'altra lucerna, come dinanti e dicto. Et face do transito sopra lo hiato dil salire, iui uerso il capo dill'animale. Et in qsto lato ācora una medesima factura di ueterrima sepultura trouai. Et la

---

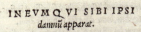

Capra lupum non sponte meo nunc ubere lacto,
Quod male pastoris prouida cura iubet.
Creuerit ille simul, mea nec post ubera pascet,
Improbitas nullo flectitur obsequio.

REMEDIA IN ARDVO MALA.
in prono esse.

Aetherijs postquā deiecit sedibus Atēn,
Iupiter heu uexat quàm mala noxa uiros.
Euolat hæc pedibus celer & pernicibus alis,
Intactumq̄, nihil casibus esse sinit.
Ergo litæ proles Iouis hanc comitantur euntem,
Sarcturæ quicquid fecerit illa mali.
Sed quia segnipedes strabæq̄ lassæq̄, senectæ,
Nihil nisi post longo tempore restituūt.

ELOQVENTIA FORTITV-
dine præstantior.

Arcum læua tenet, rigidam fert dextera clauam,
Contegit & Nemees corpora nuda leo.
Herculis hæc igitur facies? non conuenit illud,
Quod uetus & senio tempora cana gerit.
Quid q̄, lingua illi leuibus traiecta cathenis,
Quis fissa facili allicit aure uiros.

ABOVE
Woodcuts in Francesco Colonna, *Hypnerotomachia Poliphili* (Poliphilo's strife of love in a dream), printed by Aldus Manutius, Venice, 1499
V&A 1041-1886

LEFT
Hans Schäufelein, woodcuts in Andrea Alciati, *Emblemata liber* (*A Book of Emblems*), printed by Heinrich Stayner, Augsburg, 1531
V&A 271-1893

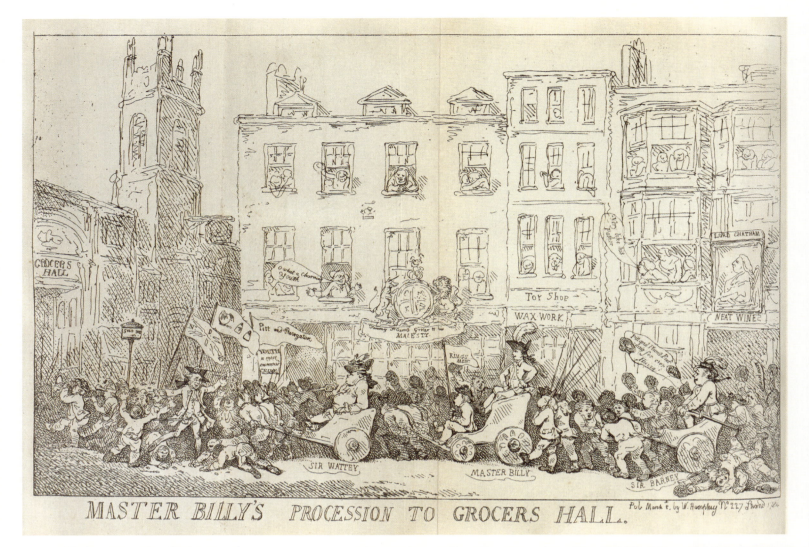

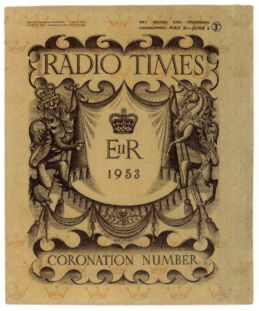
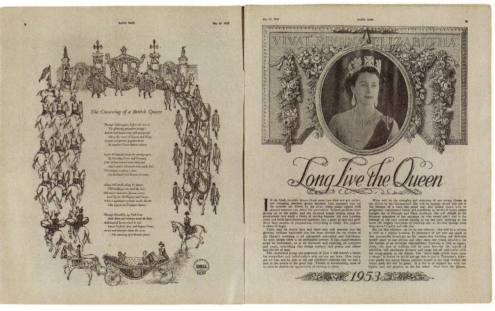

TOP
Thomas Rowlandson, 'Master Billy's Procession to Grocers' Hall', etching from J. Hartley, *History of the Westminster Election*, published by John Debrett, London, 1784
V&A L.938-1983

ABOVE LEFT AND RIGHT
Eric Fraser, Dick Hart and Norman Mansbridge, *Radio Times* 'Coronation number', published by the British Broadcasting Corporation, London, 1953
Private collection

OPPOSITE
Neville Conder, 'The Dome of Discovery', from Basil Taylor, *The Festival of Britain 1951*, published by HMSO, London, 1951
V&A 38041997044722

is itself processional, as the hero encounters triumphal parades, arches and ceremonial floats in his quest for erotic fulfilment (or maybe spiritual enlightenment). Many of these elements feature in the illustrations, which would have been well known to a cultured elite. Andrea Alciati's *Emblemata liber* (p.203 bottom), first published in 1531, and Cesare Ripa's *Iconologia* of 1593 both gave form to abstract concepts, so could be used by the designers of festivals. The 'emblems' in Alciati's work are a combination of a proverb or motto with an image and a (more or less) explanatory verse, while the *Iconologia* is essentially a dictionary of symbolism in which concepts such as virtues or countries are given pictorial representations that could be used by artists.

The imagery of festival books is not limited to the actual festival. Maximilian I, Holy Roman Emperor (reigned 1508–19), was a master manipulator of his image. He employed the best artists of his day to design a triumphal entry that only ever appeared on paper. Albrecht Dürer devised an image of a monumental arch and carriage, while Hans Burgkmair and others designed 137 blocks that, when printed, formed a view of a procession approximately 54 metres (177 feet) long. These woodcuts would have been intended for distribution to civic authorities, to be displayed in town halls.

A person's image is clearly a ready tool for propaganda and promotion, but it can also be used for satire. Thomas Rowlandson's etching of 'Master Billy's Procession to Grocers' Hall' (opposite top) shows the British prime minister William Pitt the Younger arriving at Grocers' Hall to receive the freedom of the City of London. Alongside other Rowlandson prints, this etching was used to illustrate a rather dry text on a controversial general election of 1784, which saw Pitt consolidate his control of the House of Commons.

The development of popular publishing from the nineteenth century meant that more people had access to illustrated accounts of national events. Coronations, state visits and royal weddings were all covered in the new illustrated newspapers. This coincided with the increasing democratization of festivals. City, state and church no longer held the monopoly on public spectacle. Festivals are now held to celebrate artistic, sporting or scientific achievement (below); court entertainments have developed into publicly accessible theatre, opera and ballet (p.202); eminent cultural figures have replaced hereditary elites as objects of our esteem; royal weddings are still popular, but so are those of celebrities. It can often be a publication itself that makes an event public. Mass media can allow the whole country, or even the world, to participate in some way, whether it is through reading about a celebrity wedding in a magazine or watching a coronation live on television (opposite bottom).

To fully understand any publication, it is necessary to know not only who issued it but also for whom it was intended. Official publications present the official message, but commercial publications may be no less biased. Modern publications serve many of the same purposes as the earliest festival books. A celebrity wedding that appears in a magazine is legitimated and recorded for posterity; programmes help audiences understand events; souvenirs remind attendees of the occasion or serve as a surrogate for those who did not attend. The celebrity magazine may be an unlikely descendant of the festival book, but then the modern celebrity is an unlikely descendant of Renaissance nobility.

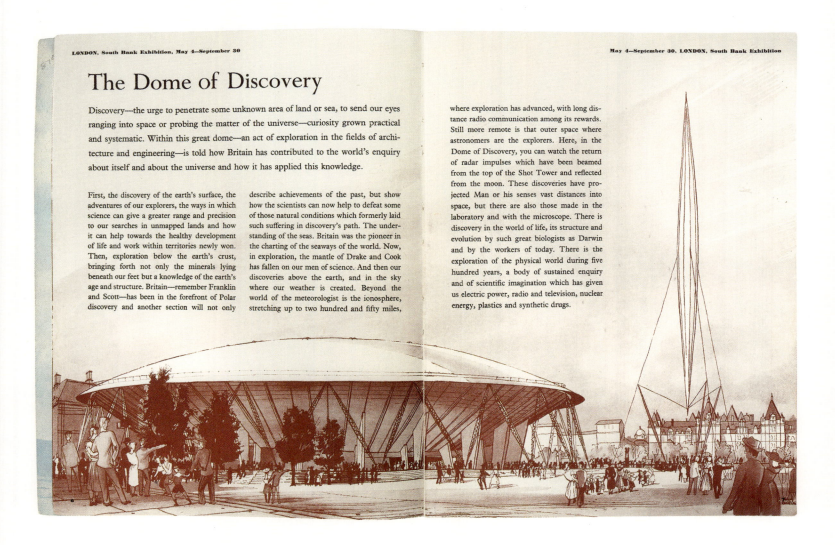

C'est l'ordre qui a esté tenu à la nouvelle et joyeuse entrée

que treshault, tresexcellent, & trespuissant Prince, le Roy treschrestien Henry deuxiesme de ce nom, a faicte en sa bonne ville & cité de Paris, capitale de son royaume, le seziesme jour de juing M. D. XLIX

(The events held at the new and joyous entry, which the very high, very excellent and very powerful prince, the very Christian King Henry, second of that name, made into his good town and city of Paris, capital of his kingdom, on the sixteenth day of June 1549)

PRINTED BY JEAN DALLIER, PARIS, 1549

11 WOODCUTS

V&A L.5040-1980

1.

2.

This book records the ceremonial entry in 1549 of Henri II, King of France, into Paris, in which he was received by the civic authorities. Most of the 11 woodcut illustrations depict the temporary constructions created for the procession. Although the symbolism can seem obscure to the modern reader, sources can be found in contemporary literature. For example, the figure of the 'Gallic Hercules' (1), in which the power of eloquence over force is shown by the chains issuing from the mouth of the hero, is found in Andrea Alciati's *Emblemata liber* of 1531 (p.203 bottom), whereas the rhinoceros carrying an obelisk (3) can be related to an illustration in the *Hypnerotomachia Poliphili* of 1499 (although in the earlier work the animal is an elephant; p.203 top). The influence of the *Hypnerotomachia* can also be seen in the style of the illustrations: the stark simplicity of the architectural lines is offset by the more fluid rendering of the organic elements. The preponderance of architectural detail is counterbalanced by the most dazzling plate in the volume: that of the captain of the guard (2). This is a true tour de force, recognized as a fine example of sixteenth-century French woodcut. [PP]

L'ENTREE DV ROY

Mais pour n'oublier les hieroglyphes, Premierement il y auoit vn lyon & vn chien de front, reposans chacun vn pied sur vne couronne de France Imperiale, estant au milieu d'eux vn liure antique fermé à gros fermoirs, dedans le liure vne espée nue trauersante de bout en bout: vn serpent tortillé en forme de couleuure, vn croissant large, duquel les cornes reposoyēt sur deux termes: vn globe sur marche d'vn pied tiré du naturel, vne poupe de nauire & vn trident, vn œil ouuert, vnes fasces consulaires, vn rond ou cercle, vn pauois, vn ancre de long, deux mains croisées sur des rameaux d'oliuier: vne corne d'abondance, dessus laquelle tomboit pluye d'or, vn cerf, vn d'aulphin, vne couronne de l'aurier, vne lampe antique allumée, vn mors de cheual, & puis le timon d'vn nauire, qui signifioyēt en s'addressant au Roy, Force & vigilance puissent garder vostre Royaume: Par conseil, bonne expedition, & prudence soyent voz limites estenduz, si qu'à vous soit soubmise toute la ronde machine de la terre, & que dominez à la mer, ayāt tousiours Dieu pour vengeur & deffenseur contre voz ennemys: par ferme paix & concorde, en affluence de tous biens longuement & sainement triumphateur, viuez, regissez & gouuernez.

En la premiere face du stilobate y auoit vn tableau placqué, dedans lequel estoit escrit en lettre d'or, sur vn fons noir, ce quatrin disant en la personne de France,

Longuement a vescu & viura la memoire
D'Hercules, qui tant de monstres surmontez:
Les peuples fiers & forts par moy France domtez
Furent, sont & seront m'a perdurable gloire.

Telle estoit la dedication de ce trigone sacré à la majesté Royale. Mais à fin que la figure supplie à ce qui pourroit auoir esté omis, elle est icy representée.

Descriptio publicae gratulationis, spectaculorum et ludorum, in adventu Sereniss. Principis Ernesti archiducis Austriae

(A description of the public thanksgiving, of the spectacles and the games, at the entry of the most serene prince Ernst Archduke of Austria)

JOANNES BOCHIUS

PRINTED BY THE PLANTIN PRESS, ANTWERP, 1595

ENGRAVINGS BY PIETER VAN DER BORCHT AFTER MAARTEN DE VOS

V&A Piot 506

The city of Antwerp commissioned the Plantin Press to produce this book commemorating the entry into the city of Archduke Ernst of Austria, the new Governor of the Spanish Netherlands. The founder of the press, Christophe Plantin, had pioneered the use of engravings for book illustration and, after his death in 1589, the practice was continued by his son-in-law Jan Moretus. The engraver, Pieter van der Borcht, was a long-time Plantin collaborator. His plates depicting the temporary structures (1) and floats designed by Maarten de Vos are printed alongside descriptions of their symbolism written by the city official Joannes Bochius. As the engravings were printed on the reverse of letterpress pages, the flow of the book is not broken by blank pages, as is common in books illustrated with engravings. The motif of the elephant supporting a column had by this time become familiar (2). In this case we are told that the statue atop the column represents Austria holding a winged Victory (in tribute to Archduke Ernst). Other illustrations show scenes of the festivities, including the 'triumphal bonfires' erected in the city square by the guilds (3). [PP]

1.

2.

3.

Pompa introitus honori serenissimi principis Ferdinandi Austriaci, Hispaniarum Infantis ... a S.P.Q. Antverp

(Ceremonial entry in honour of the most serene prince Ferdinand of Austria, Infante of Spain ... by the council and people of Antwerp)

JEAN-GASPARD GEVAERTS

PRINTED BY JOANNES MEURSIUS, ANTWERP, 1641

ETCHINGS AND ENGRAVINGS BY THEODOOR VAN THULDEN AND OTHERS AFTER PETER PAUL RUBENS

V&A 38041800392490

1.

2.

3.

Although its economy was in decline, the city of Antwerp still managed to put on magnificent celebrations and one of the most spectacular was held for Ferdinand of Austria in 1635. The programme for the festivities was devised by Jean-Gaspard Gevaerts, a scholar and city functionary, while the artistic elements were designed by his friend the painter Peter Paul Rubens. The same pair worked on this monumental book, which is over 50 cm (20 in.) high (1). The etchings, most of which reproduce Rubens's designs, were executed by Theodoor van Thulden, who had been one of the team working under the artist on the festival. Although this volume is dedicated to Ferdinand, it is also a celebration of Rubens, who by this time was famous across Europe. He is clearly named on the title page (3), and the illustrations dominate the book. The large format means that bigger plates than would normally be seen as illustrations in a book can be accommodated. The allegorical paintings that Rubens executed on the many stages and arches are also reproduced in detail. Delays with the text set back publication and unfortunately Rubens died before the book appeared. [PP]

Les Plaisirs de l'isle enchantée

(The pleasures of the enchanted island)

PRINTED BY THE IMPRIMERIE ROYALE, PARIS, 1674

ETCHINGS BY ISRAEL SILVESTRE

V&A 38041800377301

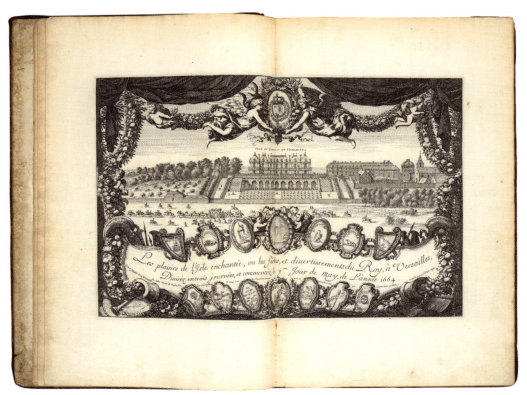

1.

2.

Between 7 and 13 May 1664, Louis XIV of France, the 'Sun King', held the first of three theatrical festivities at Versailles. This was not a ceremony with an overt message and historical symbolism, but an entertainment that displayed the king's taste. Louis was a noted patron of the arts, not least in his reinvention of Versailles itself from a modest hunting lodge into the grandest of palaces, although, as we can see from the title page (1), the transformation had only just begun. Both Louis and his brother, Philippe, duc d'Orléans, participated in performances as dancers or actors. The theme on this occasion was 'the enchanted isle', an episode from Ludovico Ariosto's sixteenth-century epic poem *Orlando Furioso*. Nine double-page etchings by the court engraver Israel Silvestre depict some of the entertainments (3), which included a performance (2) of a new comedy by the playwright Molière, *La Princesse d'Élide* (*The Princess of Elis*), music by the court composer Jean-Baptiste Lully, and fireworks (4). Although in part the record of a grand party, this volume can also be seen in the context of other publications from the royal press documenting the king's art collections. In this case, the volume documents his patronage of the performing arts. [PP]

210 • FESTIVALS

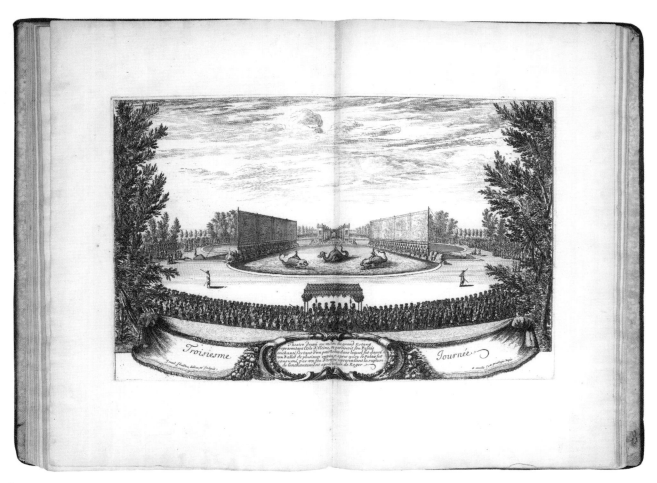

3.

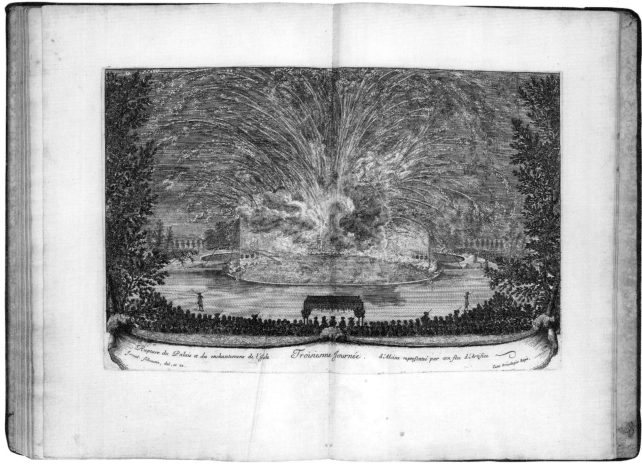

4.

FESTIVALS 211

The Coronation of his Most Sacred Majesty King George the Fourth

Solemnized in the Collegiate Church of Saint Peter Westminster upon the Nineteenth day of July MDCCCXXI. Undertaken by His Majesty's especial command, by the late Sir George Nayler, Garter Principal King at Arms, and since his decease completed from the official documents

SIR GEORGE NAYLER

PUBLISHED BY HENRY GEORGE BOHN, LONDON, 1837

AQUATINTS, COLOURED BY HAND, ETCHINGS AND WOOD ENGRAVINGS BY VARIOUS ARTISTS AFTER JAMES STEPHANOFF, FRANCIS STEPHANOFF, CHARLES WILD AND THOMAS UWINS

V&A 38041800441149

Sir George Nayler was an officer of the College of Arms who served at the coronation of George IV in 1821. His illustrated account of the coronation, 'undertaken by His Majesty's especial command', was intended to be published in five parts, but by his death in 1831 only two had been completed. The bookbinder and printer John Whittaker had also prepared a commemorative publication, which was more luxurious, with hand-coloured aquatint plates and text printed in gold. However, despite a substantial grant, Whittaker was bankrupted by the expense. Enter the enterprising publisher Henry George Bohn, who acquired the unsold copies of both works. He combined the two sets of plates and engaged Sir William Woods and Charles George Young, both also officers of the College of Arms, to help complete the text. The illustrations by the brothers James and Francis Stephanoff show many of the attending dignitaries in their ceremonial costumes (3), while Charles Wild depicted some of the ceremony's key moments (1, 2). By the time the work was published, George IV had died and his successor William IV would die in the same year. In fact, it appeared just in time for the coronation of Queen Victoria in 1838. [PP]

1.

2.

3.

The Tournament or The Days of Chivalry Revived

RICHARD DOYLE

PUBLISHED BY JOSEPH DICKINSON, LONDON, 1840

LITHOGRAPHS BY RICHARD DOYLE

V&A 480-1885

1.

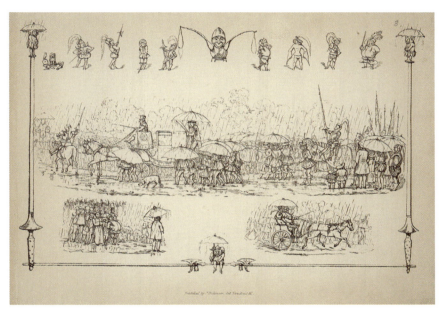

2.

The nineteenth century saw a vogue for all things medieval, seen, for example, in the architecture of the House of Commons and the novels of Walter Scott. Perhaps the most extravagant manifestation of this craze was the tournament staged by the Earl of Eglinton at his castle in Ayrshire, Scotland. Prospective 'knights', kitted out in 'authentic' armour, rehearsed in London before heading to Scotland in August 1839 for three days of jousting, banquets and balls. A suite of nine lithographs by the history painter Edward Corbould, respectfully dedicated to the earl, gives a romantic view of both the tournament and history, as do the illustrations in a commemorative book written by James Aikman. But as this volume shows, the event was ripe for parody (1): grown men (aristocrats no less) parading around in full medieval garb, torrential rainstorms (2) and gridlock in the country lanes (the event was open to the public but was massively oversubscribed). This is the first published work by Richard Doyle, who would later spend seven years at *Punch* magazine, and there is an unmistakeable similarity in styles. Doyle accentuates the faux medievalism with borders reminiscent of the often-humorous marginalia found in medieval illuminated manuscripts (2 and 3). [PP]

3.

Souvenir Programme

Given by the Theatrical & Musical Professions as a Tribute to Miss Ellen Terry on the Occasion of her Jubilee, Tuesday afternoon June 12th 1906

PRINTED AND PUBLISHED BY J. MILES & CO., LONDON, 1906

V&A 38041001202662

Ellen Terry was one of the greatest actresses of her age and perhaps the most celebrated. The gala event celebrating her 50-year career included performances by the tenor Enrico Caruso and the actresses Lillie Langtry and Mrs Patrick Campbell, as well as Terry herself. A scene from William Shakespeare's *Much Ado About Nothing* included performances from members of her family and featured scenery designs and dance arrangements by her son, Edward Gordon Craig. The printed programme is not only a souvenir, to remind those present of the evening, but also a chance for graphic artists to add to the tribute. The dance from *Much Ado* is evoked in an illustration by Byam Shaw (3); the cover design (1) is by William Nicholson (a well-known poster artist and painter who had taught Gordon Craig the art of wood engraving); the title page and ornaments throughout are by the book illustrator Walter Crane (2). In place of the triumphal arches of the Renaissance ceremonial entry celebrating the victories of kings, we have reproductions of paintings by the great society portraitists of the day showing the star in her most celebrated roles (4). [PP]

1.

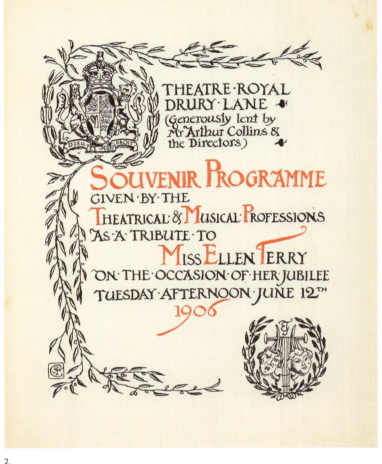

2.

3.

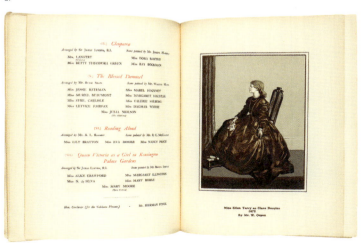

4.

The Sphere
Special Coronation Number
PUBLISHED BY THE SPHERE AND TATLER, LONDON, 1911

V&A 777-1911

Royal and state occasions have featured in illustrated newspapers since *The Illustrated London News* reported on Queen Victoria's costume ball at Buckingham Palace in its first issue in 1842. Special editions of a paper allow major events to be covered in much greater depth, with explanations and historical context. They are often issued in advance of the event, to allow readers to anticipate what will happen. That was the case with this special edition of *The Sphere* for the coronation of King George V. A range of illustrative styles are used. The section on 'Some historic coronations' includes reproductions (2) from the coronation book of George IV (p.212). Illustrations of the actual coronation of George V are necessarily imagined scenes. Watercolours commissioned from the well-known painter and teacher Byam Shaw give an 'artist's impression' of how the ceremony would look (1). Informative graphics were supplied by Blake Bourke, an otherwise unrecorded artist who also designed the heraldic cover and decorative borders for this issue (3). He was perhaps on the staff of the paper. [PP]

1.

2.

3.

FESTIVALS 215

Guide

Pleasure Gardens, 1951,
Battersea Park, Festival of Britain

PUBLISHED BY FESTIVAL GARDENS LIMITED,
LONDON, 1951

EDITED AND DESIGNED BY STANLEY BARON
AND RUARI McLEAN

V&A 38041800017972

1.

2.

3.

4.

The Festival of Britain in 1951 was described as a 'tonic to the nation': a celebration of British culture, looking forward from the dark days of the Second World War to a bright new future, symbolized by the space-age Skylon on London's South Bank. Upstream from the flagship South Bank Exhibition were the Festival Pleasure Gardens in Battersea Park. In contrast to the publications accompanying many of the Festival events, which are uniform in design, the guidebook for the Pleasure Gardens is more playful. Illustrated in a variety of styles by some of the gardens' designers, it features John Piper's design for the grand vista (1), Osbert Lancaster's entrance design (3) and, on the cover, Hans Tisdall's piazza (2). If one of the purposes of illustration is to add luxury to a product, it is interesting to note that, apart from Tisdall's striking cover design, the only colour in this publication is in the advertisements. The Pleasure Gardens were, however, a commercial concern, and the distinction between advertisement and editorial content can be blurred. The advertisement for the Guinness brewing company by the graphic design partnership Lewitt-Him (Jan Le Witt and George Him) shows the 'festival clock' that they designed for the gardens (4). [PP]

We Want the Queen

HUGO VICKERS

PUBLISHED BY DEBRETT'S PEERAGE, LONDON, 1977

PHOTOGRAPHS BY JOHN STERLING

V&A L.5426-1981

The Silver Jubilee of Queen Elizabeth II in 1977, marking 25 years of her reign, was celebrated across the country, and throughout the Commonwealth, in thousands of individual events. This book documents the work of the London Celebrations Committee. The prominent publisher's name on the title page (not to mention the coronet) suggests an Establishment publication (1). Indeed, the text is by Hugo Vickers, who became a celebrated biographer and commentator on royal events. But the photographs by John Sterling are journalistic. There are no staged portraits of dignitaries. Shots of the crowds dominate (2). When the Queen is seen, it is often from a distance, through the rear window of a car, or partially obscured (3). Details of the royal engagements are reserved for the text; the photographs show the events as ordinary people would have seen them. The success of the London Celebrations Committee can be measured by the size of the crowds. This is a celebration of celebration. [PP]

1.

2.

3.

FESTIVALS 217

Andrew Logan's Miss World '78 Souvenir Programme

PUBLISHED BY ANDREW LOGAN [?], LONDON, 1978

V&A 38041997101316

The artist Andrew Logan staged the first Alternative Miss World in his studio in Hackney, London, in 1972. According to the event's website, it is 'a fancy dress contest inspired by Crufts' (a British dog show). Fashion, performance art and drag collide in a celebration of diversity and alternative aesthetics. Fame, celebrity, spectacle and festival itself are all ripe for satire or celebration. The fourth event, as recorded here, was held in a circus tent on London's Clapham Common and co-hosted by the outrageous American actor Divine and fashion journalist-turned-erotic novelist Molly Parkin. The idea that we need not be beholden to Establishment aesthetics (Miss World was a competition created for the Festival of Britain in 1951) is reflected in the riotous punk design of this souvenir publication designed by Dick Jewell, then a recent printmaking graduate from the Royal College of Art. Part programme, part fanzine, it features a collage of photographs from previous events, tributes from friends and family, and biographical information on the artist with typed or hand-written text. [PP]

1.

2.

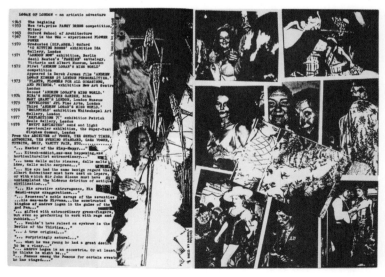

3.

Vaguely Lost in Shangri-La

Photographs from the Glastonbury Festival

BARRY LEWIS

PUBLISHED BY FLOOD GALLERY PUBLISHING, LONDON, 2017

V&A 38041017047861

1.

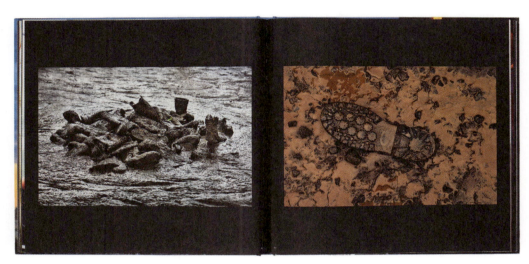

2.

3.

Today the word 'festival' is more likely to evoke images of camping in muddy fields and open-air rock concerts than stately processions of court and civic dignitaries. Glastonbury is, perhaps, the epitome of the modern festival: a celebration of community, self-expression and creativity, rather than an affirmation of political power structures. Any serious fan of the festival will tell you that 'it's not just about the music', and the photographer Barry Lewis spent several years documenting just about everything there but the music. Just like Poliphilus, the hero of the *Hypnerotomachia* (p.203 top), we progress through a fantastic dreamscape of strange architecture and even stranger people. The title refers to an area of the festival, named after the fictional Himalayan utopia of James Hilton's *Lost Horizon* (1933), but the book's epigraph from Dante's *Divine Comedy* suggests we are passing through the gates of hell. If this is hell, it is not because it is evil; rather, it is a lusty, pagan world beyond the control of the established order. Dante's 'Inferno' is home to many characters we may admire, including the great lovers of history. We can forget for a moment that Glastonbury has become part of the new Establishment. [PP]

FESTIVALS 219

11
World's Fairs

World's Fairs

Ella Kilgallon

World's fairs or universal expositions showcase the arts, culture and technological advances of nations. While some have a lasting impact – such as the Great Exhibition in London of 1851 – they are essentially ephemeral. Although some architectural features occasionally remain *in situ*, most fairs exist only for a matter of months. Therefore, illustrated catalogues and guides are important souvenirs and records, giving the occasion an enduring presence long after the pavilions have been dismantled and the crowds have gone home. Intended as a faithful record of the objects on display and the buildings that housed them, the illustrations in exposition publications are usually highly accurate, even technical, but occasionally also fantastical.

World's fairs, defined by international participation, owe their origins to the national fair, a phenomenon that began in France in the decade after the Revolution of 1789. Utopian in its projection of French life and industry, the 1798 fair sought to express national confidence – a theme that would characterize all future expositions. The flurry of French fairs that followed inspired similar events across Europe and America. It was London, however, that hosted the first world's fair: the Great Exhibition. Opening on 1 May 1851, it welcomed six million visitors to a specially built glass emporium, the Crystal Palace, with over 100,000 exhibits. The brainchild of Prince Albert and Henry Cole (the future director of the South Kensington Museum, which eventually became the V&A), it was staged to celebrate progress and encourage trade. Once the exhibition had closed, however, the illustrated books were the spectacle's afterlife. These publications, commissioned by official committees, private publishers and even commercial companies, helped to disseminate the technology and cement the styles and tastes on display. And those unable to visit could experience the wonders of the exposition (or at least its constructed image) through the medium of print.

An entanglement of nationalism and internationalism, world's fairs promoted global peace and international rivalry – all centred on the idea of progress. New printing presses were among the technologies on display in the Machinery Courts of the 1851 Great Exhibition – the court that drew the greatest crowds. At *The Illustrated London News* stand, a new vertical printing machine, designed by Augustus Applegath, was in action throughout the exhibition. Much to the delight of visitors, the machine-printed news-sheets could be taken away as souvenirs. Elsewhere at the exhibition, 'Lithographers to the Queen' Day and Son showed their technique for creating vibrant lithograph plates of up to 13 colours. This new technology was chosen to illustrate a more weighty souvenir: a catalogue of the 'choicest specimens' selected by Sir Matthew Digby Wyatt (right and pp.226–7). While Digby Wyatt's book detailed objects at the fair, other souvenir publications captured the event in the round. More than any other, *Dickinson's Comprehensive Pictures of the*

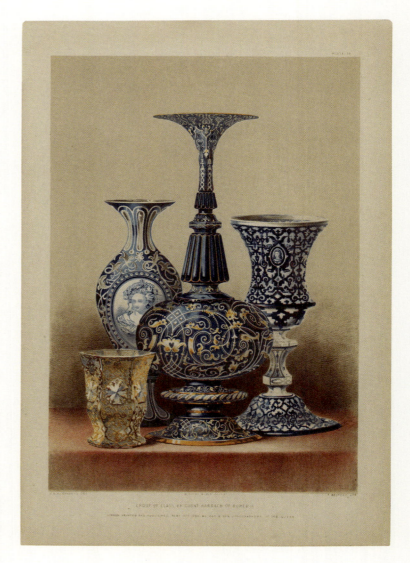

ABOVE
'Group of glass by Count Harrach of Bohemia', plate 38 from Matthew Digby Wyatt, *The Industrial Arts of the Nineteenth Century: A series of illustrations of the choicest specimens produced by every nation at the Great Exhibition of the Works of Industry*, London, 1851–3
V&A 38041800841371

Great Exhibition of 1851 placed the viewer within the richly decorated exhibition halls of the Crystal Palace, decked with ornate objects and filled with people from around the world (below).

The Great Exhibition of 1851 established the illustrated book as an essential record of a world's fair. Thereafter, all large-scale exhibitions were accompanied by a selection of publications, each vying to be the definitive record. Competition between expositions, and publishers, encouraged a spectrum of illustrated books to cater to different audiences. While chromolithography was celebrated for its ability to replicate tones and textures, it was a time-consuming and expensive process. The cheaper and therefore more democratic printing method was wood engraving. This versatile option suited the more encyclopedic exposition catalogues, which demanded hundreds of illustrations to record the vast selection of objects on display.

The official catalogue of the London International Exhibition of 1862, the much larger but lesser-known successor to the Great Exhibition, embedded scores of illustrations among the text (p.229). In an exhaustive catalogue of four volumes, the illustrations detailed everything from cast-iron gutters and cattle troughs to precious metals. It was intended as a resource that could be made widely available and therefore produced on cheaper paper. Affordability was also a key concern for the *Illustrated Newspaper* publisher, Frank Leslie, who produced a catalogue of the Centennial Exposition held in Philadelphia in 1876, the second ever in the United States (p.230). He positioned his publication as the democratic alternative to those made for the earlier London and Paris (1855) shows, which 'far exceed[ed] the purse of the ordinary book-buyer'. Leslie's observation was not wrong. Publications filled with expensive colour plates were the preserve of royal patrons and a few choice institutions.

LEFT
'The Exterior of The Crystal Palace, Great Exhibition Building of 1851' and 'The Indian Court', lithographs, coloured by hand, from *Dickinson's Comprehensive Pictures of the Great Exhibition of 1851*, London, 1854
V&A 38041800859084 (top) and 19536:11 (bottom)

WORLD'S FAIRS 223

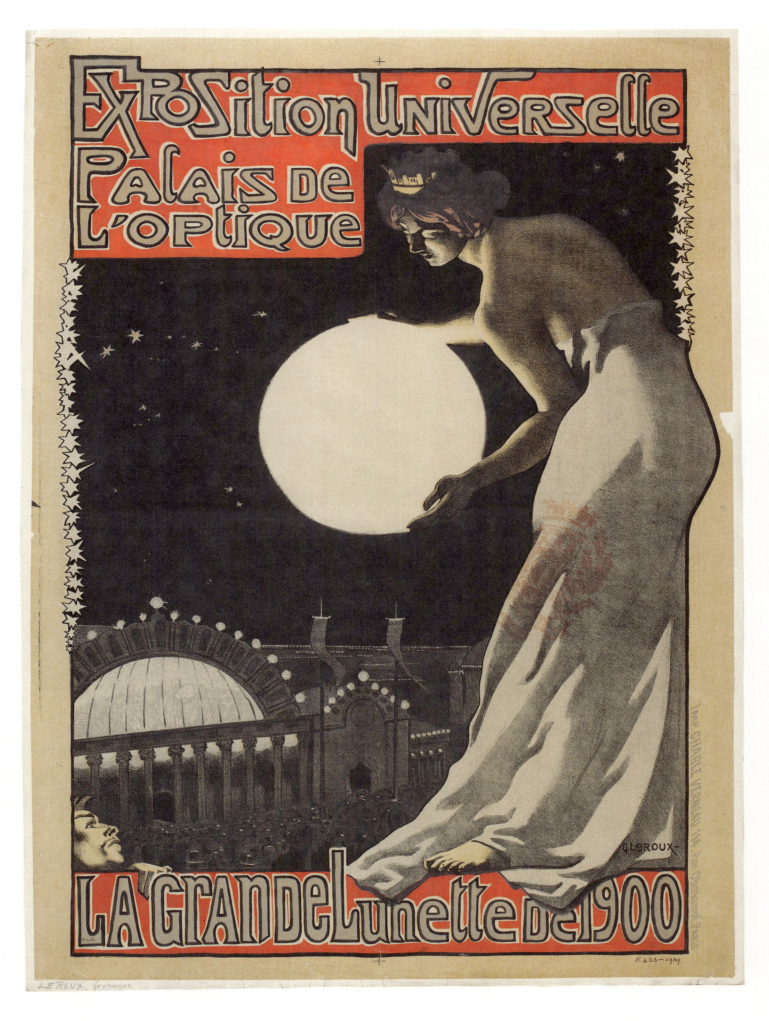

A compromise between colour and quantity of images shaped future world's fairs' catalogues, and publications often settled on a combination of illustrative techniques. While engravings were best suited to capturing fine details, colour plates tended to be favoured for rendering monumental architecture. By the time of the 1900 *Exposition Universelle* in Paris, the focus of world's fairs had shifted away from industry and towards leisure. Illustrated souvenir books no longer sought to record every product on display and instead captured the ambience of the fair. Electricity was the great invention being championed in 1900 and it was used throughout the exposition to create impressive light displays that illuminated the fair at night. Much like it was in George Paul Leroux's poster advertising the event (opposite), the spectacle of light was reflected in the accompanying catalogues. Illustrated predominantly with engravings, the *Encyclopédie du siècle* is notable for its double-page, fold-out chromolithographs (pp.232–3). Dreamlike scenes captured buildings such as the Palais de L'Électricité sparkling against the night sky. This new world vision, filled with colour and electric light, continued to define the world's fairs of the twentieth century, both on site and in print.

Just as engravings and lithographs presented an artist's interpretation of the world's fair, photographs, too, captured an official, constructed image. As early as 1889, committees hired official photographers, such as the Neurdein brothers in Paris, to document the event. By the World's Columbian Exposition in Chicago of 1893, photography inside the fair was strictly controlled and amateurs had to pay to take photographs. Photographic souvenir books, published in landscape format, presented impressive vistas and surreal streetscapes. Privileging the exhibition architecture and the products (and sometimes people) on display, photographers took their pictures early in the morning before the crowds descended. The result was photobooks, like the one made for the *Exposición Internacional de Barcelona* (1929), which presented a stark landscape of national pavilions almost entirely devoid of visitors (below).

As the twentieth century progressed, encyclopedic-style catalogues were no longer necessary. The exhibition buildings, captured during construction or from aerial angles, became the spectacle worth documenting. Fragments of exposition architecture that shape our cities hint at the extraordinary event for which it was created. But it is in the illustrated books – filled with artists' impressions, technical drawings and imaginary landscapes – where the energy, ambitions and magnitude of the world's fairs come alive.

OPPOSITE
George Paul Leroux, colour lithograph poster for the *Exposition Universelle Palais de l'Optique*, 1900
V&A E.423-1939

RIGHT
Photograph of the Danish Pavilion, from *Exposición Internacional de Barcelona: MCMXXIX*, Barcelona, 1929
V&A 38041001071117

Pabellón de Dinamarca Pavillon du Danemark Danish Pavillion Dänischer Pavillon

The Industrial Arts of the Nineteenth Century

A series of illustrations of the choicest specimens produced by every nation at the Great Exhibition of the Works of Industry

MATTHEW DIGBY WYATT

PUBLISHED BY DAY AND SON, LONDON, 1851–3

2 VOLUMES, 158 CHROMOLITHOGRAPHS; ILLUSTRATED BY FRANCIS BEDFORD, JOHN CLAYTON, EDWARD DALZIEL, GEORGE DALZIEL, PHILIP HENRY DELAMOTTE, HENRY NOEL HUMPHREYS, HENRY CLARKE PIDGEON, W.E. POZZI, H. RAFTER, JOHN SLIEGH, FREDERICK SMALLFIELD, ALFRED STEVENS AND JOHN ALFRED A. VINTER

V&A 38041800133225 and 38041800133233

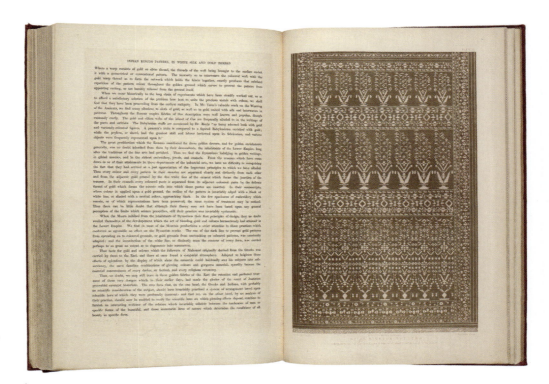

1.

2.

Made in collaboration with 13 artists, this was one of several souvenir books produced during the Great Exhibition of 1851. This was the first world's fair of the Industrial Age and the catalogue reflected its ambitions: made at speed using the relatively new technique of chromolithography, it was a testament to progress and collaboration. Both the publisher, Day and Son, and the binder, David Batten, were exhibitors and the catalogue gave them a chance to demonstrate their expertise further. The 158 chromolithograph plates, using between 7 and 13 colours, illustrate an astonishing variety of materials, from mosaics to jade vases and crimson silk. In the spirit of the Industrial Age, and 'as many of our readers may possess but imperfect ideas of the labour involved in this operation', the author begins with a detailed explanation of the process of production. For the initial 1,300 copies, the reader is informed, 1,069 lithographic stones were made to print onto the 7,892 kg (917,400 lbs) of paper that was pulled through the printing press a total of 1,350,500 times. The book, like the exhibition itself, was an enormous feat to be celebrated. [EK]

3.

4.

5.

WORLD'S FAIRS 227

1851

Or, The adventures of Mr. and Mrs. Sandboys, their son and daughter: who came up to London to 'enjoy themselves', and see the Great Exhibition

HENRY MAYHEW

PUBLISHED BY DAVID BOGUE, LONDON, 1851[?]

🕮

10 ETCHINGS BY GEORGE CRUIKSHANK

V&A Forster 5987

While official catalogues were an opportunity to celebrate the world's fair, this satirical novel reflected tensions between the spectacle itself and the experience of the average fair-goer. Henry Mayhew, a social reformer and founder of *Punch* magazine, tells of the misadventure of a family visit to the Great Exhibition in 1851. While the novel details the experiences of the Sandboys family, double-page illustrations by the caricaturist George Cruikshank present a more global perspective. A bird's-eye view of the earth topped by a commanding Crystal Palace imagines peoples of the world descending on London (1); a street scene from the city itself shows a jubilant crowd of bodies and carts processing towards Hyde Park (2); and in stark contrast the empty streets of Manchester are adorned with 'Gone to the Show' signs (3). Each illustration, while intended as satire, also gives an impression of the scale and significance of the event (4). Entry to the Great Exhibition was not restricted by class, meaning millions of people from Britain and abroad had the opportunity to attend. This coming together of classes and nationalities provided ample material for Mayhew, whose novel captures the crowds and chaos, mishaps and cultural encounters. [EK]

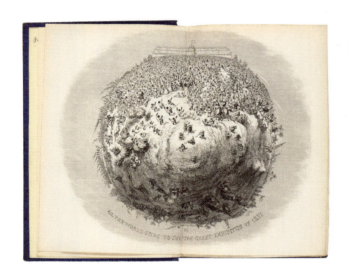

1.

2.

3.

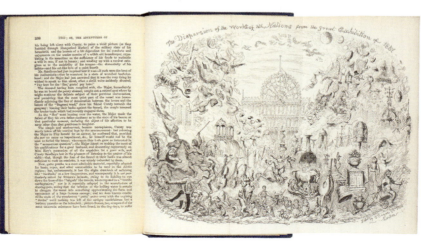

4.

The International Exhibition of 1862

The Illustrated Catalogue of the Industrial Department. British Division (Vol. II)

PRINTED FOR HER MAJESTY'S COMMISSIONERS BY CLAY, SON & TAYLOR, LONDON, 1862

ENGRAVINGS, SOME COLOURED

V&A Forster 2931

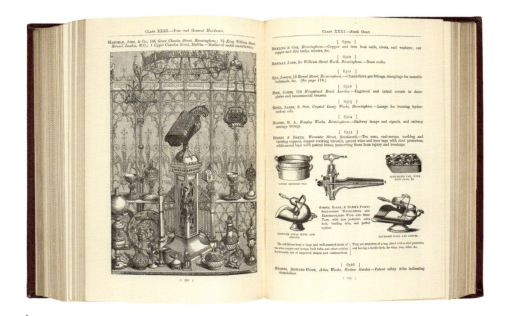

1.

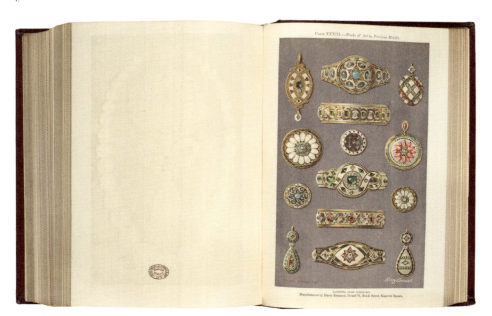

2.

3.

London's International Exhibition of 1862 has always been overshadowed by its more celebrated predecessor, the Great Exhibition of 1851. The latter was the first international trade exhibition that provided the basis and inspiration for the V&A's collections. Although it is not as well known, the 1862 exhibition was equally successful, attracting more than six million visitors, and presenting an international array of designs and applied artworks by some 28,000 exhibitors from 36 countries. The catalogues of these early international exhibitions are very much like modern auction listings, meticulously recording every object exhibited. The four volumes of this catalogue (the second of which is illustrated here) offer an encyclopedic insight into mid-nineteenth-century designs and manufacturing techniques. The numerous engravings deliver a close-to-true-life representation of the objects, presenting the applications and expertise of the makers in astounding detail (1). The plates detailing 'Works of Art in Precious Metals' (2) are captivating examples of coloured engraving and early colour printing that provide a genuine feel for the objects. Richly illustrated, the four volumes bear witness to the progress and development of art, design and manufacturing by the 1860s (3). [JR]

Frank Leslie's Historical Register of the United States Centennial Exposition, 1876

Embellished with nearly eight hundred illustrations drawn expressly for this work by the most eminent artists in America

FRANK H. NORTON

PUBLISHED BY FRANK LESLIE'S PUBLISHING HOUSE, NEW YORK, 1877

WOOD ENGRAVINGS AND CHROMOLITHOGRAPH TITLE PAGE

V&A 38041800501942

The United States Centennial Exposition was held on the centenary of American independence and aimed to establish the young nation's place in the world. Furthermore, taking place only 11 years after the end of the American Civil War (1861–5), it sought to create a united national identity centred on pioneer spirit and republican values. The *Historical Register* captured these combined motives in both price and print. An affordable price required a cheaper printing technique, and excluding the title page (1), the illustrations were all wood engravings. Drawn in precise detail, they captured the monumental architecture and engineering, from the double-cylinder steam engine that powered the exhibition (3) to the vast Machinery Hall in the final stages of construction (2). While the engravings faithfully documented the fair, the opening chromolithograph made explicit claims about America's place within the perceived global hierarchy: an allegorical female figure of the country presents the achievements of her nation to Europe, Asia and Africa, while kneeling to her right is a figure representing Native Americans. In the use of allegory the illustrator employed damaging racial stereotypes that supported the idea that Europe and, now, the United States were the rightful leaders of the world. [EK]

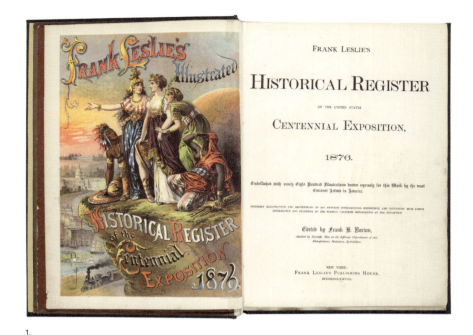

1.

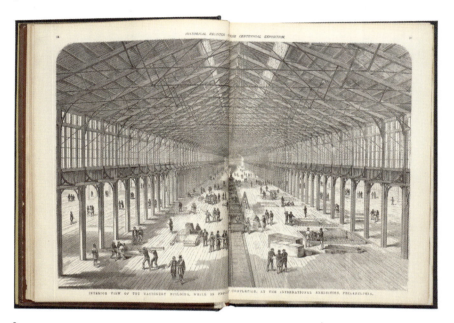

2.

3.

Art and Handicraft in the Woman's Building of the World's Columbian Exposition, Chicago, 1893

MAUD HOWE ELLIOTT

PUBLISHED BY GOUPIL AND CO., PARIS AND NEW YORK, 1893

BLACK-AND-WHITE ILLUSTRATIONS BY VARIOUS ARTISTS

V&A L.63/1914-1913

The European world's fair had centred on the question of man's place in the world. A significant contribution of the American expositions was the creation of a space for women. Designed by the 21-year-old architect Sophia G. Hayden, the Woman's Building at the World's Columbian Exposition in Chicago showcased art, literature, music and science. While the building and its sculptural decoration were largely destroyed after the fair, the accompanying catalogue became an invaluable record. Edited by the prize-winning author Maud Howe Elliott, it also captured the ambitions of the women behind the project. Progress and an 'instinct for expansion', the reader is told, defined the American woman. The art of illustration was celebrated as a site of particular progress with a roll call of the nation's best women illustrators. The French painter Madeleine Lemaire was one of the few non-American women to be celebrated, and it was her watercolour that was chosen for the exhibition poster, used as the catalogue cover (1). Lemaire's painterly cover, depicting a woman artist surrounded by the tools of her trade, quietly sang of progress. [EK]

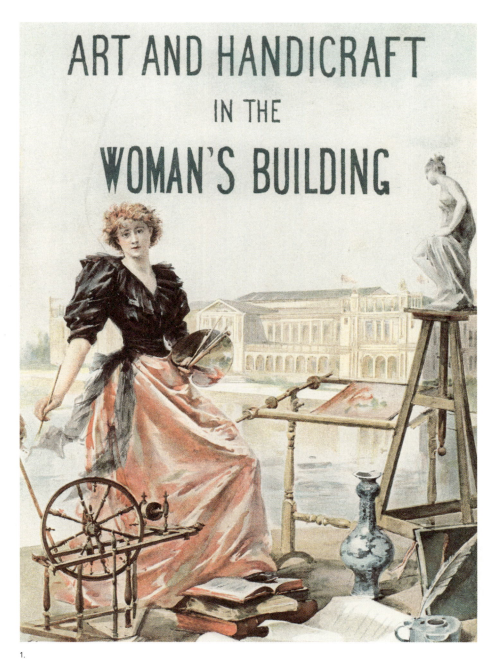

1.

2.

3.

4.

Encyclopédie du siècle. L'Exposition de Paris 1900

(The encyclopedia of the century. The Paris Exposition 1900)

PUBLISHED BY MONTGRÉDIEN ET CIE, PARIS, 1900

3 VOLUMES, GRAVURE, BLACK-AND-WHITE PHOTOGRAPHY AND CHROMOLITHOGRAPHS

V&A 278:1 to 3-1899

1.

2.

France hosted five of the most important international exhibitions in the nineteenth century, and the *Exposition Universelle* of 1900 was the last and most ambitious. By that year Paris was globally acknowledged as a centre for great exhibitions and had long been a magnet for the art lover. About 50 million visitors flocked to Paris to experience the culture and atmosphere of the participating nations. The purpose of the exhibition was to 'sell' an experience, which situated striking international designs within the geographical and cultural milieux that had produced them. This mission was elegantly conveyed in the beautifully illustrated catalogues. They combine gravure illustrations, black-and-white photography and chromolithographs. Gravure printing was a method widely used to print large volumes of magazines or catalogues, whereas chromolithographs became the most successful of several methods of colour printing developed in the nineteenth century, employed in these volumes on double-page spreads and fold-out pages. These highly decorative publications evoke the spirit of the Belle Époque and underline the position of Paris at the nexus of a global empire at the *fin de siècle*. [JR]

3.

The Greatest of Expositions Completely Illustrated

Official views of the Louisiana Purchase Exposition

PUBLISHED BY THE OFFICIAL PHOTOGRAPHIC COMPANY OF THE LOUISIANA PURCHASE EXPOSITION, ST LOUIS, MISSOURI, 1904

ILLUSTRATIONS REPRODUCED FROM GOERZ LENS PHOTOGRAPHS, MADE BY WILLIAM H. RAU, DIRECTOR OF THE OFFICIAL PHOTOGRAPHIC COMPANY, 288 PAGES, 327 PHOTOGRAPHS

V&A L.5518-1989

From the advent of photography in 1841 world's-fair catalogues used the technology to capture the places and objects on display (1). At the Louisiana Purchase Exposition, intended to celebrate the expansion of America into territories that reached from the Mississippi River to the Rocky Mountains, an official photographic company was established to capture the event. The theme of nationalist expansion defined the fair and the person chosen to record it was the documentary photographer William H. Rau (1855-1920). Rau had made his name photographing the Pennsylvania Railroad and the Spanish-American War (1898), and he brought this style of observation to the exposition. In one double-page spread, animals and people are presented side by side: a taxidermy dog called 'Owney' is seen in a glass case, while two Patagonian men, Gescheco and Bonifacio, stand posed for the camera (2). Since the Paris Exposition of 1889 people, rather than products, had become one of the main attractions, and exposition catalogues were filled with faces from across the globe. These portraits are a reminder that most international fairs presented the world through a Western, often colonial, gaze. [EK]

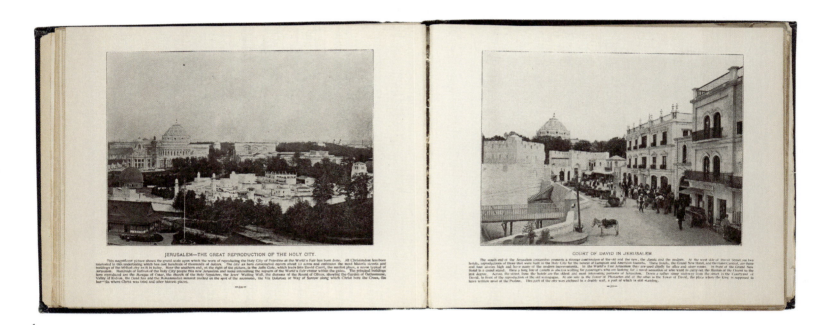

1.

2.

Intérieurs en couleurs France: cinquante planches en couleurs

(Colour interiors France: fifty colour plates)

PUBLISHED BY ÉDITIONS ALBERT LÉVY, PARIS, 1926

12 UNNUMBERED PAGES, 50 COLOUR PLATES

V&A L.6525-1979

An important feature of the *Exposition Internationale des Arts Décoratifs et Industriels Modernes* (Paris, April–October 1925) was the display by major designers, manufacturers and department stores of rooms as curated exhibits. *Intérieurs en couleurs France* showcases 50 plates of French interior design. Fresh, vibrant colours are captured through the separation process, using filters and screens to create the tiny ink dots that make up three-colour process prints. The groundbreaking display spaces are all brought to life with an immediacy that survives to this day. They include iconic, low, obtuse-angled chairs and neat built-in storage in 'Fumoir' ('Smoking room', 1); a contemporary take on traditional check flooring with stylish, yet functional olive-green utilities in 'Cuisine' ('Kitchen', 2); and the sleek, muted palette of greys, purples and blues and luxurious materials reflected by fan-shaped mirrors in 'Salle à manger' ('Dining room', 3). The cover by Boris Grosser also presents an Art Deco-imbued geometric composition blocked in silver (4). A foreword by the art historian Léon Deshairs outlines the work's aims, marking it now as an example of early interior design publishing focused on the concept of colour. [FW]

1.

2.

3.

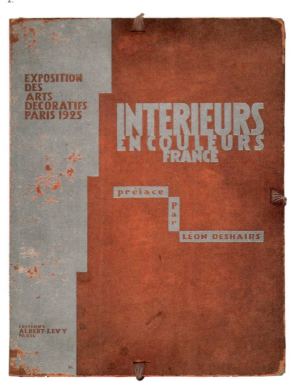

4.

The Official Pictures of a Century of Progress Exposition, Chicago 1933

JAMES WEBER LINN

PUBLISHED BY THE REUBEN H. DONNELLEY CORPORATION, CHICAGO, 1933

12 PAGES OF COLOUR PLATES, 144 PAGES OF BLACK-AND-WHITE HALF-TONE PHOTOGRAPHIC REPRODUCTIONS; PHOTOGRAPHS PREDOMINANTLY BY KAUFMANN & FABRY CO.

V&A 38041001071117

1.

2.

The Century of Progress Exposition presented a futuristic vision of hope during a time of severe economic depression. This accompanying publication includes over 150 pages of images – several utilizing the newly prevalent four-colour relief process. The large-format colour plates capture the predominantly Art Deco buildings, showcasing, for instance, the Electrical Building's (1) dynamic mix of innovative artificial materials and the groundbreaking height-adjustable suspended dome of the Travel and Transport Building (2). The interpretations by an artist allow for details such as the aurora borealis (3), sometimes visible in Chicago, and the *Graf Zeppelin* airship, which landed as a temporary exhibit, to be included as desired. The official black-and-white exhibition photography contrasts with the few commissioned colour illustrations – its extensive use perhaps reflective of the book's publication during the Great Depression. The many shots taken were reproduced in black-and-white half-tones, reducing costs, while offering extensive coverage of the fair. The exhibition saw the unprecedented phenomenon of companies being allowed to exhibit free of charge. Chrysler Motors' epochal building and those of other companies are captured inside and out (4). However, the compromise becomes clear when the lavish interior murals, with titles such as 'Progress' and 'Metal Industries', are reduced to monochrome. [FW]

THE CHRYSLER MOTORS BUILDING AND PROVING TRACK

THE FEDERAL BUILDING AND COURT OF STATES FROM THE LAGOON

THE HALL OF SCIENCE, FROM THE BRIDGE

THE GENERAL MOTORS BUILDING, AGAINST THE BACKGROUND OF THE AURORA BOREALIS

3.

4.

WORLD'S FAIRS 237

Expo 67

L'album-mémorial de l'Exposition universelle et internationale de première catégorie tenue à Montréal du vingt-sept avril au vingt-neuf octobre mil neuf cent soixante-sept

(The commemorative album for the category one universal and international exposition held in Montreal, 27 April – 29 October 1967)

JEAN-LOUIS DE LORIMIER

PUBLISHED BY THOMAS NELSON & SONS (CANADA) LIMITED, 1968

V&A 38041011014180

This large commemorative album, published a year after the closure of Expo 67, demonstrates the appetite for reflection on a celebrated event in Canada's history. Dynamic aerial photography provides an impressive overview of the islands that made up the exhibition site (1). Non-military use of planes for aerial photography has taken place since the end of the First World War, with a primary focus on mapping. The significant cost of commercial usage was perhaps considered warranted for this commemorative publication: aerial views offered a connection to the expansive (though simultaneously gendered) exhibition theme 'Man and his World'. Panoramic shots reveal the magnitude of the pavilions, including the USSR's (3), standing somewhat symbolically on an opposing island to the 20-storey geodesic bubble shape of R. Buckminster Fuller's United States Pavilion (2). The global unrest of the era feels further reflected by eye-catching fisheye lens photography – only recently available for popular use – of what the organizers described as the cumulation of the exhibition's theme. This was 'Labyrinth', a five-storey building where visitors could take a journey through the story of humanity from birth to old age, from cave dweller to astronaut, generating their own bird's-eye view by gazing down a 40-foot drop to one of the two huge central screens (4). [FW]

1.

2.

3.

4.

Nihon Bankokuhaku no kenchiku

(*The Edifice in Expo '70*)

PUBLISHED BY ASAHI SHINBUNSHA, TOKYO, 1970

136 PAGES OF PLATES, PLUS FOLD-OUT

V&A L.129-1971

Nihon Bankokuhaku no kenchiku emphasizes the materials, colour and scale of many of the Expo buildings, key to the fair's iconic vision of modernity. The colourful, organically inspired structures of many of the post-war Japanese Metabolist buildings are reproduced photolithographically from high-saturation colour photographs. This collection predates the explosion in artistic fever around colour photography that came from the United States in the mid-1970s. The vibrant immediacy provided by the highly saturated colours and the intimacy of the book format are used to great effect in this tribute to an exhibition drenched in technologically pioneering work (1). Details include a close-up of the Swiss Pavilion's award-winning aluminium *Tree of Light* (3) and views of the giant space frame spanning the central treelike core of the Symbol Zone (2) – a homage to the Crystal Palace of 1851 and in keeping with the Metabolist vision for the fair. [FW]

1.

2.

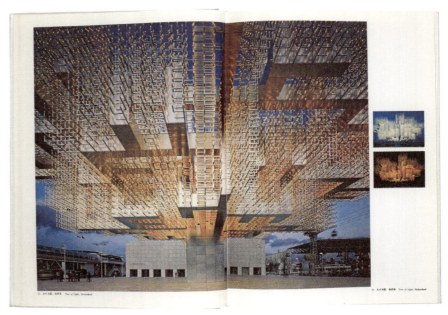

3.

12

Fashion

Fashion

Bernadette Archer and Anna Vlasova

The concept of 'fashion' as we know it today is thought to have emerged in western Europe as a cultural phenomenon in the Renaissance. Also at this time, the advent of printing, coinciding with the age of European exploration and an interest in other lands and their peoples, led to a proliferation of illustrated 'costume books', popular throughout sixteenth-century Europe. The clothing styles of countries depicted in books such as *Recueil de la diversité des habits* (A collection of the various styles of clothing, 1562) and *Habitus praecipuorum populorum* (The costumes of the principal peoples, 1577) marked the wearers' social status and regional identity. The peak of the genre was Cesare Vecellio's *Degli habiti antichi et moderni di diverse parti del mondo* (1590, p.246), intended as a sourcebook for artists and to appeal to a general audience.

Seventeenth-century depictions of fashionable dress tended to appear as prints, rather than in bound volumes, by artists such as Jacques Callot and Abraham Bosse in France and Wenceslaus Hollar in England (right). In the second half of the century *portraits en mode* – images of nobles, actors and opera singers in fashionable dress – were produced under the auspices of King Louis XIV. Their popularity throughout Europe meant *la mode française* dominated European courts.

The latter half of the eighteenth century saw the founding of various fashion magazines in France and England. Individual prints continued to be popular too, and 'fashion plates' were distributed either in the new journals or sold unbound. The latter were fine, often hand-coloured prints that went beyond simply recording contemporary attire and were intended to guide women on their choice of dress. The regularity of magazines meant that new styles could be promoted on a monthly or more frequent basis and the journals soon became essential to the transmission of fashion ideas. French fashions still dominated throughout Europe, but when the Revolution temporarily dethroned France as the arbiter of style, England took the lead. Produced in London from 1794 to 1803, Nikolaus Heideloff's lavish *Gallery of Fashion* (opposite top) recorded dress styles of 'ladies of rank and fashion' in the form of luxurious hand-coloured aquatints. And from 1809 to 1828 Rudolph Ackermann's influential *Repository* included hand-coloured fashion plates as a regular feature (opposite bottom) and helped shape women's taste in dress for over 20 years.

The earliest technical books on tailoring were printed in Spain between 1589 and 1640 and used diagrams to show the best way to arrange pattern pieces on cloth. Benoist Boullay's *Le Tailleur sincère*, printed in Paris in 1671 (p.245 top), included instructions on the cut of garments alongside simple pattern diagrams. It was not for another 100 years, however, that the first serious treatise on the art form – *Art du Tailleur* (1769), by François Alexandre de Garsault – was written. Published in a project for the Académie Royale des Sciences, the book features plates showing the tailor at work, equipment, diagrams of patterns and depictions of people wearing the finished garments.

ABOVE
Wenceslaus Hollar, 'Nobilis Mulier Aulica Anglicana (Lady of the Court of England)', etching from the series *Theatrum Mulierum*, London, 1643–4
V&A 20768:2/A

OPPOSITE TOP
Aquatint, coloured by hand, from *Gallery of Fashion* published by Nikolaus Heideloff, London, 1794–1803
V&A L.258-1943

OPPOSITE BOTTOM
Etchings, coloured by hand, from Rudolph Ackermann, *Repository of Arts, Literature, Commerce, Manufactures, Fashions and Politics*, London, 1809–28
V&A 38041800391948

MORNING DRESSES.

FIG. XXIII.

White and purple striped sarcenet hat, with an embroidered purple border, trimmed round the crown with a rose-coloured gauze handkerchief, occasionally tied under the chin with rose-coloured riband. The side hair frizzed into large curls; the hair behind turned up, and tied very low with a white *rosette*. A round gown of muslin with long sleeves, trimmed at the wrists with lace, and tied with rose-coloured ribands. The short sleeves over them, and the border of the gown embroidered in white. Handkerchief of plain lawn put within the gown. Gold ear-rings. Rose-coloured gloves and shoes.

FIG. XXIV.

Sky-blue beaver hat, trimmed round the crown with a broad purple riband, forming a large bow in the front. A large yellow ostrich feather placed behind the bow, inclining forwards. The hair frizzed into small curls; the side hair and the hair behind falling in ringlets upon the neck and back. Festoon necklace of coloured beads. Gold ear-rings. Petticoat of spotted muslin. Lawn handkerchief put within the gown. White and rose-coloured striped chintz gown; short sleeves, with a full cuff of white lawn trimmed at the top and bottom with a broad edging; a plaiting of the same round the neck. Yellow bow placed behind in the centre of the waist. Sky-blue gloves and shoes.

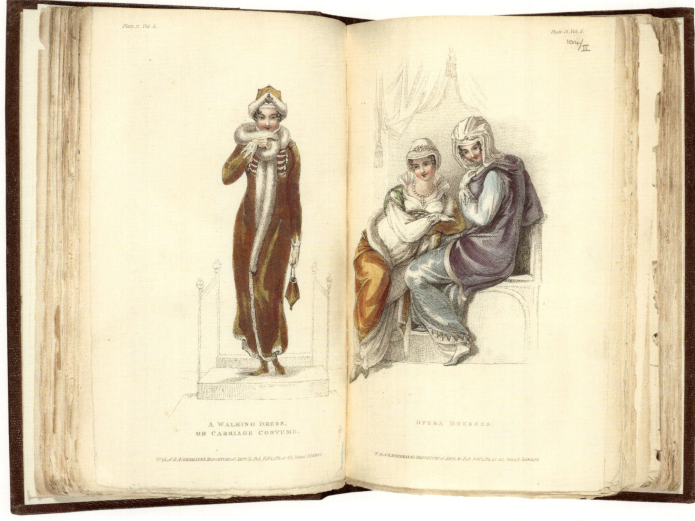

A WALKING DRESS, OR CARRIAGE COSTUME.

OPERA DRESSES.

Denis Diderot and Jean Le Rond d'Alembert's *Encyclopédie* also featured a similar section on tailoring (p.123).

In Japan the production of woodblock-printed illustrated books steadily increased from the 1620s and women's fashion was a popular genre from the outset. A favourite illustrator was Nishikawa Sukenobu (right and p.247), who often included figures wearing kimono in various indoor and outdoor settings. Like Vecellio's *Habiti*, his works were largely intended for aspiring painters but were also used by women of all social classes to learn about the latest styles.

In France and England examples of fashionable dress could also be seen in books depicting the social life of the leisured classes, in which garments were often immaculately observed from life. *Monument du costume physique et moral* (1789, p.248) presents a masterful suite of copperplate engravings of French aristocratic society just before the Revolution. Likewise, Lady Blessington's poem *The Belle of a Season* (1840, p.249) sees its heroine attired in the latest Victorian fashions. *Everyday People* (1904), a compendium of Charles Dana Gibson's humorous pen-and-ink illustrations, depicts scenes of fashionable American high society at the turn of the twentieth century (opposite bottom).

The interest in fashion as a subject for book publishing had increased steadily since the late eighteenth century, albeit with illustrations of varying quality. In the nineteenth century writers such as Charles Baudelaire turned their attention to fashion, and by the turn of the twentieth century art critics were producing works on the subject. Examples include Octave Uzanne's *Les Modes de Paris* (Paris fashions, 1898), illustrated with lithographs by François Courboin, and *Les Reines de l'aiguille* (1902, p.250) by Arsène Alexandre, with a series of exquisite etchings also by Courboin.

Fashion imagery has always been essential in promoting collections to consumers, and some particularly fine illustrated works were produced specifically for this purpose. The couturier Paul Poiret promoted his avant-garde designs by commissioning luxury albums by artists who brought a new, Modernist sensibility to fashion illustration. *Les Robes de Paul Poiret* (1908, p.251) and *Les Choses de Paul Poiret vues par Georges Lepape* (The things of Paul Poiret as seen by Georges Lepape, 1911) inaugurated a period of deluxe fashion publishing which continued until the 1930s, when fashion engraving was supplanted by photography.

Hand-drawn fashion illustration continued, however, alongside photography for the first half of the twentieth century. In *Fashion Drawing* (1955, p.252), Francis Marshall discusses the professional requirement not only to depict clothes in detail, but also to capture their beauty and refinement. The use of hand-drawn images declined with the dominance of photography, although revivals are sometimes seen. Contemporary fashion illustrators reach audiences directly on social media platforms, rather than via the publishing industry. Today, occasional ventures delight us, such as Annie Goetzinger's graphic novel *Girl in Dior* (2015, pp.256–7).

The tradition of documenting regional dress, which began with woodcuts and engravings in sixteenth-century costume books, continues in the twenty-first century. Artist-photographers offer insights into the fashion or clothing culture of specific locations through documentary photography from the street or the studio. Shoichi Aoki presented 'straight-up' portraits of Tokyo teenagers in his fanzine Fruits, later published as a book of the same name (p.253), as street style became an important element in the democratization of fashion in the late twentieth century. Likewise, shot in postcolonial West Africa, Sanlé Sory's studio portraits of stylish urbanites are a fascinating source of information for fashion historians (p.258).

In contrast to Sory's makeshift-studio portraits, the luxury art and fashion publication *Visionaire* regularly commissions celebrated fashion creatives to represent haute couture brands such as their 2010 tribute to Alexander McQueen (pp.254–5). The technical virtuosity and extravagant spectacle of such images are valued as artistic commodities in their own right, as much as for the clothes they represent.

ABOVE
Nishikawa Sukenobu, woodblock print from *Ehon tokiwagusa* (Picture book of evergreens), Kyoto, 1731
V&A E.6821-1916

OPPOSITE TOP
Title page and spread showing the diagram and the instructions for making a *casaque*-style coat, copperplate engraving from Benoist Boullay, *Le Tailleur sincère* (The sincere tailor), Paris, 1671
V&A L.1564-1932

OPPOSITE BOTTOM
Illustration from pen-and-ink drawings from Charles Dana Gibson, *Everyday People*, New York and London, 1904
V&A L.595-1967

LE TAILLEVR SINCERE,

CONTENANT CE QV'IL faut observer pour bien tracer, couper & assembler toutes les principales pieces qui se font dans la profession de Tailleur.

Par le Sieur B. BOVLLAY.

A PARIS,
Chez ANTOINE DE RAFFLÉ, Imprimeur & Libraire, ruë du Petit-Pont, au Chaudron.

M. DC. LXXI.
AVEC PRIVILEGE DV ROY.

---

68   *Le Tailleur*

POVR LA CASAQVE DE Trompette de Chevaux Legers.

IL faut observer toutes les mesmes circonstances, que dans celles de Gendarmes, à la reserve des fausses pointes du devant qui n'y sont pas necessaires, comme aussi vn collet droit, car la vuidange du col, ne sera seulement que bordée & tout le surplus doit estre la mesme chose.

Pour

Sincere.   69

POVR VN MANTEAV à Rebras.

L'ON commance par la longueur du derriere, il faut laisser pour la vuidange un douze & demy, & marquer pour la longueur du Rebras du devant, demie aulne & un seize, & apres la vuidange faite, il faut tirer un trait au droit du milieu de ladite vuidange, pour observer la longueur du derriere du manteau, & poser la ficelle sur la vuidange du costé du devant, & la porter sur la longueur du derriere & l'arrondir iusques audit costé, & pour le devant, il faut aussi poser la ficelle sur la vuidange du costé du derriere, & la porter depuis la longueur que l'on a pris pour le devant, iusques au costé marqué B, & pour le devant du manteau, il luy faut donner de carrure

F

THE JURY DISAGREES.

Degli habiti antichi, et moderni di diverse parti del mondo

(The ancient and modern clothing of different parts of the world)

CESARE VECELLIO

PUBLISHED BY DAMIAN ZENARO, VENICE, 1590

WOODCUTS BY CHRISTOPH CHRIEGER

V&A 2058-1880 (Piot 750)

The Venetian printmaker and painter Cesare Vecellio produced in 1590 what was to become an indispensable sourcebook for antique and contemporary dress of various parts of the world. Printed in a compact octavo format, woodcuts of European dress, followed by costumes from Asia and Africa, appear in heavy Renaissance frames beside the commentary on the garments, geography and customs of the country, in what Margaret Rosenthal and Ann Rosalind Jones describe as 'an informative interplay of word and image'. In his preface Vecellio highlights the great effort he devoted to creating accurate representations of the dress and the difficulty in acquiring dependable information, especially about clothing of faraway lands. He studied sculpture and frescoes to document earlier styles, collected prints and drawings of clothing, and produced his own sketches. His pivotal location in Venice, a major trading centre, also allowed him to converse with travellers to gather information on lands he could not visit. Nonetheless, Vecellio's magnum opus was not achieved without copying from artists such as Enea Vico, Jost Amman and Jean-Jacques Boissard, whose work was published in earlier costume books. [AV]

1.

2.

3.

4.

Ehon tokiwagusa

(Picture book of evergreens)

NISHIKAWA SUKENOBU

PUBLISHED IN KYOTO, 1731

3 VOLUMES, WOODBLOCK PRINTS

V&A E.6819, 6820 and 6821-1916

This three-volume publication by Nishikawa Sukenobu consists of double-page illustrations of women of different social classes. At the end of each volume a single text page gives painting and colouring instructions for aspiring painters. Although these works were essentially designed as picture manuals, the detailed illustrations of the latest fashions had a wider appeal among townspeople, who could purchase this type of publication from booksellers. The first volume (1) features high-ranking beauty icons from different periods, including court ladies of the Heian period (794–1185). The second volume shows modern townswomen enjoying outings and seasonal activities (2). The third volume (3) reveals the contemporary daily lives of courtesans in the urban centres of Kyoto, Osaka and Edo (present-day Tokyo). Sukenobu is best known for his refined depictions of fashionable women. He was the most influential and prolific book illustrator in Japan in the first half of the eighteenth century. Many of his books, including 'Picture book of evergreens', remained in print for many years, even after his death. [MY]

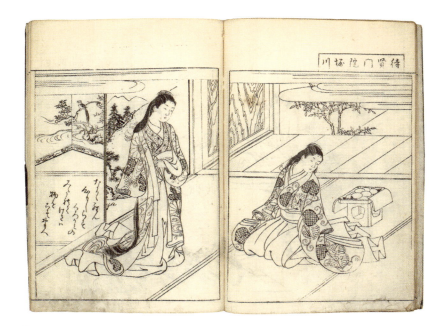

1.

2.

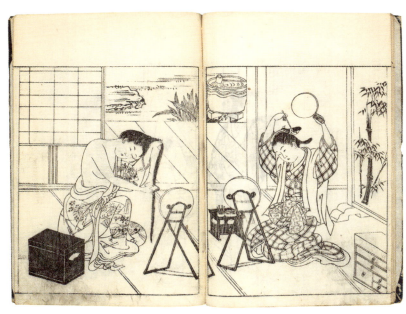

3.

FASHION 247

Monument du costume physique et moral de la fin du dix-huitième siècle, ou tableaux de la vie

(Monument of physical and moral costume of the end of the eighteenth century, or paintings of life)

NICOLAS RESTIF DE LA BRETONNE

PUBLISHED BY THE SOCIÉTÉ TYPOGRAPHIQUE, NEUWIED SUR LE RHIN, 1789

COPPERPLATE ENGRAVINGS BY JEAN-MICHEL MOREAU LE JEUNE

V&A 436-1890

Monument du costume physique et moral was conceived by the financier and art dealer Johann Heinrich Eberts as an accurate overview of refined French fashions and manners of the last quarter of the eighteenth century – when all of Europe revered the French lifestyle and its fashions in dress and interior design. It was produced 'for contemporary painters, actors, artists and for posterity' and became a swansong for the elegant way of life led by the French nobility of the *ancien régime*. The large folio of copperplate engravings by Jean-Michel Moreau le Jeune, considered the greatest French illustrator of the eighteenth century, represent sophisticated Parisian life with lightness, taste and precision in the detail of the costume and decor. The plates were first published between 1777 and 1783, accompanied by an anonymous script; however, for this 1789 edition a new text by the renowned novelist and libertine Nicolas Restif de la Bretonne was commissioned. The original descriptions of the plates were rather uninspired, but here Restif brings the scenes to life with vibrant dialogues and entertaining stories about day-to-day interactions between members of French high society. [AV]

1.

2.

The Belle of a Season: A Poem

MARGUERITE GARDINER, COUNTESS OF BLESSINGTON

PUBLISHED BY LONGMAN, ORME, BROWN, GREEN AND LONGMANS, LONDON; APPLETON & CO., NEW YORK, 1840

🕮

STEEL ENGRAVINGS AFTER ALFRED EDWARD CHALON

V&A 38041800391740

An elegant and lavishly illustrated gift book, *The Belle of a Season* presents an account of a well-born girl's entry into society in the form of a poem. Chalon was known for painting Queen Victoria after she acceded to the throne in 1837 and later became her Painter in Watercolour. Steel engravings were the usual choice for large editions such as this joint venture between two publishers, aimed at a wide distribution in England and America. Although dress is not particularly accentuated in the sentimental text by Lady Blessington, Chalon made it a prominent feature of his illustrations. He was evidently familiar with the latest fashions, as every plate features the protagonist in various social situations, appropriately dressed in styles that can be traced to those appearing in contemporary magazines. As expected, the story concludes with a wedding, where the bride is pictured in a white dress accompanied by a veil and orange blossom (2), key elements of fashionable bridal attire after Queen Victoria wore them at her wedding in 1840. [AV]

1.

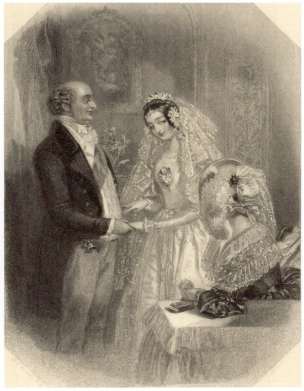

2.

3.

4.

FASHION 249

Les Reines de l'aiguille: modistes et couturières: étude parisienne

(The queens of the needle: milliners and dressmakers: Parisian study)

ARSÈNE ALEXANDRE

PUBLISHED BY THÉOPHILE BELIN, PARIS, 1902

ILLUSTRATIONS DRAWN AND ETCHED BY FRANÇOIS COURBOIN

V&A L.5015-1979

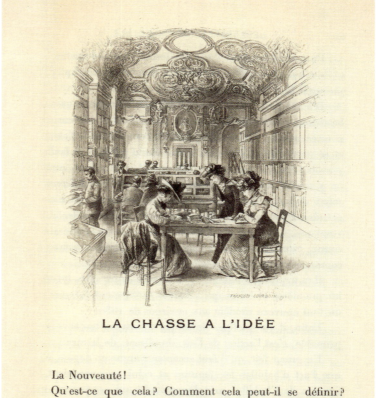

1.

Les Reines de l'aiguille is an elegant, limited-edition volume in which the delicate etchings of François Courboin, coupled with a vivid narrative by Arsène Alexandre, bring to life the Parisian fashion world at the start of the twentieth century. From the design of the garments to the relationships between the saleswomen and their clientele, the reader is offered a peek behind the scenes of the contemporary couture industry. Courboin's charming miniatures of fashionably dressed Parisian ladies appear in the plates next to scenes of seamstresses and milliners in their workshops, doing dress fittings, or absorbed in creating new designs. In contrast to the publications that depict contemporary or historical fashions, the numerous female employees take centre stage here. Alongside the professional routines of couture houses, more mundane matters are described, such as the daily arrival at work and lunch breaks when the workers flood onto the streets of the Opéra and Madeleine districts. Alexandre also draws attention to the specialist skills required, remarking that the women who design and make the garments are the artists, while those who sell them are both psychologists and masters of strategy and diplomacy. [AV]

2.   3.

Les Robes de Paul Poiret racontées par Paul Iribe

(The dresses of Paul Poiret related by Paul Iribe)

PAUL IRIBE

PUBLISHED BY PAUL POIRET, PARIS, 1908

🐚

10 POCHOIR PLATES

V&A 38041000210013

Les Robes de Paul Poiret by Paul Iribe (1883–1935) comprises 10 illustrations interpreting Poiret's dress designs of 1908. Poiret commissioned the luxury album to promote his new style of dress that jettisoned the tightly corseted models of his contemporaries in favour of a classical line that followed the natural shape and contours of the body. Inspired by the fashion of the Directoire period in France (1795–9), Poiret created ensembles featuring straight silhouettes with high waistlines that elongated the figure. The exquisite ink drawings by Iribe were reproduced using a series of hand stencils to produce dress designs with bold, flat areas of jewel-like colour that stand out dramatically against the pared-back Directoire interiors. Printed on high-quality paper and published in a limited edition of 250 copies, the successful album was followed in 1911 by *Les Choses de Paul Poiret vues par Georges Lepape* in an edition of 1,000 copies. The popularity of these two works is credited with reinvigorating the art of the fashion plate, later described as Art Deco in style. [BA]

1.

2.

3.

Fashion Drawing

FRANCIS MARSHALL

PUBLISHED BY STUDIO PUBLICATIONS, LONDON, 1955

V&A L.5493-1988

1.

2.

For *Fashion Drawing*, Francis Marshall (1901–80) was both author and artist. As one in the 'How To Do It' series published by Studio Publications in the 1940s and 1950s, Marshall's charming, companionable and sometimes humorous text is packed full of practical information on everything from artists' materials and drawing techniques to models, markets and a raft of other behind-the-scenes industry insights useful for the aspiring fashion illustrator. The text is brilliantly illustrated with Marshall's drawings (many created specially for this book) and the work of other leading fashion illustrators whom he admired. With every page layout as exquisitely conceived as the fashions depicted, the black-and-white images in the form of vignettes, sketches and finished drawings are a virtuoso presentation of a craft. *Fashion Drawing* was republished in several updated editions throughout the 1940s. This completely revised final edition with updated material on post-war fashion reached an apotheosis of elegance and was published to great success in 1955. [BA]

Fruits

SHOICHI AOKI

PUBLISHED BY PHAIDON PRESS, LONDON, 2001

V&A 38041001088897

Fruits is a collection of Tokyo street-style portraits from a popular fanzine of the same name established by the photographer Shoichi Aoki in 1994. Aoki founded the fanzine to document the exuberant and extraordinary street fashion emerging among teenagers in the Harajuku district of Tokyo. *Fruits* attracted a keen following among Japanese teenagers who were eager to discover the latest trends. The styles worn creatively combine high fashion and homemade or customized garments, and each of the subjects is presented in the same 'straight-up' style. The vibrant photographs are accompanied by amusing vox pops detailing the subject's age, occupation, the brands they are wearing and their own sometimes off-the-wall descriptions of their look in the 'point of fashion' section. The creative outfits sometimes combine traditional Japanese items of clothing such as the kimono with elements of Western dress such as American sportswear, particularly tracksuits for boys (3). The get-ups are often worn with elaborate accessories, especially bags and toys. Other notable trends included brightly coloured, dyed hair (2); platform shoes; cyber fashion; and, for girls, what came to be known as the 'Gothic-Lolita' look (1). This Phaidon photobook gathered examples from the fanzine and became a cult hit with Western audiences. [BA]

1.

2.

3.

4.

Visionaire 58 SPIRIT: A Tribute to Lee Alexander McQueen

'Couture' edition, New York, 2010

PORTFOLIO OF 18 PLATES, 2 PAGES OF ILLUSTRATED TEXT

V&A 38041014030563

The fashion and art publication *Visionaire* created a tribute to the designer Alexander McQueen (d.2010) with its 58th edition, entitled *SPIRIT*. A celebration of McQueen's life and the collections he created, the archival images gathered here from previous issues include contributions from the musician Lady Gaga (2) and the photographers Nick Knight (4) and Mario Testino. A new commission was given to the photographer Mario Sorrenti specifically for this issue. A model with hair spiked like a halo is clad in a gown from the designer's last collection, posthumously and unofficially titled *Angels and Demons* (1). She cradles a lamb on her lap in a pose resembling a *pietà*, a Christian image of lamentation and a nod perhaps to McQueen's own extensive use of religious iconography in his work. A 'Ready to Wear' edition was published alongside a limited 'Couture' edition of 75 copies. The portfolio is bound in sumptuous white Italian leather and covered with metallic brocade in a pattern from McQueen's last collection. Each illustration is printed on paper embedded with seeds, which, when planted and watered, would grow into wildflowers. [BA]

1.

2.

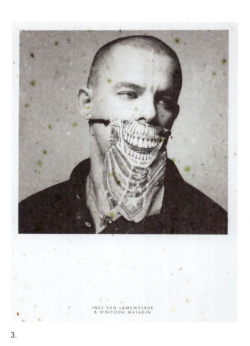

3.

NICK KNIGHT

Girl in Dior

ANNIE GOETZINGER

PUBLISHED BY NBM PUBLISHING, NEW YORK, 2015

V&A 38041016010308

1.

2.

3.

Girl in Dior describes the life of the fashion designer Christian Dior from 1947, when he opened his fashion house, to his sudden death just 10 years later in 1957. The story, both written and illustrated by Annie Goetzinger (1951–2017), her first to be translated from French into English, is told from the perspective of Clara, a fictional novice journalist hired to report on Dior's eagerly anticipated inaugural collection. Originally conceived as a comic, the work developed into a graphic novel, allowing more space to present the glamorous world of post-war fashion in more detail. Goetzinger carried out meticulous research in the Dior archives and interviewed dressmakers who had worked with the designer in order to inform her authentic and intimate portrait of the man and his work. An abundance of vignettes, text panels and speech balloons are complemented by aerial images of frantic, behind-the-scenes preparations for salon shows. Indulgent splash pages present voluminous dresses, dramatically bleeding across page spreads. The initial worm's-eye view of Dior's iconic Bar suit (3) is amplified by detailed alternative perspectives below. [BA]

256   FASHION

Studio Volta Photo

SANLÉ SORY

PUBLISHED BY FLORENT MAZZOLENI FOR TEZETA, BORDEAUX, AND YOSSI MILO GALLERY, NEW YORK, 2018

RISOGRAPH PRINTING FROM PHOTOGRAPHS BY SANLÉ SORY, DESIGNED BY SÉBASTIEN GIRARD

V&A 38041018013003

The studio portraits of Sanlé Sory (b.1943) provide a glimpse into the joyful fashion culture that emerged in the newly emancipated Republic of Upper Volta (now Burkina Faso) in the years following independence from French colonial rule in 1960. At the time studio photography served a dual purpose, since the portraits could be cropped to make the identity photos required by the administration during a period of rapid urban migration. The pictures capture youthful subjects wearing a mix of Western clothing and traditional African garments. They pose against Sory's distinctive painted backdrops (the column, the city scene with street lamp, the beach, the 1970s plane), with chequered linoleum on the floor and with their chosen studio props (the radio, the camera, the motorbike (2), an Air Afrique travel bag (1)). *Studio Volta Photo* presents 74 vintage photographs from the 1960s to the 1980s, published by the Yossi Milo Gallery on the occasion of Sory's debut gallery exhibition in New York. The homemade aesthetic of the risograph prints and spiral binding convey a personal quality and the sense of intimacy of a treasured family photo album. [BA]

1.

2.

Tim Walker: Wonderful Things

TIM WALKER AND SUSANNA BROWN
PUBLISHED BY V&A PUBLISHING, LONDON, 2019

V&A 38041019029057

1.

2.

3.

4.

Wonderful Things presents 10 series of stills and a short film by the fashion photographer Tim Walker, inspired by a diverse group of objects from the V&A collections. Each chapter chronicles a different photo shoot, beginning with the chosen V&A object being used as the springboard for a series of fantastical worlds created by Walker and his myriad collaborators. In these worlds Walker is interested in breaking down traditional boundaries by enabling more varied kinds of beauty and in representing society in its infinite diversity. In the shoot 'Why Not Be Oneself', the muse Tilda Swinton is captured in a series of candid portraits in a celebration of age and difference (1). In 'Cloud 9', Walker collaborates with models of Indian, Pakistani and Bangladeshi heritage in a richly vibrant shoot representing the cultural diversity of modern Britain (2). Unlike in traditional fashion shoots, the clothes are used to tell stories that go beyond fashion, rather than taking centre stage. In 'Handle with Care' the ghostly silhouettes of couture garments shrouded in their protective covers celebrate the wonder of collection preservation and care (3), while the knit-and-crochet-clad eco-activists in 'Soldiers of Tomorrow' (4) speak to the times we live in, using fashion and photography as tools for change. [BA]

13
Shopping

Shopping

Deborah Sutherland and Caroline Penn

Since the first stalls were set up, shopping has been embedded in our lives, and displays to attract sales have been integral to that experience. As retail spaces evolved, tempting growing numbers of consumers, not all potential customers were gazing through the windows. Increased production in England between the 1760s and 1820s – the outcome of industrial progress – prompted brass foundries, Sheffield platers and potteries to send brochures of wares depicted in engravings to Europe, America and beyond. These were the earliest catalogues containing printed illustrations selling mass-produced manufactured goods.

The essential contribution that illustration makes to trade literature is explored in this chapter – from merchants' trade cards to the 'magalogue' (a catalogue that includes written articles as well as product listings, p.273). Studies of trade literature have appraised its design, analysed its place in economic and retail history, and investigated what it can reveal about material cultures, for example W.A. Young's study of a collection of metalwork catalogues at the V&A (right). The selection here, however, considers how the illustrative elements complement and amplify the textual messages, and sometimes even replace them.

The first printed example of trade literature – a broadsheet listing priced titles by the Italian scholar-printer Aldus Manutius in 1498 – was not illustrated. Likewise, trade cards simply itemized goods available at a particular address. It was only with the advent of commercial engraving that merchants could entice customers with images of their elegant premises and quality assortments. In 1744, Benjamin Franklin's pamphlet *New Invented Pennsylvania Fire-Places* carried an advertisement

Brass Handles for Furniture, made for the French Market.

M. 101. c., *page 16*.

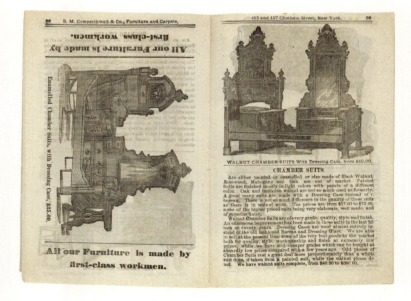

identifying agents from whom his stoves might be purchased and diagrams showing how they worked. Technical illustrations provided measurements and plans, not only to inform customers but also to inspire them. This is still done today in catalogues issued by stores such as IKEA. Medieval and Renaissance books of ornament (pp.182–3, 186) were produced for craftworkers to copy from. However, over time cabinetmakers, in particular Thomas Chippendale (p.265), adapted traditional pattern books to solicit commissions from patrons, as well as to provide specifications to other artisans. By the late eighteenth century the images in metalwork pattern books – produced for furniture makers – and catalogues of architectural components – produced for construction companies – were no longer intended as templates, but representations of items to purchase. *Sweet's Indexed Catalogue of Building Construction*, established in 1906, was an immense annual compendium of building-trade catalogues. A consumer version, the *Home Owners' Catalogs* (opposite top), comprised a selection that enabled 'Homeplanners [to] have at their fingertips … information about the many quality products … that make a house a home'.

Accurate depiction in illustrated trade literature can also be traced to the Frankfurt Fair of 1612, where the Dutch floriculturist Emanuel Sweerts introduced his *Florilegium amplissimum et selectissimum*, a catalogue comprising hand-tinted botanical plates of bulbs for sale. In the nineteenth century, catalogues published for the retail trade by household and fancy goods manufacturers and wholesalers described thousands of items. The carefully exact inventories were supplemented with captioned illustrations (pp.266–7).

Precision was not always achieved or even the prime concern. The text of the New York retailer B.M. Cowperthwait's mail-order catalogue of 1878 (opposite bottom) echoes a salesperson's encouraging patter: 'It is entirely impossible in many cases to represent on paper the important elements of QUALITY. Wood cuts [cannot] show nicety of workmanship.' Options for finishes are described, rather than shown, so that patrons could 'buy understandingly'. This need for reassurance may have arisen because mail order was a somewhat recent phenomenon. In 1872, in the United States, Montgomery Ward took advantage of developments in postal and distribution systems to reach rural consumers with his catalogues (p.271). A decade earlier, in 1861, the Welsh entrepreneur Pryce Pryce-Jones had described and depicted his woollens in catalogues sent to potential customers unable to visit his warehouse in person.

Emulating these successes, department stores issued catalogues to Europe, the colonized countries and the United States. Whether magnificent volumes or modest brochures, all were illustrated so that customers could visualize what they were buying. In Japan, during the Meiji era (1868–1912), an edict was passed requiring all public servants to wear Western clothing. The Kyōto Yōfuku Kaisha (Kyoto Western Clothing Company) pasted albumen prints of illustrations taken from European catalogues into its pages, possibly to emphasize authenticity (below).

Cheaper production meant greater quantities reaching larger audiences, but some companies exploited advances in printing processes to convey superior quality or modernity. Illustrations were printed on coated paper in sumptuous colour, for example. Photography was

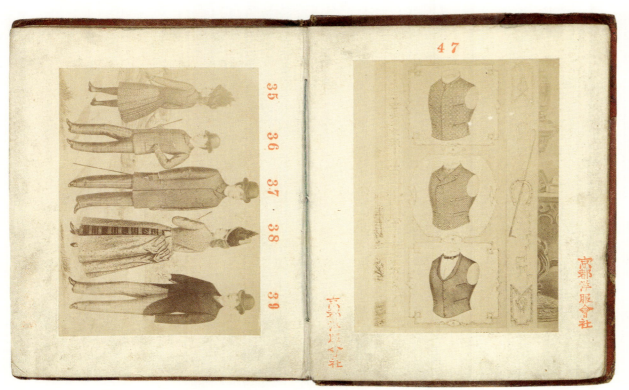

OPPOSITE LEFT
'Chamber suits', from *The Housekeeper's Guide: Illustrated Catalogue and Price List of Furniture*, New York, 1878
V&A 38041002041770

OPPOSITE RIGHT
'French Handles', from W.A. Young, *Old English Pattern Books of the Metal Trades: A Descriptive Catalogue of the Collection in the Museum*, London, 1913
V&A L.2601-1913
(From a brass-founder's catalogue, c.1785, V&A E.2259-1913)

ABOVE
'Youngstown kitchens', from *Home Owners' Catalogs [1951]*, New York, 1950
V&A 38041012068391

LEFT
Plates 35 to 39 and 47, from *Shiga Shashin* (Photography of figural images), Kyoto, 1880s
V&A L.2534-1989

SHOPPING 263

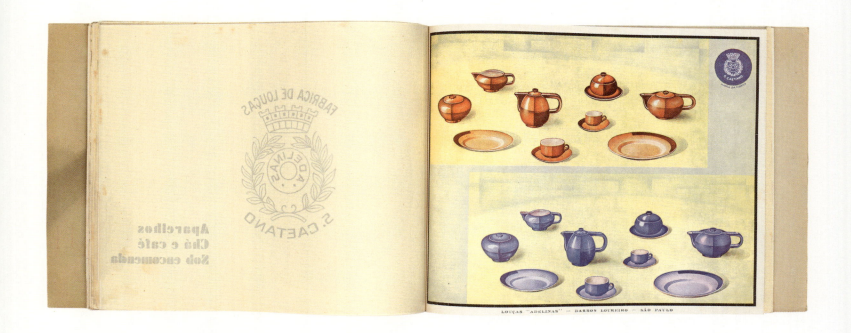

used, as well as lithography and wood engraving, sometimes executed by celebrated artists such as Raoul Dufy or Rex Whistler. Commercial artists embraced new styles and techniques of design and illustration, such as Art Deco (p.268) or photomontage (p.269).

The psychedelic imagery in *Imagination IV* (p.272), the Postmodern styling of *D.E* (p.273), and even the commonplace settings in agency mail-order catalogues such as La Redoute or Littlewoods provide a familiar aesthetic. Placing the product within the shopper's world view is a significant function of the illustrations. Sometimes just the simple addition of shadows (above) makes the goods more tangible.

In 2000, Kate Spade published a limited-edition catalogue containing a series of photographs depicting the contents of successful women's handbags (right). The women's identities are not made explicit in the main body of the catalogue, but are listed at the end alongside the image number. The (unseen) bags are glamorized by implication. Readers are encouraged to desire a lifestyle associated with owning the handbag. The images provide a sense of the product that is almost more real than seeing it on the shelf.

Illustrations sometimes represent more than the product – they 'enhance the customer's ability to imagine' and evoke the emotions associated with a brand (pp.274–5). In *A&F Quarterly* (a magalogue produced by Abercrombie & Fitch), the illustrations accompanying its articles celebrate a fantasy that might be realized by wearing the brand. Although the first Tiffany catalogue of fancy goods, published in 1845, was unillustrated, the stunning imagery in their 'Blue Books' have portrayed luxuries to which most can only aspire.

Dreams can also be ordinary, and companies such as Uniqlo or Habitat aim to 'elevate the ordinary', making good design happen on the high street as well as in high-end stores. This applies as much to the mechanisms of consumption as to the merchandise. Excellent illustration attracts an audience, in literature as in advertising, whether the product on sale is an envelope or a car. Catalogues are universal, embedded in our visual world (indeed, they may be the only illustrated books to be found in some households), and their illustrations are probably the most internationally influential.

TOP
'Louças "Adelinas": Barros Loureiro', from trade catalogue for Fabrica de Louças Adelinas, São Paulo, 1935
V&A 38041994076842

ABOVE
'ARTIST/AUTHOR 000005 [Maira Kalman]', from *Kate Spade: Contents*, New York, 2000
V&A 38041002038800

The Gentleman and Cabinet-maker's Director

Being a large collection of … designs of household furniture in the Gothic, Chinese and modern taste …

THOMAS CHIPPENDALE

PRINTED FOR THE AUTHOR, LONDON, 1754

160 COPPERPLATE ENGRAVINGS BY MATTHIAS DARLY AND JOHANNES SEBASTIAN MÜLLER

V&A 38041800767469

1.

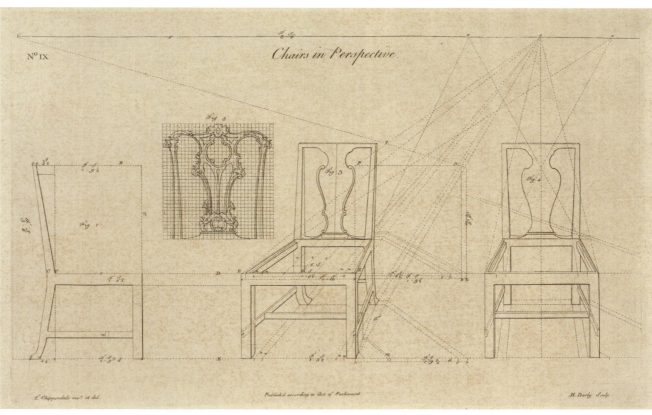

2.

Printed pattern books were widespread in Europe from the mid-sixteenth century, published for lacemakers, goldsmiths, architects and other craftspeople. This publication by Thomas Chippendale (1718–79) was ambitious in scale and purpose. It aspired to be a source of inspiration for cabinetmakers, as well as a catalogue for potential customers. The detailed designs, some annotated with measurements and ratios (2), were usually adapted by other artisans rather than copied in their entirety. The engravings in the *Director* depict the complete range of domestic furniture available at the time in Europe (1). Although the illustrations do not show furniture within the context of rooms, Chippendale was an interior designer as well as a furniture maker, advising patrons on drapery and decoration. Chippendale's workshop not only produced furniture to his published designs, but also offered clients bespoke commissions that simplified existing forms or combined features. The *Director* was hugely influential throughout Britain, Europe and colonial America, so much so that Chippendale's introduction of Chinese and Gothic elements into the fashionable French Rococo style – thereby creating the 'English Rococo' – became synonymous with his name. [CP]

SHOPPING   265

Illustrated pattern-book of furniture …

… carpets, rugs, linoleums, floor cloths, curtains, window blinds, table linen, towellings, blankets, etc: bedsteads and bedding, church, camp, ship, and garden furniture, pianofortes, organs, harmoniums, etc.: also of pictures, looking-glasses, cornices, paper hangings, etc., etc.

SILBER & FLEMING LTD

PRINTED BY J.S. VIRTUE AND CO. LTD, LONDON, 1880S

ENGRAVINGS BY J. AND G. NICHOLLS; LITHOGRAPHS BY ALLBUT & DANIEL AND PAWSON & BRAILSFORD OF SHEFFIELD
1910 PAGES IN 3 VOLUMES, ILLUSTRATED THROUGHOUT, SOME COLOUR

V&A 11 to 12 and 16-1898

The magnificent volumes published by Silber & Fleming, 'manufacturers, importers and warehousemen and agents', are archetypal illustrated trade catalogues. The company offered a vast range of household products and fancy goods to retailers across the British Empire and North America. Appropriately for publications intended to assist buyers at one remove, each page is carefully designed to allow the maximum quantity of information. The detailed images enhance the text, which is legible even at the smallest type size. Impressive examples of nineteenth-century book production, the catalogues effectively utilized the best available printing processes of the time: electrotyping, wood engraving and lithography. Chromolithographs and gilding are employed wherever this might improve representation and desirability. Graded sizes of some products are reminiscent of early metalwork pattern books. Colour guides and paper product samples are occasionally inserted between pages. Some illustrations show the product being used, inviting readers to imagine themselves in a hammock or on a bicycle, for example (6 and 7). Others are diagrammatic and include dimensions. In order to both impress and reassure, the frontispiece of the second volume depicts the firm's premises (1) – a trade literature trope that started with trade cards and continues into the twenty-first century, even online. [DRS]

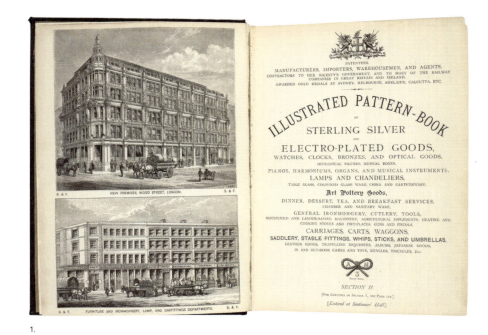

1.

2.

3.

4.

5.

6.

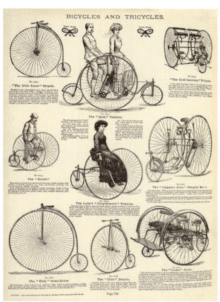

7.

8.

9.

10.

11.

SHOPPING   267

Indépendance

(Independence)

SOCIÉTÉ ANONYME DES AUTOMOBILES PEUGEOT

PRINTED BY DRAEGER FRÈRES, PARIS, 1933

35 ILLUSTRATED PAGES, 27 COLOUR PAGES, 8 UNNUMBERED PAGES OF PLATES; ILLUSTRATED BY PIERRE BRISSAUD, EDY LEGRAND AND REYNALDO LUZA

V&A 38041989046487

In 1933 Peugeot launched its 'aerodynamic' range of vehicles, publishing this brochure to coincide with that year's Salon de l'Automobile (Paris Motor Show). The illustrations and text sought to evoke nostalgia and patriotic sentiment as a backdrop to the elegant new style. *Indépendance* also highlighted the new-found freedom that driving a Peugeot offered women (1). One of Reynaldo Luza's double-page spreads claims *'Conduire une Peugeot, c'est Être à la Mode'* ('To drive a Peugeot is to be in fashion'). The car can hardly be seen but the woman driving exudes sophistication.

All three of the contributing artists were renowned painters and fashion illustrators in Paris, although Luza was born in Lima, Peru. Their contrasting, yet equally expressive approaches celebrate the ambition of Peugeot's well-established family business. The charming line drawings by Pierre Brissaud tell the history of Peugeot (2), Edy Legrand captures the Art Deco spirit of glamour in shades of grey (3), and the clean, sweeping shapes in Luza's stunning colour illustrations epitomize streamlined design (4). [CP]

1.

2.

3.

4.

Gebr. Fretz A.G., Zurich

HERBERT MATTER

PUBLISHED BY GEBRÜDER FRETZ, ZURICH, 1933

6 ILLUSTRATED PAGES IN COLOUR

V&A 38041800794588

The Swiss printers Gebrüder Fretz promoted their services – letterpress, lithography and offset lithography, photogravure and a range of binding styles – in a booklet that showcased these processes and presented the company as highly advanced. The Modernist graphic designer Herbert Matter pioneered the concept of 'Foto-graphik', or photomontage, using it in this catalogue in three colours to express both technical expertise and modernity. The asymmetrical layout and layered images generate dynamic arrangements of all the pictorial elements, including line drawings, photographs and typography as an illustrative device. Although the text is placed within a grid, it is interwoven with the images. The illustrations wind their way through the pages, suggesting the printing presses in action. It is almost possible to hear the clack of type being composed and feel the paper going through the rollers. In just a few exceptional pages, the illustrations in this catalogue provide product information, reinforce the firm's reputation for innovation and evoke in the reader a sense of being in the printer's workshop. [DRS]

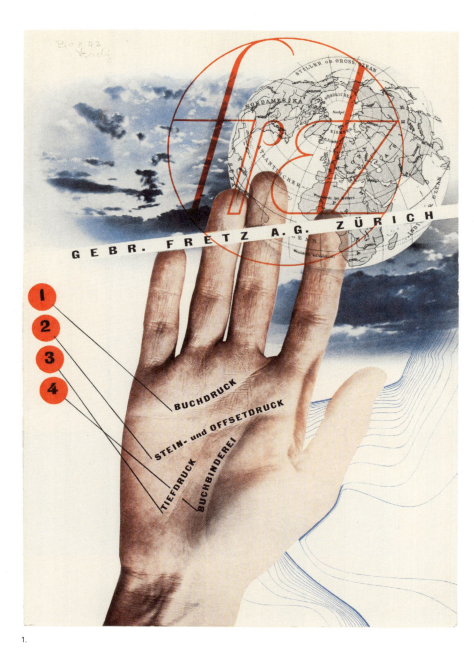

1.

2.

3.

4.

Schweppes Devonshire Cider: Cider Throughout the Ages

ANNA K. ZINKEISEN

PUBLISHED BY SCHWEPPES LTD, LONDON, 1930S

❧

12 ILLUSTRATED PAGES IN COLOUR; DESIGNED AND PRINTED BY HUDSON & MORRISON LTD

V&A 38041800780322

1.

In the early twentieth century women were increasingly targeted as influential consumers in the domestic sphere. The amusing anecdotes in Schweppes' catalogue are worthy of the influential British satirical magazine *Punch*. It portrays situations with which this particular audience might have identified – clever women managing difficult men. The lively vignettes by Anna Zinkeisen capture the tongue-in-cheek tone in a few fluid lines. Ruffles, curls and clouds mimic cider's bubbliness. The Schweppes colours of green and gold are used in the illustrated border of the final puff piece (1) and on the cover (2). Skilful posing and characterization of the figures simultaneously convey authentic historic dress and a modern manner, suggesting chic fancy-dress parties and the invigorating effects of Schweppes cider. Zinkeisen worked as both a commercial artist and a society portrait painter. The inclusion of her signature on the illustrations, which was not common practice at the time, clearly indicates the market at which this booklet was aimed. [DRS]

2.

Montgomery Ward, Chicago: Spring and Summer 1952

PUBLISHED BY MONTGOMERY WARD, CHICAGO, ILLINOIS, 1952

968 ILLUSTRATED PAGES, MOSTLY IN COLOUR; PRINTED BY R.R. DONNELLY AND SONS COMPANY

V&A 38041995078011

The American entrepreneur Aaron Montgomery Ward founded his mail-order business in 1872, with a broadsheet inventory of just under 200 products. Customers in remote locations welcomed having access to consumer goods, especially after the introduction in 1896 of Rural Free Delivery in the United States. By 1952 the Montgomery Ward catalogue was almost 1,000 pages long. Ample text was squeezed onto the page to guarantee readers were not without any necessary detail. There were also diagrams to help customers choose the right fit. To achieve both affordability and accuracy, high-quality images were printed on cheap newsprint using 'modern high-speed printing methods', and illustrations were reused for items that appeared in every seasonal volume. With the constant aim of increasing sales, the pictorial styles within the 'wish book' – as it affectionately became known – were as varied as the products themselves, and included pencil drawings, gouache and photographs reproduced in different ways, from photogravure to offset lithography. Colour was used judiciously: in women's fashion, to appeal to youthful consumers, or where a range of available colours was a strong selling point. [CP]

1.

2.

3.

4.

5.

6.

Imagination IV: Envelope

TOM KAMIFUJI

PUBLISHED BY CHAMPION PAPERS INC., HAMILTON, OHIO, 1964

ART DIRECTED BY RON SANDILANDS AND JOHN AMON

V&A 38041800385742

Envelope was the fourth in the *Imagination* series of catalogues published by the American paper company Champion Papers between 1963 and 1988. Several well-established artists were commissioned to illustrate their samplers, transforming them from booklets of blank paper into works of art that demonstrated the product's versatility. Each issue had a different theme, which was explored using various printing techniques, including lithography, gravure, silk screen, embossing and photography. The catalogue opens with the statement: 'This book is devoted to the proposition that envelopes deserve attention.' It contains over 100 unique designs utilizing simple, yet distinctive visual devices for a succession of imagined businesses. Making the envelope a part of the message through vivid colour, witty illustrations and die-cuts bring a potentially mundane product to life. Tom Kamifuji, a Japanese–American illustrator, designer and graphic artist, was known for his bold, colourful screen-prints, a familiar feature of Southern Californian Pop Art in the 1960s and 1970s. [CP]

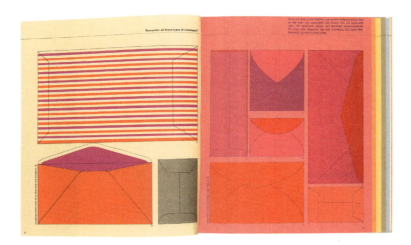

1.

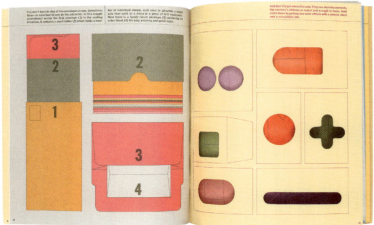

2.

3.

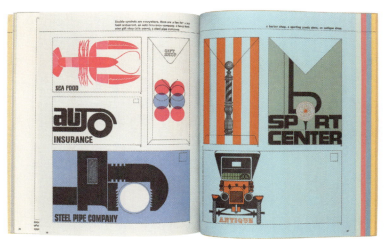

4.

D.E driade edizioni

Furnishings for the home of the third millennium

PUBLISHED BY DRIADE S.P.A., MILAN, 1996–8

101 ILLUSTRATED PAGES; ART DIRECTED BY ADELAIDE ACERBI

V&A 38041800379240, 38041800379257, 38041800379265

1.

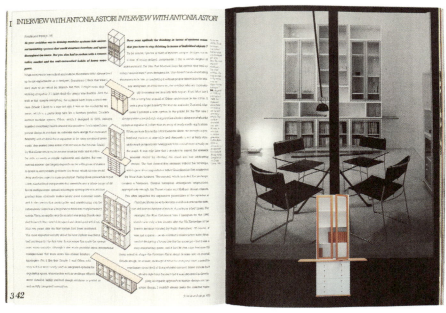
2.

3.

Driade is an Italian furniture company with a reputation for innovative design, manufacturing and marketing. Its co-founder Adelaide Acerbi created the Postmodern magalogue *D.E*, to reveal the company's design process in more detail, thus appealing to an increasing consumer awareness of design in the 1990s. For example, in an interview with the furniture designer Antonia Astori, her fellow founder, the illustrations and layout echo the structure of Astori's modular cabinets (2). *D.E driade edizioni* integrated many elements of Postmodernism, which revels in the deliberate clashing and confusion of styles; the design of different articles within each issue is inconsistent. Occasionally the composition is almost chaotic (1). The expectation that clear visuals convey form and function is ignored. Sometimes text is printed over pictures, or images are layered with seemingly minimal consideration for legibility. At times the products are not even immediately recognizable. Another component of the Postmodern aesthetic is pastiche. For example, mail-order catalogues are referenced on crowded pages where as many illustrations as possible are presented, and the text is obliged to snake around the images. Just as Chippendale's *Director* depicts his designs (p.265), *D.E* often includes sketches by the designers (3), thereby involving the consumer in the act of production. [CP]

Habitat

PUBLISHED BY HABITAT, LONDON, 1966

ILLUSTRATED BY JULIET GLYNN SMITH

V&A AAD/1995/12

People places culture ... home

PUBLISHED BY HABITAT, LONDON, 1999

199 ILLUSTRATED PAGES; ART DIRECTED BY SUE SKEEN, DESIGNED BY STUART SMITH AND PHOTOGRAPHED BY MARTIN MORRELL

V&A 38041800379273

From 1964 Habitat – the high-street homeware chain founded by Sir Terence Conran – adhered to the principle that good, affordable design is an essential aspect of everyday life. The inaugural Habitat catalogue was a single, folded broadsheet, depicting a selection of products in rows of black-and-white line drawings reminiscent of nineteenth-century catalogues (1). The text was informal, appropriate to the rustic pictorial style and the warm, simple aesthetic of the store. Habitat catalogues consciously presented emerging lifestyle trends, so issues from different decades are immediately recognizable. In keeping with the design-conscious 1990s, the millennial issue (2 to 7) shows chinaware sets on the familiar grid, but against a chequerboard or strips of flat, bright colour. Playful illustrative elements have been added to break the rigidity. They suggest real individuals scribbling down their own ideas. Real life is also illustrated through twentieth-century design classics portrayed in quirky photography, sometimes blurred or messy to imply active use; or in photographs taken at odd angles, where the product is barely discernible but the pleasures of living with Habitat products are clear. [DRS]

1.

2.

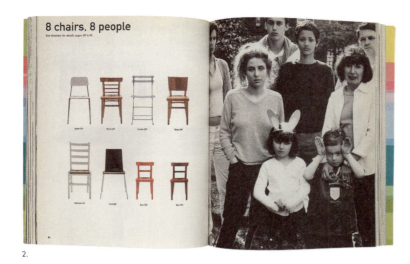

3.

4.

5.

6.

7.

SHOPPING 275

Gidi gidi bu ugwu eze/ Unity is Strength: Kenzo Folio No. 01

PUBLISHED BY KENZO, PARIS, 2017

2 BROADSHEET INSERTS, 32 ILLUSTRATED PAGES IN COLOUR; PHOTOGRAPHED BY RUTH OSSAI, DIRECTED BY AKINOLA DAVIES JR AND STYLED BY IBRAHIM KAMARA

V&A 38041017033481

Ruth Ossai's photography is in part inspired by West African studio portraits. In 2017, when there was a swell of interest in African inspirations within the Global North fashion world, Kenzo commissioned two artists of British–Nigerian heritage to create an integrated print and online catalogue. Akinola Davies Jr directed the overall look, using the metaphor of a beauty pageant to challenge Western standards of beauty (4 and 5). He deliberately chose to work only with professional creatives based in Nigeria. The models in *Folio No. 01* live in the Igbo town of Nsukka, where the campaign was shot. A visual inventory insert imitates the posters found on the walls in dressmakers and hair salons in many African countries (2). There is little text in the catalogue. The illustrations allow the models to tell their own stories, reflecting real-life rituals of youth that are both specific to the community and resonate with anyone, anywhere: trying out new hairstyles; dancing; taking part in traditional ceremonies (1, 4); driving (3); and dressing up. In the age of online shopping, trade catalogues need to elicit an emotional response to the brand, while keeping the product at the core of the message. The images in this hybrid catalogue do exactly that. [DRS]

1.

2.

276 SHOPPING

3.

4.

5.

SHOPPING 277

NOTES

1. William Morris, *The Ideal Book: A Paper by William Morris read before the Bibliographical Society, London, June 14, 1893* (London, 1908), p.13. Morris used the term 'picture book'.

2. For a definition of a book see C.T. Onions, *et al.* (eds), *The Shorter Oxford English Dictionary on Historical Principles* (third edition, Oxford, 1944; reprinted with corrections, Oxford, 1975), p.217: 'a collection of sheets of paper or other substance, blank, written, or printed, fastened together so as to form a material whole'.

3. For an overview of *livres d'artiste*, drawn from the NAL's collections, see Hogben and Watson, 1985.

4. For an excellent recent study (870 images in 29 chapters), described in its preface as 'a global overview of illustration practices from before the development of written language to the digital age. ... the first textbook on the topic ... aimed at undergraduate illustration students', see Doyle, Grove and Sherman, 2019.

5. Quoted in Bland, 1969, p.163. See also Anne-Marie Logan and Michiel C. Plomp, *Peter Paul Rubens. The Drawings* (New York, 2005) p.14.

6. Edward Hodnett, *Francis Barlow: First Master of English Book Illustration* (London, 1978), p.10.

7. Edmond and Jules de Goncourt, *L'Art du dix-huitième siècle*, 3 vols (Paris, 1880–2), *passim*.

8. Julius Bryant, 'James "Athenian" Stuart. The Architect as Landscape Painter', *V&A Online Journal* (Autumn 2008), no. 1, unpaginated (http://www.vam.ac.uk/content/journals/research-journal/issue-01/)

9. David Bindman, *Blake as an Artist* (Oxford, 1977).

10. Julius Bryant, *Turner: Painting the Nation* (London, 1996), pp.15–21, and Julius Bryant, *The English Grand Tour: Artists and Admirers of England's Historic Sites* (London, 2005), *passim*.

11. Forrest Reid, *Illustrators of the Sixties* (London, 1928), republished as *Illustrators of the Eighteen-Sixties* (London, 1975), p.1.

12. British Library, BL MS 46700.

13. Lewis Carroll, *Alice's Adventures in Wonderland* (London, 1865), pp.1–2.

14. Matthew Sturgis, 'Aubrey Beardsley and Oscar Wilde', *The Wildean*, 13 (July 1998) pp.15–27: p.22.

15. Bryant, James and Watson, 2015, pp.62–4.

16. 'The Sunday Times Bestsellers: General Hardbacks', *The Sunday Times, Culture* (3 April 2022), p.24, where Mackesy's book is no. 2, after 129 weeks in the top ten.

FURTHER READING

GENERAL

Alan Bartram, *Five Hundred Years of Book Design* (London, 2001)

Otto Benesch, *Artistic and Intellectual Trends from Rubens to Daumier as shown in Book Illustration* (Cambridge, MA, 1943)

James Bettley (ed.), *The Art of the Book: From Medieval Manuscript to Graphic Novel* (London, 2001)

David Bland, *A History of Book Illustration: The Illuminated Manuscript and the Printed Book* (London, 1958; second edition, London, 1969)

Julius Bryant, Elizabeth James and Rowan Watson (eds), *Word & Image. Art, Books and Design from the National Art Library* (London, 2015)

Gerard Curtis, *Visual Words: Art and the Material Book in Victorian England* (Aldershot, 1999)

Susan Doyle, Jaleen Grove and Whitney Sherman (eds), *History of Illustration* (New York, 2019)

Paul Goldman, *Victorian Illustration: The Pre-Raphaelites, the Idyllic School and the High Victorians* (Aldershot, 1996)

John P. Harthan, *The History of the Illustrated Book: The Western Tradition* (London, 1981)

Edward Hodnett, *Five Centuries of English Book Illustration* (Aldershot, 1988)

Carol Hogben and Rowan Watson (eds), *From Manet to Hockney: Modern Artists' Illustrated Books* (London, 1985)

Alan Horne, *The Dictionary of 20th-Century British Book Illustrators* (Woodbridge, 1990)

Simon Houfe, *The Dictionary of 19th-Century British Book Illustrators and Caricaturists*, third edition (Woodbridge, 1994)

A. Hyatt Mayor, *Prints and People: A Social History of Printed Pictures* (New York, 1971)

Derek Jones (ed.), *Censorship: A World Encyclopedia* (London, 2001)

Bill Katz, *A History of Book Illustration. 29 Points of View* (Metuchen, NJ, 1994)

T.M. MacRobert, *Fine Illustrations in Western European Printed Books* (London, 1969)

William Morris, *The Ideal Book: Essays and Lectures on the Arts of the Book*, ed. W.S. Peterson, (Berkeley, CA, 1982)

Anna Nyburg, *Émigrés: The Transformation of Art Publishing in Britain* (London, 2014)

Gordon N. Ray, *The Illustrator and the Book in England from 1790 to 1914* (New York, 1976)

D. Roylance, *European Graphic Arts: The Art of the Book from Gutenberg to Picasso* (Princeton, NJ, 1986)

Rowan Watson and Valerie Holman (eds), *Art Publishing and Art Publics Today*, transcript of a one-day conference organized by the National Art Library and Wimbledon School of Art (London, 1989)

1 RELIGION

Christiane Gruber, 'Between Logos (Kalima) and Light (Nur), Reproductions of the Prophet Muhammad in Islamic Painting', in *Muqarnas* 26 (2009), pp.229–62

Christopher de Hamel, *The Book: A History of the Bible* (London and New York, 2001)

Lynn Hunt, Margaret Jacob and Wijnand Mijnhardt, *The Book that Changed Europe: Picart and Bernard's Religious Ceremonies of the World* (Cambridge, 2010)

Silvia Naef, *Y a-t-il une «question de l'image» en Islam?* (Paris, 2015)

F.E. Peters, *The Voice, the Word, the Books: The Sacred Scriptures of the Jews, Christians, and Muslims* (Princeton, 2007), esp. Chapter 8, 'Picturing the Word'

2 NATURAL HISTORY

Ann Shelby Blum, *Picturing Nature: American Nineteenth-Century Zoological Illustration* (Princeton, 1993)

Ray Desmond, *Great Natural History Books and their Creators* (London, 2003)

Florike Egmond, *Eye for Detail: Images of Plants and Animals in Art and Science, 1500–1630* (London, 2017)

Judith Magee, *Art of Nature: Three Centuries of Natural History Art from Around the World* (London, 2017)

Therese O'Malley and Amy R.W. Meyers, *The Art of Natural History: Illustrated Treatises and Botanical Paintings, 1400–1850* (New Haven and London, 2008)

Gill Saunders, *Picturing Plants: An Analytical History of Botanical Illustration* (London, 1995; revised 2009)

3 TRAVEL

Malcolm Andrews, *The Search for the Picturesque: Landscape Aesthetics and Tourism in Britain, 1760–1800* (Aldershot, 1989)

Jeremy Black, *The British Abroad: The Grand Tour in the Eighteenth Century* (New York, 1992)

David Brafman, 'Facing East: The Western View of Islam in Nicolas de Nicolay's "Travels in Turkey"', *Getty Research Journal*, no. 1 (2009), pp.153–60

Jaś Elsner and Joan-Pau Rubiés, *Voyages and Visions: Towards a Cultural History of Travel* (London, 1999)

Rüdiger Joppien and Bernard Smith, *The Art of Captain Cook's Voyages* (New Haven, CT, 1985-8)

Olivier Loiseaux, Gilles Fumey and Freddy Langer, *Image and Exploration: Early Travel Photography from 1850 to 1914* (London and New York, 2019)

Constance Martin, *Distant Shores: The Odyssey of Rockwell Kent*, with essays by Richard V. West, exh. cat., Norman Rockwell Museum, Stockbridge, MA (Chesterfield, Berkeley and Stockbridge, MA, 2000)

Tijana Rakic and Jo-Anne Lester (eds), *Travel, Tourism and Art* (London, 2016)

Da Zheng, *Chiang Yee: The Silent Traveller from the East – A Cultural Biography* (New Brunswick, NJ, 2010)

4 FABLES AND FOLK TALES

Ulrich Boner and Paul Kristeller (introduction), *Der Edelstein* (facsimile of 1461 edition, Berlin, 1908)

Karen L. Bowen and Dirk Imhof, *Christopher Plantin and Engraved Book Illustrations in Sixteenth-Century Europe* (Cambridge, 2008)

Alan Dundes (ed.), *The Study of Folklore* (Englewood Cliffs, NJ, 1965)

James Hamilton, *Arthur Rackham: A Life with Illustration* (London, 1995)

Derek Hudson, *Arthur Rackham: His Life and Work* (London, 1960)

Maximiliaan P.J. Martens (ed.), *Bruges and the Renaissance: Memling to Pourbus* (Ghent, 1998), esp. Eva Tahon, 'Marcus Gheeraerts the Elder', pp.231-8

John J. McKendry (ed.), *Aesop: Five Centuries of Illustrated Fables* (New York, 1964)

Bernard O'Kane, *Early Persian Painting: Kalila and Dimna Manuscripts of the Late Fourteenth Century* (London and New York, 2003)

Philip M. Peek and Kwesi Yankah, *African Folklore: An Encyclopedia* (London, 2009)

Anne Stevenson Hobbs, *Fables* (London, 1986)

Thompson Stith, *The Folktale* (New York, 1946)

5 LITERATURE

Elizabeth Bergmann Loizeaux, *Twentieth-Century Poetry and the Visual Arts* (Cambridge, 2008)

Simon Eliot, Andrew Nash and Ian Willison, *Literary Cultures and the Material Book* (London, 2007)

Rodney Engen, *The Age of Enchantment: Beardsley, Dulac and their Contemporaries, 1890-1930* (London, 2007)

Oleg Grabar, *Masterpieces of Islamic Art: The Decorated Page from the 8th to the 17th Century* (Munich and New York, 2009)

Ian Haywood, Susan Matthews and Mary Shannon, *Romanticism and Illustration* (Cambridge, 2019)

Lorraine Janzen Kooistra, *Poetry, Pictures, and Popular Publishing: The Illustrated Gift Book and Victorian Visual Culture, 1855-1875* (Athens, OH, 2011)

Maxime Leroy, *A Study of Authorial Illustration: The Magic Window* (Newcastle upon Tyne, 2019)

Melissa McCormick, *The Tale of Genji: A Visual Companion* (Princeton, NJ, 2018)

Fiona Pearce and David Wootton, *The Illustrators: The British Art of Illustration, 1786-2003* (London, 2003)

Peter Sharratt, *Bernard Salomon: Illustrateur Lyonnais* (Geneva, 2005)

Michael Steig, *Dickens and Phiz* (Indiana, 1978)

Peter Whitfield, *Illustrating Shakespeare* (London, 2013)

6 ART MAKING

James Ayres, *The Artist's Craft: A History of Tools, Techniques, and Materials* (Oxford, 1985)

James Ayres, *Art, Artisans and Apprentices: Apprentice Painters and Sculptors in the Early Modern British Tradition* (Oxford and Philadelphia, 2014)

Barbara C. Bowen, 'Geofroy Tory's "Champ Fleury" and Its Major Sources', *Studies in Philology*, vol. 76, no. 1 (1979), pp.13-27

Katie Chenoweth, *The Prosthetic Tongue: Printing Technology and the Rise of the French Language* (Philadelphia, 2019)

Chelsea Foxwell, 'Mediated Realism in Kuwagata Keisai's Illustrated Book of Birds From Abroad', *Journal18*, no. 4 (2017), https://www.journal18.org/2232 (accessed 20 February 2022)

Antony Griffiths, *The Print Before Photography: An Introduction to European Printmaking 1550-1820* (London, 2016)

Morrison Heckscher, 'Lock and Copland: A Catalogue of the Engraved Ornament', *Furniture History*, vol. 15 (1979), pp.1-23

Jennifer Montagu, *The Expression of the Passions, The Origin and Influence of Charles Le Brun's 'Conférence sur l'expression générale et particulière'* (New Haven, 1994)

Tirthankar Roy, *The Crafts and Capitalism: Handloom Weaving Industry in Colonial India* (2020)

7 ART HISTORY

James Elkins, *Stories of Art* (New York, 2002)

Chelsea Foxwell, 'Access Granted: Art-Historical Art and Woodblock-Printed Books in Eighteenth-Century Japan', in *Ars Orientalis* (2019), vol. 49, doi.org/10.3998/ars.13441566.0049.006 (accessed 9 February 2022)

Anthony J. Hamber, *'A Higher Branch of the Art': Photographing the Fine Arts in England, 1839-1880* (Amsterdam, 1996)

Francis A. Haskell, *The Painful Birth of the Art Book: Walter Neurath Memorial Lectures, 19* (London, 1987)

Christopher Lloyd, *Art and Its Images: An Exhibition of Printed Books Containing Engraved Illustrations After Italian Painting* (Oxford, 1975)

Robin Myers, Michael Harris and Giles Mandelbrote (eds), *Publishing the Fine and Applied Arts, 1500-2000* (London and New Castle, DE, 2021)

Rodney Palmer and Thomas Frangenberg (eds), *The Rise of the Image: The History of the Illustrated Art Book* (Aldershot, 2003)

Elizabeth Pergam, 'Selling Pictures: The Illustrated Auction Catalogue', *Journal of Art Historiography* (2014), vol. 11, arthistoriography.wordpress.com/11-dec14/ (accessed 9 February 2022)

Richard Shone and John-Paul Stonard (eds), *The Books That Shaped Art History: From Gombrich and Greenberg to Alpers and Krauss* (London, 2013)

Ingrid R. Vermeulen, *Picturing Art History: The Rise of the Illustrated History of Art in the Eighteenth Century* (Amsterdam, 2010)

8 ARCHITECTURE

Mario Carpo, *Architecture in the Age of Printing: Orality, Writing, Typography and Printed Images in the History of Architectural Theory*, trans. Sarah Benson (Cambridge, MA, 2001)

Eileen Harris and Nick Savage (eds), *British Architectural Books and Writers, 1556-1785* (Cambridge 1990)

Vaughan Hart and Peter Hicks (eds), *Paper Palaces: The Rise of the Renaissance Architectural Treatise* (New Haven and London, 1998)

The Mark J. Millard Architectural Collection, 4 vols (Washington, DC, 1993-2000)

Adolf K. Placzek (ed.), *Avery's Choice: Five Centuries of Great Architectural Books – One Hundred Years of an Architectural Library, 1890-1990* (New York, 1997)

Royal Institute of British Architects, *Early Printed Books, 1478-1840: Catalogue of the British Architectural Library Early Imprints Collection*, 5 vols (London 1994-2003)

André Tavares, *The Anatomy of the Architectural Book* (Zurich, 2016)

9 ORNAMENT AND PATTERN

Amelia Calver, *The V&A Sourcebook of Pattern and Ornament* (London, 2021)

Auguste Racinet, *The World of Ornament* (Cologne, 2018)

Michael Snodin, *The V&A Book of Western Ornament* (London, 2006)

Peter Thornton, *Authentic Decor: The Domestic Interior 1620-1920* (London, 2000)

Peter Thornton, *Form and Decoration* (London, 2000)

Tim Travis (ed.), *The V&A Book of Colour in Design* (London, 2020)

Elizabeth Wilhide, *The Complete Pattern Directory: 1500 Designs from All Ages and Cultures* (New York, 2018)

10 FESTIVALS

Anna C. Knaap and Michael C.J. Putnam (eds), *Art, Music, and Spectacle in the Age of Rubens: The Pompa introitus Ferdinandi* (Turnhout, 2013)

J.R. Mulryne, Helen Watanabe-O'Kelly and Margaret Shewring (eds), *Europa triumphans: Court and Civic Festivals in Early Modern Europe* (Aldershot, 2004)

Roy Strong, *Art and Power* (Woodbridge, 1984)

'Treasures in Full: Renaissance Festival Books', 253 digitized Renaissance festival books from the British Library collection, www.bl.uk/treasures/festivalbooks/ (accessed 9 February 2022)

Helen Watanabe-O'Kelly and Anne Simon, *Festivals and Ceremonies: A Bibliography of Works Relating to Court, Civic and Religious Festivals in Europe 1500-1800* (London, 2000)

11 WORLD'S FAIRS

Paul Greenhalgh, *Fair World: A History of World's Fairs and Expositions, From London to Shanghai, 1851-2010* (London, 2011)

Anna Jackson, *EXPO: International Expositions 1851-2010* (London, 2008)

Ives Maes, *The Future of Yesterday* (Antwerp, 2013)

12 FASHION

Catherine Flood and Sarah Grant, *Style and Satire: Fashion in Print 1777-1927* (London, 2014)

Hollar to Heideloff: An Exhibition of Fashion Prints Drawn from the Collections of Members of the Costume Society and held at the Victoria and Albert Museum (London, 1979)

Alice Mackrell, *An Illustrated History of Fashion: 500 Years of Fashion Illustration* (London 1997)

Margaret Rosenthal and Ann Rosalind Jones, *The Clothing of the Renaissance World: Europe, Asia, Africa, the Americas: Cesare Vecellio's Habiti Antichi et Moderni* (London, 2008)

Eugénie Shinkle (ed.), *Fashion as Photograph: Viewing and Reviewing Images of Fashion* (London 2008)

Sacheverell Sitwell, *Gallery of Fashion, 1790-1822: from Plates by Heideloff and Ackermann* (London, 1949)

13 SHOPPING

Robin Cherry, *Catalog: The Illustrated History of Mail-Order Shopping* (New York, 2008)

Richard Coopey, Sean O'Connell and Dilwyn Porter, *Mail Order Retailing in Britain: A Business and Social History* (Oxford, 2005)

Dianna Edwards and Robert Valentine, *Catalog Design: The Art of Creating Desire* (Gloucester, MA, 2003)

Pages d'or de l'edition publicitaire: catalogues illustrés au service des entreprises, exh. cat., Bibliothèque Forney (Paris, 1987)

Lawrence B. Romaine, *A Guide to American Trade Catalogs, 1744-1900* (New York, 1990)

Neville Thompson, 'Trade Catalogues in the Winterthur Library', in *The Magazine Antiques*, vol. 161 (January 2002), pp.206-11

Jonathan Z. Zhang, 'Why Catalogs are Making a Comeback', *Harvard Business Review* online (11 February 2020), hbr.org/2020/02/why-catalogs-are-making-a-comeback (accessed 9 February 2022)

CONTRIBUTORS

Bernadette Archer is the Online Services Librarian at the National Art Library (NAL) at the V&A. She has a particular interest in the fashion collections and co-authored the chapter 'The Fashion Archive' in *Word & Image: Art, Books and Design from the National Art Library* (2015).

Nicholas Barnard is a Curator of South Asian Art in the Asian Department at the V&A. He specializes in South Asian sculpture and jewellery and the arts of the Jain religion.

Sarah Beattie is an Assistant Curator of Designs and previously a Cataloguer, specializing in prints and drawings at the V&A. She was Research Assistant for the exhibition *Winnie-the-Pooh: Exploring a Classic* (2017).

Annemarie Bilclough is the Frederick Warne Curator of Illustration at the V&A. She has co-curated several exhibitions, including *Beatrix Potter: Drawn to Nature* (2022), *Alice: Curiouser and Curiouser* (2021) and *Winnie-the-Pooh: Exploring a Classic* (2017).

Julius Bryant is Keeper Emeritus of the V&A. As Keeper of the Word and Image department (2005–21) he was responsible for the V&A's collections of paintings, prints, drawings, photographs and designs, and for the NAL and the Archive of Art and Design.

Juliet Ceresole is an Assistant Curator at the V&A and worked with the NAL collections for seven years before moving into exhibition loans. She contributed to the publication *The V&A Book of Colour in Design* (2020).

Catriona Gourlay is the Assistant Curator of the NAL collections. She curated the V&A display *Landscape and Language in Artists' Books* (2019–22).

Sarah Grant is a Curator of Prints, including the national collection of engraved ornament, at the V&A.

Ruth Hibbard is a Curator at the V&A working on prints, drawings and illustration collections. She co-curated the display *Printing a Modern World* (2018), and contributed to *Word & Image: Art, Books and Design from the National Art Library* (2015) and *The V&A Book of Colour in Design* (2020).

Olivia Horsfall Turner is the Senior Curator of Architecture and Design at the V&A. A historian, writer and broadcaster, she looks after the museum's collection of design drawings, which documents the creative process in art, architecture and design from the fourteenth century to the present day.

Elizabeth James is the Senior Librarian in charge of collections at the NAL. A contributor to and editor of a number of V&A books, she researches, teaches and publishes on museum publications, book illustration and artists' books.

Ella Kilgallon is the Property Curator of Kedleston Hall for the National Trust and was previously Assistant Curator of Designs at the V&A.

Emily Knight is the Assistant Curator of Paintings and Drawings at the V&A. She contributed to the publication *The V&A Book of Colour in Design* (2020) and curated the display *Sir James Thornhill: Exploring Lines* (2021–2).

Hannah Lyons is a PhD Candidate at Birkbeck, University of London, and the V&A. Previously, she was Assistant Curator at Tate Britain and Christ Church Picture Gallery, Oxford University.

Elizabeth Miller is a former Senior Curator of Prints at the V&A, and the author of the museum's catalogue of sixteenth-century Italian ornament prints.

Caroline Penn is the Reading & Study Rooms Manager at the V&A. She was previously the Assistant Project Manager of the V&A Illustration Awards and has produced several events at the V&A around the NAL collections.

Patrick Perratt is the Acquisitions Manager at the NAL. He was responsible for cataloguing the Library's Piot Collection of festival books.

Jana Riedel is the Research Projects Officer at the V&A Research Institute (VARI). Previously, she completed her doctoral research at the V&A on Prince Albert of Saxe-Coburg and Gotha as collector, educator and cultural transferant.

Gill Saunders is the Senior Curator of Prints at the V&A. She has written widely on art and design, and her publications include *Picturing Plants: An Analytical History of Botanical Illustration* (1995/2009), *Recording Britain* (2011) and books on Edward Bawden and his circle.

Lucy Shaw is currently pursuing an AHRC-funded PhD on British Neo-Romantic art at the University of Birmingham. She was formerly an Assistant Curator and Cataloguer at the V&A, working on prints, drawings and illustration collections.

Deborah Sutherland has curated the trade literature and related collections in the NAL since 2000. She co-curated the display *Printing a New World* and contributed to *The Phaidon Archive of Graphic Design* (2012), *Word & Image: Art, Books and Design from the National Art Library* (2015) and *The V&A Book of Colour in Design* (2020).

Anna Vlasova is an Assistant Librarian at the NAL with responsibility for the fashion and textiles collections. She holds an MA in the History of the Book and has a special interest in the hand-press period.

Marc Ward is the Serials Librarian at the NAL, looking after its vast collection of magazines and comics.

Frances Willis, Assistant Librarian at the NAL, enhances access to its collections through a varied group visits programme. She has curated several displays at the V&A, most recently *Prince Albert: Science & the Arts on the Page* (2019).

Xueqing Xi is a historian specializing in printing and book history. She undertook the joint V&A/Royal College of Art History of Design MA degree course, and is currently researching for a PhD at the University of Edinburgh.

Masami Yamada is a Curator in the Asian Department at the V&A, with responsibility for Japanese *ukiyo-e* woodblock prints, netsuke, lacquerware and contemporary crafts.

Catherine Yvard is the Collections Curator at the NAL. A specialist in late medieval Western European manuscripts and Gothic ivory sculpture, she has published extensively on these topics.

ACKNOWLEDGMENTS

This ambitious study began in 2018 with a suggestion from Julian Honer and Susannah Lawson of Thames & Hudson, as part of the publisher's partnership with the V&A. A core objective of the project, and one that made it even more of a joy, was to embrace it as an opportunity for librarians and curators across the V&A's Word and Image department to share and expand upon our specialist knowledge of different fields of the art of the illustrated book, through choosing and discussing key examples from the collections of the National Art Library at the V&A. Curators from the Asia Department and from Research, and V&A/RCA research students, also made vital contributions.

Hannah Newell and Jane Ace managed the project for V&A Publishing, the latter taking on the lion's share with contagious good humour. Thanks are also due to Coralie Hepburn, Managing Editor, and Tom Windross, Head of Content, at the V&A, and Melissa Mellor at Thames & Hudson. Sarah Yates also provided an excellent copy-edit and Charlie Smith oversaw the elegant design. With the onset of the Covid-19 pandemic, staff were dispersed, either on furlough or working from home. The editors are greatly indebted to the section authors and their teams of contributors for their enthusiasm, creativity and perseverance through national 'lockdowns'. Once the V&A reopened its offices to staff, Catriona Gourlay masterfully managed the photography campaign, marshalling hundreds of books to the photo studio and back. All credits go to photographer Sarah Duncan, assisted by Kieron Boyle, for cheerfully facing this tidal wave and making every book look its best. We are especially grateful to the contributors who have carried on researching and writing despite the impact of the pandemic on the V&A's resources and on their own positions. Many of the books illustrated came to the V&A as gifts and bequests, either individually or as part of larger collections; for reasons of space, it has not been possible to acknowledge the generosity of donors in each caption but further information can be found in the NAL catalogue. All along, as the project grew, we realized that each section is worthy of a book in itself, and we look forward to seeing many offspring from *The Art of the Illustrated Book*.

JB, EJ, CY

PICTURE CREDITS

p.18: Taken from *Eyewitness Travel: India* published by DK. Copyright © Dorling Kinderley Ltd. p.19: © Tom Phillips. All rights reserved, DACS 2022. p.20: © Sukita. p.21: From *The Boy, the Mole, the Fox and the Horse* by Charlie Mackesy, published Ebury. Copyright © Charlie Mackesy, 2019. Reprinted by permission of The Random House Group Ltd. pp.38 and 39: © Estate of Ben Shahn/VAGA at ARS, NY and DACS, London 2022. p.41: © The Late Estate of Broomberg & Chanarin. All Rights Reserved, DACS 2022. p.80: © DACS 2022. p.81: Courtesy Mónica Alcázar-Duarte. p.85: Courtesy Frederick Warne & Co. p.94: © ADAGP, Paris and DACS, London 2022. p.98: © 1974 Helen Siegl. All rights reserved. p.99 Poetry © Estate of Roy Fisher. Images and fabrication © Ron King. pp.112 and 113: © Salvador Dalí, Fundació Gala-Salvador Dalí, DACS 2022. pp.114 and 115: © ADAGP, Paris and DACS, London 2022. p.116: By permission of the Estate of Leonard Baskin. © Estate of Leonard Baskin. Poem © The Estate of Ted Hughes. p.118: © Paula Rego, Courtesy Victoria Miro Gallery. p.119: Jila Peacock, *Ten Poems from Hafez* © Sylph Editions, 2006, pp. 26-7, 30-31, 32-3. p.139: Courtesy REAS Studio. pp.155 and 156: Courtesy Phaidon Press. p.157: Photo by Arnold Newman Properties/Getty Images. p.158: © Romare Bearden Foundation/VAGA at ARS, NY and DACS, London 2022. © ARS, NY and DACS, London 2022. © Estate of Robert Gwathmey/VAGA at ARS, NY and DACS, London 2022. © John T. Biggers Estate/VAGA at ARS, NY and DACS, London/Estate Represented by Michael Rosenfeld Gallery 2022. pp.164 and 216: Hans Tisdall Artist and Illustrator 1910-1997. p.177: © F.L.C./ADAGP, Paris and DACS, London 2022. p.178: Courtesy MIT Press. p.218: Andrew Logan. p.219: Barry Lewis. pp.240-41 and 256-7: *Une Jeune Fille en Dior* © Dargaud 2013, by Goetzinger, www.dargaud.com, All rights reserved © 2015 NBM for the English translation. p.252: © ADAGP, Paris and DACS, London 2022. p.253: Shoichi Aoki, Courtesy Phaidon Press. p.254: Matthew Williams; Mario Sorrenti/Art Partner; Inez and Vinoodh/Trunk Archive; Nick Knight/Trunk Archive. p.258: Sanlé Sory. p.259: © Tim Walker Studio. p.273: © Driade. pp.276-7: Courtesy Ruth Ossai.

V&A photography by Sarah Duncan. All photographs V&A, except p.67, bottom: Senate House Library and p.85, top: Herzog August Bibliothek, Wolfenbüttel.

The following list, arranged by page and figure number, provides the specific Victoria and Albert Museum object numbers for those works referenced only by a number range.

p.29, fig. 1: V&A A.L.792:1-1894; fig. 2: V&A A.L.792:2-1894. pp.34–5, fig. 1: V&A 38041800167330; fig. 2: V&A 38041800760472; fig. 3: V&A 38041800497687. p.36, fig. 1: V&A E.365-1956; fig. 2: V&A E.366-1956; fig. 3: V&A E.367-1956; fig. 4: V&A E.373-1956. p.37, figs 1-2: V&A 846-1888; fig. 3: V&A 847-1888. p.40, fig. 1: V&A 38041800379323; fig. 2: V&A 38041800379315. pp.48–9, figs 1-3: V&A 38041800377400. p.52, fig. 1: V&A 38041800586893; fig. 2: V&A 38041800586547. p.54, figs 1-2: V&A 38041800377541; figs 3-4: V&A 38041800554628. p.56, fig. 1: V&A 38041800159931; fig. 2: V&A 38041800160061. p.57, fig. 1: V&A L.1254-1939; figs 2-3: V&A L.1255-1939. p.75, figs 1-2: V&A E.2629-1925; fig. 3: V&A E.2628-1925. p.94, figs 1-2: V&A L.161:1-1984; fig. 3: V&A L.161:2-1984. pp.128–9, fig. 1: V&A E.4780:12-1916; fig. 2: V&A E.4780:15-1916; fig. 3: V&A E.4780:19-1916; fig. 4: V&A E.4780:8-1916; fig. 5: V&A E.4780:9-1916. p.131, fig. 1: V&A E.5035-1907; fig. 2: V&A E.5038-1907; fig. 3: V&A E.5036-1907. p.146, fig. 1: V&A L.1304-1903; fig. 2: V&A L.1306-1903; figs 3-4: V&A L.1305-1903. p.147, fig. 1: V&A 38041800386211; fig. 2: V&A 38041800386229. pp.148–9, figs 1–2 and 4: V&A 38041800386351; fig. 3: V&A 38041800495491. p.150, fig. 1: V&A 38041800386310; figs 2-3: V&A 38041800898215. pp.152–3, figs 1 and 3: V&A 38041800386252; fig. 2: V&A 38041800386245. p.157, fig. 1: V&A L.5339a and b-1985; fig. 2: V&A L.5339b-1985. p.172, figs 1-4: V&A 38041800989097. p.174, figs 1-4: V&A 38041800393019. pp.190–1, figs 1-2: V&A 38041800499097; fig. 3: V&A 38041800499048. p.192, figs 1-2: V&A 134:2-1883. p.198, fig. 1: V&A 38041800377509. pp.226–7, figs 1 and 3: V&A 38041800133225, figs 2, 4 and 5: V&A 38041800133233. pp.232–3, figs 1-3: V&A 278:1-1899. p.247, fig. 1: E.6819-1916; fig. 2: E.6821-1916; fig. 3: E.6820-1916. pp.260–1: V&A 38041800491318. pp.266–7, figs 1, 2, 4, 6, 7 and 8: V&A 16-1898; figs 3 and 9: V&A 11-1898; figs 5, 10 and 11: V&A 12-1898. p.273, fig. 1: V&A 38041800379257; fig. 2: V&A 38041800379240; fig. 3: V&A 38041800379265.

Captions for chapter openers:

pp.6-7: Detail from *Britannia illustrata*, 1707 (p.13)

pp.22-3: Detail from *Cérémonies et coutumes religieuses*, 1723-43 (p.34)

pp.42-3: Detail from *Conchology*, 1811 (p.55)

pp.62-3: Detail from *Vues des Cordillières*, 1810 (p.72)

pp.82-3: Detail from *XXIV Fables*, 1959 (p.97)

pp.100-101: Detail from *Bleak House*, 1852-3 (p.109)

pp.120-21: Detail from *A Tracte Containing the Artes of Curious Paintinge Carvinge & Buildinge*, 1598 (p.127)

pp.140-41: Detail from *A Second Series of the Monuments of Nineveh*, 1853 (p.151)

pp.160-61: Detail from *Darstellung und Geschichte des Geschmacks*, 1796-9 (p.174)

pp.180-81: Detail from *L'Ornement polychrome*, 1869-87 (p.192)

pp.200-201: Detail from *Les Plaisirs de l'isle enchantée*, 1674 (p.211)

pp.220-21: Detail from *The Official Pictures of a Century of Progress Exposition*, 1933 (p.236)

pp.240-41: Detail from *Girl in Dior*, 2015 (p.256)

pp.260-61: Moulded glassware from Illustrated *Patternbook of Furniture*, 1880s (p.266)

INDEX

Page numbers in *italic* refer to the captions

XXIV Fables 96, *96, 97*
90 Albums du Père Castor 18
1851: Or, The adventures of Mr. and Mrs. Sandboys 228, *228*

A&F Quarterly 264
Abercrombie & Fitch 264
Académie Royale de Peinture et de Sculpture 125, 130
Acerbi, Adelaide 273
Ackermann, Rudolph 14–15, *185*, 242, *242*
Adam, Robert and James 172, *172, 173,* 187
Adprint 18
Aesop 84, 85, *85,* 86, 88, *88,* 89, 91–2, *92,* 96
Aesopics 12
Aesop's Fables 92, *92*
Aesthetic Movement 16, 110
The Age of Adam 18
Aikman, James 213
Albert, Prince Consort 176, 189, 222
Albin, Eleazar 44, *46,* 47
Alcazar-Duarte, Monica 81, *81*
Alciati, Andrea 203, 205, 206
Aldine Press 10
Alexander McQueen 20
Alexandre, Arsène 244, *250, 250*
Alice's Adventures in Wonderland 16, *17,* 18
Allbut & Daniel 266
Alvise, Giovanni and Alberto 86
Amar Chitra Katha 40, *40*
The American Landscape 14
Amman, Jost 246
Anansi Company 99, *99*
Anatomy of the Horse 13
Antiquities of Athens 13
Antwerp 10–11, 13, 208, 209
Aoki, Shoichi 244, *253, 253*
Applegath, Augustus 222
aquatints 14–15, 55, 65, 175
Araeen, Rasheed 144, *145*
Aranei 44
Architectonisches Alphabet 163, *163*
Architectura von Außtheilung, Symmetria und Proportion der funff Seulen 168, *168*
The Architectural Press 78
Archive of Modern Conflict 41
The Arion Press 104
Ariosto, Ludovico 210
Aris, Brian 202
Arnold, Johann Friedrich 72
The Art and Craft of Lino Cutting and Printing 138, *138*
Art and Handicraft in the Woman's Building ... 231, *231*
Art Deco 195, 235, 236, 251, 264
Art du Tailleur 242

Art Nouveau 44, 60
Art Through the Ages 144
Art Without Epoch 156
Arts and Crafts movement 8, 16, 91
Arundel, Thomas Howard, 2nd Earl of 12
Asahi Shinbunsha 239
Ashbee, C.R. 16
Astori, Antonia 273
Atelier Bow-Wow 162
Atlas Coelestis 12
Audsley, William James and George Ashdown 193, *193*
Audubon, John James 47, *56, 56*
The Aurelian 45, 58, *58, 59*
Un autre monde 16

Baby's Own Aesop 91, *91*
Badmin, Stanley Roy 47, 61, *61*
Baedeker, Karl 65
Balbus 163, *164*
Balzac, Honoré de 15
Barlach, Ernst 16
Barlow, Francis 12, 87, 88, *88,* 89
Barnes, Joseph 127
Baron, Stanley 216, *216*
Barrie, James 18
Bartolozzi, Francesco 54
Baskin, Leonard 116, *116*
Batsford, B.T. 18, 138
Batsford, Brian Cook 18
Batten, David 226
Battersea Park, London 216, *216*
Baudelaire, Charles 244
Bawden, Edward 16
Baxter, Glen 18
BBC 204
Beardsley, Aubrey 16, 110, *110*
Beaton, Cecil 18
Beaulieu, Edmondo 148, *148*
Beckham, David 202
Bedford, Francis 190, 226
Beilby, Ralph 53, *53*
The Belle of a Season 244, 249, *249*
Bellin, Jacques-Nicolas 70, *70*
Bemojake 81
Benlowe, Edward 12
Bensley, Thomas 71, 175
Bentley, R. 13
Bernard, Jean-Frédéric 34, *34, 35*
Berndt, J.C. 163
Bernini, Gian Lorenzo 10
Besler, Basilius 48, *48*
Betjeman, John 18, 65–6, *66,* 78
Bewick, Thomas 14, 15, 47, 53, *53,* 118
Bible 10, 12, 16, 24, 28, *28,* 29, *29,* 37, *37,* 41, *41*; *Biblia pauperum* 24, 26; *Biblia polyglotta* 10; 'Cambridge Bible' 12; 'Coverdale Bible' 10; *Dalziel's Bible Gallery* 16; Luther's translation 10, 26
Bibliographisches Institut 60
Bidpai 84, *84,* 98, *98*
Bilibin, Ivan 102, 111, *111*

The Birds of America 47, 56, *56*
Black 158, *158*
Blake, Quentin 18
Blake, William 14, 36, *36*
Bleak House 109, *109*
Blessington, Lady 244, 249, *249*
Bligh, Elizabeth and William 55
block books 9, 24
Blossfeldt, Karl 196, *196, 197*
Blum, Hans 168
Boccaccio, Giovanni 13
Bochius, Joannes 208, *208*
Bogue, David 228
Bohn, Henry George 58, 188, 212
Boissard, Jean-Jacques 246
Bokushi, Suzuki 75, *75*
Bonaparte, Josephine 44–5, *54*
Boner, Ulrich 84–5, *85,* 96
Bonpland, Aimé 72, *72, 73*
'Book of the Dead' 24, *24*
The Book of Hours of Emperor Maximilian I 10
Book of Job 14, *15*
Book of Nonsense 104, *104*
A Book of Sundry Draughtes 186, *186*
books of hours 24, *24,* 31, *31*
Borcht, Pieter van der 208, *208*
Bordon, Benedetto 10
Bosse, Abraham 242
Boucher, François 13, 102, *102,* 182
Boullay, Benoist 242, 244
Bouquet, Louis 72
Bourke, Blake 215, *215*
Bowie, David 20, *21*
Bowyer, Robert 71
The Boy, the Mole, the Fox and the Horse 21, *21*
Boydell, John 14
Bracci, Giuseppe 148
Bradbury & Evans 109
Briggs, Raymond 18
Brissaud, Pierre 268, *268*
Britannia illustrata 12, 13
British Museum, London 55, 142, 148, 151
British Oology 45, 46
British Photographers 18
Broakes, Victoria 20, *21*
Brontë, Charlotte 93, 104, 118, *118*
Broomberg, Adam 41, *41*
Brothers Dalziel 16, *17,* 104, 226
Brown, Ford Madox 16
Brown, Susanna 259, *259*
Browne, Hablot Knight ('Phiz') 15, 109, *109*
Brunfels, Otto 44, *45*
Brunhoff, Jean de 18
Brunhoff, Maurice de 202
Bryant, William Cullen 14
Buddhism 24
Buffon, comte de 53
Bunkeidō 75
Burgkmair, Hans 205
Burne-Jones, Edward 8

Burney, Fanny 108, *108*
Byron, Lord 14

Cadell, T. 74
Calcar, Jan Stephan van 10
Caldecott, Randolph 16
Callot, Jacques 11, 242
Camilla of Aragon 202
Campbell, Colen 14
Camporesi, Pietro 185
The Canterbury Tales 9
Capote, Yoan 159, *159*
Cardon, Antoine A. 148
Caricatures 18
Carradori, Francesco 123, *123*
Carrington, Noel 61, 154, *154*
Carroll, Lewis 16, *17,* 18
Cars, Laurent 102
Cassatt, Mary 16
Castro, Fidel 159, *159*
catalogues 20, 21, 262–4, 266
Catholic Church 31, 32, 33
Caxton, William 9
Caylus, comte de 147
Caymocx, Balthasar 168
Centennial Exposition, Philadelphia (1876) 223, 230, *230*
Century of Progress Exposition, Chicago (1933) 236, *236, 237*
Cérémonies et coutumes religieuses 34, *34, 35*
Cervantes, Miguel de 16, 102, 112, *112, 113*
Cervino, Elizabeth 159, *159*
Cesari, Giuseppe 147, *147*
Cesariano, Cesare 165
C'est l'ordre qui a esté tenu à la nouvelle et joyeuse entrée ... 206, *206, 207*
Cézanne, Paul 159
Chagall, Marc 94, *94*
Chalon, Alfred Edward 249, *249*
Chambers, Ephraim 123
Chambers, William 169
Champ fleury 126, *126*
Champion Papers Inc 272
Chanarin, Oliver 41, *41*
Chang, Shuhong 199, *199*
chapbooks 11, 14
Chapman and Hall 143
Chaucer, Geoffrey 8, *8,* 9
The Chemistry of Light and Photography 137, *137*
Chesterton, G.K. 92
Chiang Yee 79, *79*
Chicago 225, 231, 236
Chieh Tzu Yuan Hua Chuan 128, *128, 129*
children's books 11, 16–18, 85
Chippendale, Thomas 9, 13–14, 131, 262, 265, *265,* 273
Chodowiecki, Daniel 13
Chōjiya Heibei 75
Chōjū ryakugashiki 132, *132*
Les Choses de Paul Poiret vues par Georges Lepape 244, 251

Chrieger, Christoph 246, *246*
Christianity 24–6
chromolithography 15, 16, 143, 176, 184, 190, 223
Circle Press 99
Cistercian order 26
Clarissa 13
Clark, John 133, *133*
Clarke, John 55, 71
Claude Lorrain 14
Clay, Son & Taylor 229
Clayton, John 226
Clerck, Carl *44*
Cleyn, Francis 12
Cobden-Sanderson, Thomas J. 16
'Codex Mendoza' 72
Cole, Henry 190, 222
A Collection of Ceilings 187, *187*
Collection of Etruscan, Greek and Roman Antiquities ... 148, *148, 149*
A Collection of Fables 11
Collection of Monuments and Decorations of Architecture in Rome 189
Collins, William 18
collotypes 38
Colonna, Francesco 10, 202–5, *203*, 206, 219, *219*
Columbia University Press 198
Comenius, John Amos 11
Communist Party (China) 95
Compound Frame 117, *117*
Conchology 45, 55, *55*
Conder, Neville 204
Conran, Sir Terence 274
Constable, John 14
Constructivism 179
Cook, Captain James 64, *64*
Copernicus, Nicolaus 12
Copland, Henry 131, *131*
copperplate engravings 10
Corbould, Edward 213
Corinth, Lovis 16
Corneille, Pierre 12, 13
Cornwall (Shell Guide) 18, 65–6, *66*
The Coronation of his Most Sacred Majesty King George the Fourth 212, *212*
Cortona, Pietro da 11
Cotta'schen (J.G.) Buchhandlung 134
Country Life Ltd 79
Courboin, François 244, 250, *250*
Cowell, W.S. 61
Cowperthwait, B.M. 263
Cox, David 136, *136*
Coyett, Baltazar 50
Coypel, Charles Antoine 102
Craig, Edward Gordon 114, 214
Cranach, Lucas the Elder 10, 26, 32
Cranach Presse 16
Crane, Walter 16, 85, 91, *91*, 214, *214*
Crawford, Dr Ian 81
Crès, G. et Cie 177
Creswick, Thomas 16, 104
Crow 116, *116*

Crozat, Pierre 142, 147, *147*
Cruikshank, George 15, 228, *228*
Cuba Talks 159, *159*
Cube, J.W. von *45*
Curtis, William *45*, 52, *52*
cyanotypes 47
Cyclopedia 123

Dahl, Roald 18
Dalí, Salvador 16, 102, 112, *112, 113*
Dallier, Jean 206
Dante 16, *18*, 20, 102, *102*, 150, 219
Dante's Inferno 18, 20
Darly, Matthias 265, *265*
Darstellung und Geschichte des Geschmacks der vorzüglichsten Völker 174, *174*
Darwin, Charles 47, *47*, 60
Davent, Léon 68
David Bowie Is 20, 21
Davies, Akinola Jr 276
Davison, Thomas 74
Day and Son 190, 226
De architectura libri decem 165, *165*
D.E driade edizioni 264, 273, *273*
De historia stirpium commentarii insignes 10
De humani corporis fabrica 10
Debrett, John 204
Debrett's Peerage 217
Decameron 13
Degas, Edgar 16
Degli habiti antichi et moderni ... 242, 244, 246, *246*
Delacroix, Eugène 14, *15*, 21
Delamotte, Philip Henry 226
Della Bella, Stephano 12
Della magnificenza ed architettura de' Romani 170, *170, 171*
DeMille, Cecil B. 37
Descartes, René 130
Descriptio publicae gratulationis ... 208, *208*
Description géographique de la Guiane 70, *70*
Deshairs, Léon 235
Designs of Inigo Jones 14
Designs by Mr. R. Bentley for Six Poems by Mr. T. Gray 13
Desplaces, Louis 147
Dickens, Charles 15, 109, *109*
Dickinson, Emily 117, *117*
Dickinson, Joseph 213
Dickinson's Comprehensive Pictures of the Great Exhibition of 1851 222–3, *223*
Diderot, Denis 13, 70, 123–4, *123*, 244
Didot family 15, 70, 192
Dietterlin, Wendel 168, *168*
Dight, Walter 186
Dior, Christian 244, 256, *256*
Directoire style 251

Discoveries in the Ruins of Nineveh and Babylon ... 151
Divine 218
Divine Comedy 102, *102*, 150, 219
DK Eyewitness Travel: India 18
Dominican order 28
Don Quixote 16, 102, 112, *112, 113*
Donatello 182
Donnelly (Reuben H.) Corporation 236
Doré, Gustave 16, 37, *37*
Dorling Kindersley (DK) *18*, 20, 66
Dorp, Maarten van 85
Dorset Shell Guide 78, *78*
Doubleday, Page & Co. 92
Doves Press 16
Doyle, Richard 213, *213*
Draeger Frères 268
'Dresden Codex' 72, 73
Driade 273, *273*
Dufy, Raoul 264
Dugdale, William 12
Dulac, Edmund 18, 93, *93*
Dumas, Alexandre 15
Dunhuang Tang dai tu an xuan 199, *199*
Dupuis, Grégoire 90
Durand, Asher B. 14
Dürer, Albrecht 10, *11*, 126, 182, *182*, 205
Dutch East India Company 12, 57

Eastlake, Sir Charles 134
Eberts, Johann Heinrich 248
Ebury Press 21
Der Edelstein 84–5, *85*, 96
Éditions Albert Lévy 195, 235
Edmund Dulac's Fairy-Book 93, *93*
Edwards, Sydenham 52
Eglinton, Earl of 213
Ehon tokiwagusa 244, *244*, 247, *247*
Eichenberg, Fritz 16
electrotypes 15
Elizabeth II, Queen 217, *217*
Elkin Mathews & John Lane 110
Elliott, Maud Howe 231, *231*
emblem books 11
Emblemata liber 203, 205, 206
Emblemes 11
encyclopedias 123–4
Encyclopédie 13, 70, 123–4, *123*, 244
Encyclopédie du siècle. L'Exposition de Paris 1900 225, 232, *232, 233*
Endter, Michael 11
Engelmann, Gottfried 15
English Cathedrals 20
English Church Monuments 18
English Country Houses 18
English Landscape Scenery 14
The English People 18
English Women 18
engravings 11, 34, 48; copperplate 10; line 16; steel 14, 74; stipple 14; wood 15–16, 223
Enitharmon Editions 118
Enlightenment 13, 64, 123–4

Entwurff einer Historischen Architectur 13
Epstein, Jacob 16
Eragny Press 16
Erklärung der zu Goethe's Farbenlehre gehörigen Tafeln 134, *134, 135*
Ernst, Archduke of Austria 208
Esbatement moral des animaux 87, *87*
Esdaile, Katharine 18
Essex House Press 16
Esther scrolls 24, 26
etchings 11; photo-etching 91; relief etchings 36
Euclid 10
European Space Agency 81
Evans, Edmund 16, 91
Evelina 108, *108*
Everyday People 244, *244*
Expo 67, Montreal (1967) 238, *238*
Expo 70, Tokyo (1970) 239, *239*
Exposición Internacional de Barcelona (1929) 225, *225*
Exposition Internationale des Arts Décoratifs, Paris (1925) 235, *235*
Exposition Universelle, Paris (1900) 225, *225*, 232, *232, 233*
The Expression of the Emotions in Man and Animals 47, *47*

Faber and Faber 116
Fables (Aesop) 85, 86, 88, *88*, 89, 91–2, *92*, 96
Fables (Feng) 95, *95*
Fables (Gay) 13
Fables (La Fontaine) 16, 94, *94*
Fables of Bidpai 98, *98*
Fables nouvelles (La Motte) 90, *90*
Fabrica de Louças Adelinas 264
Fairy Tales of the Allied Nations 93
Fallours, Samuel 50
Fashion Drawing 244, 252, *252*
Faust 14, *15*, 21
Feng Xuefeng 95, *95*
Ferdinand, Cardinal-Infante 11
Ferdinand of Austria 209
Ferdowsi 102
Ferwerda, Abraham 51
Festival of Britain, London (1951) 204, 216, *216*, 218
Feuchtwang, Eva 18–20, 158
Fini, Leonor 114, *114, 115*
First World War 93
Fischer von Erlach, Johann Bernhard 13
Fisher, Roy 99, *99*
Flamsteed, John 12
Flaxman, John 14
Flight, Claude 138, *138*
Flood Gallery Publishing 219
Flora Londinensis 45, 52, *52*
Florilegium amplissimum et selectissimum 263
Foges, Wolfgang 18
Folio Society 16
Folkema, Jacob 51
Foreign Languages Press 95

Forster, Georg 64
Fortnum, C. Drury E. *143*
Franceschi, Francesco de' *166*
Franciscan order 28, 33
François I, King of France 126
Frank Leslie's Historical Register of the United States Centennial Exposition, 1876 230, *230*
Frankfurt Fair (1612) 263
Franklin, Benjamin 262
Fraser, Eric 204
Frederick, Prince of Wales 169
French Revolution 14, 64, 242
Fresco Decorations and Stuccoes of Churches & Palaces in Italy 189, *189*
Frith, Francis 77, *77*
Frog Went A-Courtin 18
Fruits 244, 253, *253*
Fry, Ben 139
Fuchs, Leonhart 10
Fuller, R. Buckminster 238
Fuller, S. and J. 136
Füllmaurer, Heinrich 10
Fuseli, Henry 14

Gaga, Lady 254, *254*
Gainsborough, Thomas 13
Galileo Galilei 12
Galle, Philippe 87
Gallery of Fashion 242, *242*
Ganjavi, Nizami 102, 106, *106*, *107*
Gardner, Helen 144
Garima Gospels 24
Garrick, David 71
Garsault, François Alexandre de 242
Gaubisch, Urban 32
Gauguin, Paul 16
Gay, John 13, 85
Gebr. Fretz A.G., Zurich 269, *269*
Gedde, Walter 186, *186*
Gedenkwaerdige gesantschappen 12
Gefn Press 117
A General History of Quadrupeds 14, 47, 53, *53*
Genji monogatari emaki 102, *102*
Gentleman and Cabinet-maker's Director 9, 13–14, 131, 265, *265*, 273
George IV, King 212, 215
George V, King 215
Gerlach, Martin 124, *124*
Germani Fidelissimi 86
La Gerusalemme liberata 13
Geschichte der Kunst des Altherthums 142, *143*
Gessner, Conrad 87
Gevaerts, Jean-Gaspard 209, *209*
Gheeraerts, Marcus the Elder 87, *87*, 96
Giacomelli, Hector 37
Gibson, Charles Dana 244, *244*
Gidi gidi bu ugwu eze ... 276, *276*, *277*
Gilbert, Stuart 145
Gillot, Claude 90
Gilpin, William 64, 65, 71, 136

Giltsch, Adolf 60
Giovanni Gioconda da Verona, Fra 165, *165*
Girl in Dior 244, 256, *256*, *257*
Giulio Romano 10, 189, *189*
I Giunti 146
Giusti, Gordana Fontana 179, *179*
Glastonbury Festival 219, *219*
Glossary of Ecclesiastical Ornament and Costume 188, *188*
Glynn Smith, Juliet 274, *274*
Goethe, Johann Wolfgang von 14, *15*, 21, 134, *134*, *135*
Goetzinger, Annie 244, 256, *256*, *257*
Gogol, Nikolai 104, *104*
Golden Cockerel Press 16
Goldscheider, Ludwig 20, 144, 156, *156*
Gombrich, Ernst 18, 20, 144, 155, *155*
Goncourt, Edmond and Jules de 13
Gonzalez, Osvaldo 159
Gooden, Stephen 16
Gorey, Edward 18
Gormenghast 18
Göschen, G.J. 174
The Gossiping Photographer at Hastings 77, *77*
Gothic Revival 184, 188, 193
Gould, John 47
Goupil and Co. 231
Gourmont, Giles 126
Grahame, Kenneth 18
The Grammar of Ornament 174, 184, 190, *190*, *191*, 192
Grand Tour 13, 14, 64, 187
Grandville (J.I.I. Gérard) 16
graphic novels 18, 244, 256, *256*, *257*
Gravelot, Hubert-François 13
Gray, Thomas 13
Great Exhibition, London (1851) 184, 222–3, *222*, *223*, 226, *226*, *227*, 228, *228*, 229
The Greatest of Expositions Completely Illustrated 234, *234*
Greenaway, Kate 16
Greff, Jeronimus 11
Griffo, Francesco 10
Grimm, Jacob and Wilhelm 84
Grosser, Boris 235, *235*
Gruner, Ludwig 151, *151*, 176, *176*, 189, *189*
Guide (Festival of Britain) 216, *216*
Gutenberg, Johann 9, 29, 162
Gutensohn, Johann Gottfried 189

Habitat 264, 274, *274*, *275*
Habitus praecipuorum populorum 242
Hadid, Zaha 179, *179*
Haeckel, Ernst 44, 60, *60*
Hafez 119, *119*
Haggadah shel Pesach 38, *38*, *39*
Halfpenny, William and John 169, *169*
Hall, John 64
Hamilton, Sir William 142, 148
Hamlyn, Paul 20

Hancarville, Pierre d' 148, *148*, *149*
Harris, Moses 45, 58, *58*, *59*
Hart, Dick 204
Hartley, J. 204
Hassonville, Gaspar de 31
Hastings 77
Havell, Robert Jr 56
Hayden, Sophia G. 231
Haydock, Richard 127
Hayman, Francis 13, 114
Hayward Gallery Publishing 145
Heath, William 108, *108*
Heideloff, Nikolaus 242, *242*
Die heimliche offenbarung Johannes 11
Heinemann, W. 92
Helm, Margaretha 182
heliotypes 47
Helmut Newton 20
Henri II, King of France 206, *206*
Herbarum vivae eicones 44, 45
Hesperides 11
Hevelius, Johannes 12
Hewitson, William C. 45, 46
Heyns, Peeter 87
Hill, Oliver 163, 164
Hills, Henry Jr 88
Hilton, James 219
Him, George 18, 216
Himid, Lubaina 145
Hinduism 40
Hiroshige, Andō 16
Histoire de l'art par les monumens 150, *150*
Histoire des arts industriels au moyen âge 143, 152, *152*, *153*
Histoire de Babar 18
Histoire naturelle 53
Histoires ou contes du temps passé 12
Historia animalium 87
Historia Naturalis 142, *142*
Historiae of Foure Footed Beastes 12
Historiae Naturalis de Quadrupedipus 12
History of Art 144
A History of British Birds 14, 47, 118
History of St Paul's Cathedral 12, *12*
History of the Westminster Election 204
Hittorff, A. 189
HMSO (His Majesty's Stationery Office) 204
Hockney, David 159
Hodder & Stoughton 93
Hodges, William 64, *64*
Hoffman, Heinrich 15
Hogarth, William 13
Hokuetsu seppu 75, *75*
Hokusai, Katsushika 16
Holbein, Hans 10, 150, 182
Hollar, Wenceslaus 12, *12*, 242, *242*
Holy Bible 41, *41*
The Holy Carpet of the Mosque at Ardebil 194, *194*
Home Owners' Catalogs 262, 263
Hooke, Robert 12
Hoole, Charles 11

Hooper, William Harcourt 8
Horovitz, Béla 20
Horsley, J.C. 16
Hortus Eystettensis 44, 48, *48*, *49*
The Housekeeper's Guide 263
Huang Yongyu 95
Hughes, Ted 116, *116*
Hugo, Victor 15
Hullmandel, Charles James 15
Humboldt, Alexander von 72, *72*, *73*
Humphreys, Henry Noel 226
A Humument 20
Hunt, William Holman 16, 104
The Hunting of the Snark 18
Hürlimann, Martin 20
Hutton, Clarke 154, *154*
Hypnerotomachia Poliphili 10, 202–5, *203*, 206, 219, *219*

Icones historiarum Veteris Testamenti 10
Iconologia 205
Idylls of the King 16
The Illustrated London News 15, 215, 222
Illustrated pattern book of furniture ... 266, *266*, *267*
Imagination IV 264, 272, *272*
Imprimerie Royale, Paris 11, 147, 210
In Search of England 65
Indépendance 268, *268*
The Industrial Arts of the Nineteenth Century 222, *222*, 226, *226*, 227
Inferno 16, 18, 20
Ingres, J.-A.-D. 68
Insel Verlag 18
instructive guides 122–4
Intérieurs en couleurs France 235, *235*
International Exhibition, London (1852) 229, *229*
Iribe, Paul 251, *251*
Islam 24, 34, 102
Istruzione elementare per gli studiosi della scultura 123, *123*
Italian Masters in German Galleries 144
Italy 74, *74*

Jainism 30
Jamaican Song and Story 99
Jane Eyre 104, 118, *118*
Janson, H.W. 144
Janus Press 98
Jekyll, Walter 99
Jennings and Chaplin 74
Jewell, Dick 218, *218*
Johanknecht, Susan 117, *117*
Johannot, Tony 15
Johnstone, W.G. 47
Jones, Owen 174, 176, 184, 190, *190*, *191*, 192
Jones, V.S. Vernon 92, *92*
Jones and Co. 108
Jonston, John 12
Judaism 24, 34, 38
Jukes, Francis 64, 65

Kaléidoscope, ornements abstraits 195, *195*
Kalman, Maira 264
Kalpasutra 30, *30*
Kamifuji, Tom 272, *272*
Kaufmann & Fabry 236
Kawachiya Mohei 75
Kawahara Keiga 47, 57, *57*
Kcho 159, *159*
Keisai, Kuwagata 132, *132*
Kelmscott Press 8, *8*, 16
Kent, Rockwell 66, *66*
Kent, William 14
Kentridge, William 104, *104*
Kenzo 276, *276*, *277*
Kessler, Harry Graf 16
Khusraw u Shirin 102, 106, *106*, *107*
Kilburn, William 52
Kilian, Wolfgang 48
Kinder- und Hausmärchen 84
King, H.S. & Co. 137
King, Ronald 99, *99*
Kip, Johannes 12, *13*
Kirchner, Ernst Ludwig 16
Knight, Nick 254, *254*
Knoop, Johann Hermann 45–7, 51, *51*
Knyff, Leonard 12, *13*
Koberger, Anton 9–10, 29, *29*
Koolhaas, Rem 162, *163*
Koran 24, 26
Kris, E. 18
Krol, Abram 96
Krylov, Ivan 85
Kunst- und Fleiss-übende Nadel-Ergötzungen 182
Kunstformen der Natur 2, 44, 60, *60*
Kyōsui, Iwase 75
Kyōto Yōfuku Kaisha 263

La Fontaine, Jean de 16, 85, 90, 94, *94*, *96*, *96*, *97*, *98*
La Motte, Antoine Houdar de 90, *90*
La Redouté 264
Labarte, Jules 143, 152, *152*, *153*
The Ladies Amusement 184, *185*
Ladybird Books 47
Lancaster, Osbert 216, *216*
Lane, Allen 18
Langewiesche, K. 18
Langstaff, John 18
Larionov, Mikhail 202
Layard, Austen Henry 151, *151*
Le Brun, Charles 125, 130, *130*
Le Corbusier 177, *177*
Le Keux, John Henry *15*
Le Rond d'Alembert, Jean 13, 123–4, *123*, 244
Le Sueur, Nicolas 147
Le Witt, Jan 216
Lear, Edward 47, 104, *104*
Learning from Las Vegas 178, *178*
Leclerc, Sébastien 12–13
Leech, John 15
Lees-Milne, James 18

Legrand, Edy 268, *268*
Leicester Galleries, London 93
Leighton, Frederic 16
Lemaire, Madeleine 231, *231*
Leonardo da Vinci 44, 182
Lepape, Georges 244, 251
Lépicié, Nicolas Bernard 102
Leroux, George Paul 225, *225*
Leslie, Frank 223
Lewis, Barry 219, *219*
Lewitt, Jan 18
Li Liufang 128, *128*, *129*
Li Yu 128
Liber chronicarum see 'Nuremberg Chronicle'
Liber studiorum 14
Life and Opinions of Tristram Shandy 13
Ligniville, Eve de 31
Les Liliacées 44–5, 54, *54*
Limited Editions Club 16
Linn, James Weber 236
Linnell, John 14
linocuts 138
lithography 14, 152
The Little Red Engine Gets a Name 18
Littlewoods 264
Liu Xiaodong 80, *80*
Lock, Matthias 131, *131*
Locke, John 36
Logan, Andrew 218, *218*
Loggie di Rafaele nel Vaticano 184, *185*
Lomazzo, Giovanni 127, *127*
London 13, 18, 79, *79*
London: A Pilgrimage 16
London Celebrations Committee 217
London International Exhibition (1862) 223, 229
Lorenzo da Viterbo 150
Lorimier, Jean-Louis de 238
Lose, Friedrich 176, *176*
Lost Horizon 219
Louis XIV, King of France 210, 242
Louis XV, King of France 13, 90
Louis Vuitton 80
Louisiana Purchase Exposition (1904) 234, *234*
Loutherbourg, Philip James de 71, *71*
Lucas, David 14
Lully, Jean-Baptiste 210
Luther, Martin 10, 26, 32, *32*
Luttrell, Henry 74
Lux claustri 11
Luza, Reynaldo 268, *268*

Macchiavelli, Giacomo 150
Mackesy, Charlie 21, *21*
McKnight Kauffer, Edward 16, 18
McLean, Ruari 216
Maclise, Daniel 15
McQueen, Alexander 20, 244, 254, *254*, *255*
Made in Tokyo 162
Maiolica 143
Malory, Thomas 9

Malraux, André 144, *145*, 155, 158
Mame, Alfred et Fils 37
Mansbridge, Norman 204
Manutius, Aldus 10, *203*, 262
Mao Zedong 95
Mariette, Pierre-Jean 147, *147*
Marsh, Geoffrey 20, *21*
Marshall, Francis 244, 252, *252*
Martiel, Carlos 159
Martyn, John 44
'Master Cristofano' 146, *146*
Matisse, Henri 16
Matter, Herbert 269, *269*
Mau, Bruce 162, *163*
Maximilian I, Emperor 205
Mayhew, Henry 228, *228*
Mayne, Roger 65
Medina, John Baptist 12
Meissonier, Ernest 15
Melanchthon, Philip 32, *32*
Melanesian Design 198, *198*
Menzel, Adolph 16
Merian, Maria Sibylla 45, *45*
Metabolists 239
Metamorphoses 105, *105*
Méthode pour apprendre à dessiner les passions 125, 130, *130*
Meursius, Joannes 209
Michelangelo 37, 144, 146, 156, *156*
Michelangelo 144, 156, *156*
Micrographia 12
Mies van der Rohe, Ludwig 178
Miles, J. & Co. 214
Millais, John Everett 16, 104
Milne, A.A. 18, 21
Milton, John 12, 16
Miss World '78 Souvenir Programme 218, *218*
MIT Press 178
Modernism 18, 178, 184, 269
Les Modes de Paris 244
Molière 12, 102, *102*, 210
Monacelli Press 163
Monograph on the Silk Fabrics of Bengal 124–5, *124*
Montanus, Arnoldus 12
Montgomery Ward 263, 271, *271*
Montgrédien et Cie 232
Monument du costume physique et moral 244, 248, *248*
Morandi, Giorgio 159
Moreau, Jean-Michel le Jeune 248, *248*
Morel, A. et Cie 152
Morelli, Giovanni 143, *144*
Moretus, Balthasar 10–11
Moretus, Jan 208
Moronobu, Hishikawa 16
Morrell, Martin 274
Morris, William 8, *8*, 16, 91
Morte d'Arthur 9
Morton, H.V. 65
Moxon, Edward 16, 74, 104
Mueller, Hans A. 16

Muhammad, Prophet 24
Mukerji, Nitya Gopal 124–5, *124*
Müller, Johannes Sebastian 265, *265*
Mulready, William 16, 104
Munch, Edvard 16
Murasaki Shikibu 102, *102*
Murray, John 64, 65, 151, 176, 189
Museum of Modern Art, New York 144, 157
Muziano, Girolamo 147, *147*

Napoleonic Wars 14, 111
Nash, John 16, 18, 65
Nash, Paul 16, 18, 65, 78, *78*
A Natural History of Birds 46, 47
The Nature Printed British Sea-Weeds 47
Nayler, Sir George 212, *212*
Nelson, Thomas & Sons (Canada) 238
Neoclassicism 64, 184, 187
Neue Sachlichkeit 196
Neurath, Walter 18–20, 158
Neurdein brothers 225
A New Book of Ornaments 131, *131*
The New Colonists 81, *81*
New Invented Pennsylvania Fire-Places 262
Newton, Helmut 20
Newton, Sir Isaac 12, 134
Nicholls, J. and G. 266
Nicholson, Ben 18
Nicholson, William 214, *214*
Nicol, George 187
Nicolay, Nicolas de 68, *68*, 69
Nierendorf, Karl 196
Nihon Bankokuhaku no kenchiku 239, *239*
Nineveh and its Remains 151
Noble, Thomas 133, *133*
Nonesuch Press 16
Norton, Frank H. 230, *230*
The Nose 104, *104*
Nuremberg 9–10, 29
'Nuremberg Chronicle' 8, 9–10, *9*, 29

Observations on the River Wye 64, 65, 71
Observations on the Theory and Practice of Landscape Gardening 175, *175*
Œuvre complète 177
The Official Pictures of a Century of Progress Exposition, Chicago, 1933 236, *236*, *237*
Ogilvy, John 12
OK! magazine 202
Old English Pattern Books 263
One Hundred Views of Mount Fuji 16
Ophir, Adi 41
Orbis sensualium pictus 11
Orlando Furioso 210
Orléans, Philippe, duc d' 210
Orme, Edward 133
L'Ornement polychrome 184, 192, *192*
Ortus sanitatis 44, *45*
Orwell, George 18
Ossai, Ruth 276, *276*, *277*
The Other Story 144, *145*

Ottaviani, Giovanni 185
Ovid 105, *105*

Pai, Anant 40
Palladio, Andrea 162, *162*
Panchatantra 84, 98, *98*
Pannemaker, Adolphe François 37
Paradise Lost 12, 16
Paris 11, 13, 15, 31, *163*, 225, 232, 235
Parkin, Molly 218
Passional Christi und Antichristi 32, *32*
Les passions de l'âme 130
pattern books 124, 181–99, 262, 265
Paul et Virginie 15
Pawson & Brailsford 266
Peacock, Jila 119, *119*
Peake, Mervyn 18
Pelican History of Art 158
The Pencil of Nature 15
Penguin Books 18, 154
People places culture ... home 274, *274*, *275*
'Perfection of Wisdom in 8,000 Verses' 24, *24*
Perrault, Charles 12
Perrault d'Armancourt, Pierre 12
Perry, George 45, 55, *55*
Peter Pan in Kensington Gardens 18
Petrutius, Petrus Jacobus 33
Peugeot 268, *268*
Pevsner, Nikolaus 18, 65
Pfister, Albrecht 9, 84–5
Die Pflanze in Kunst und Gewerbe 124, *124*
Phaidon Press 20, 155, 156, 253
Philadelphia 223
Philips, Jan Casper 51
Phillips, Tom 18, 20, 21
Philosophiæ naturalis principia mathematica 12
The Photographers' Gallery, London 81
photography 15, 47, 65, 137, 143–4
photomontage 66, 264, 269
Pi Sheng 9
Piaud, Antoine Alphée 37
Piazzetta, Giambattista 13
Picart, Bernard 34, *34*-5
Picasso, Pablo 16, 157
Piccolpasso, Cipriano 122–3, *123*
Pickett, William 71
Picture Book: Selected Insects 16
Picturesque Architecture in Paris ... 15
The Picturesque Scenery of Great Britain 71
Pidgeon, Henry Clarke 226
Pignatari, Carmine 148
Pillard, Adélaïde and Maurice 195, *195*
Pillement, Jean 184, *185*
Piper, John 18, 65, 216, *216*
Piranesi, Giovanni Battista 168, 170, *170*, *171*
Piroli, Tommaso 150
Pisan, Héliodore Joseph 37
Pissarro, Lucien 16
Pitt, William the Younger 204, 205
Plaats, François van der 130

Les Plaisirs de l'isle enchantée 210, *210*, *211*
Plans, Elevations, Sections, and Details of the Alhambra 176
Plantin, Christophe 10, 208
Pleasure Gardens, Battersea Park, London 216, *216*
Pleiades Books 164
Pliny the Elder 142, *142*
Plutarch 202
pochoir 195, 251
Poem of the Pillow 16
Poems (Rogers) 15
Poems (Tennyson) 104, *104*
Poiret, Paul 244, 251, *251*
Poissons, écrevisses et crabes ... 45, 50, *50*
Poitevin process 152
Polychromatic Decoration as Applied to Buildings in the Mediæval Styles 193, *193*
Pomologia 45–7, 51, *51*
Pompa introitus ... Ferdinandi 11, 209, *209*
Pompadour, Madame de 13
Pop Art 178, 272
Popular Art in Britain 154, *154*
Posthumous Papers of the Pickwick Club 15
Postmodernism 264, 273
Potter, Beatrix 16–18, 85, *85*, 104
Poussin, Nicolas 11
Powell, Richard J. 158, *158*
Pozzi, W.E. 226
Practical Perspective Exemplified on Landscapes 133, *133*
Pre-Raphaelites 14, 16, 104
Price, Uvedale 136
"Primitivism" *in 20th Century Art* 157, *157*
La Princesse d'Élide 210
Principles of Art History 143, *144*
private press movement 16
Process Compendium 2004–2010 139, *139*
Pryce-Jones, Pryce 263
Puffin Books 18, 47, 61, 154
Pugin, A.W.N. 188, *188*

Quarles, Francis 11
Les quatre premiers livres des navigations ... 68, *68*, *69*
I quattro libri dell'architettura 162, *162*

Racine, Jean 12
Racinet, Auguste 184, 192, *192*
Rackham, Arthur 18, 85, 92, *92*
Racknitz, Joseph Friedrich zu 174, *174*
Radio Times 'Coronation number' 204
Rafter, H. 226
Raimondi, Marcantonio 142, 146
Random House 112
Raphael 37, 142, 182, 184
Ratdolt, Erhard 10
Rau, William H. 234, *234*
Ravilious, Eric 16
Reas, Casey 139, *139*
Recueil de la diversité des habits 242
Recueil d'estampes ... 147, *147*

Redouté, Pierre Joseph 44–5, 54, *54*
Reeve, Richard 136, *136*
Reformation 10, 26, 29, 32
Rego, Paula 104, 118, *118*
Reichard, Gladys A. 198, *198*
Les Reines de l'aiguille 244, 250, *250*
Relations de divers voyages curieux 12
relief etchings 36, *36*
Ren min mei shu chu ban she 199
Renaissance 142, 146, 150, 165, 168, 202, 205, 242, 262
Renard, Louis 45, 50, *50*
Repository of Arts 242, *242*
Repton, Humphry 175, *175*
Restif de la Bretonne, Nicolas 248, *248*
Revett, Nicholas 13
Reynard the Fox 84
Reynolds, Joshua 14
Rhetorica Christiana 33, *33*
Richardson, George 184, 187, *187*
Richardson, Samuel 13
Richelieu, Cardinal 11
Richter, Louise *144*
Ricketts, Charles 16
Rimicium (Rinuccio da Castiglione) 85
Ripa, Cesare 205
Riza Abbasi 102, 106, *106*, *107*
Rizzoli International 159
Les Robes de Paul Poiret 244, 251, *251*
Robinson, Vincent and Company 194
Robson & Sons 194
Rococo style 13, 131, 184, 265
Rodogune 13
Rogers, Samuel 14, 15, 74, *74*
Rojankovsky, Feodor 18
The Romantic and Picturesque Scenery of England and Wales 71, *71*
Romantic movement 14, 84
Romney, George 14
Ross, Diana 18
Rossetti, Dante Gabriel 14, 16, 104, *104*
Rossi, Properzia de' 146
Roth, Martin 20, *21*
Rouillé, Guillaume 68
Routledge, George & Sons 91
Rowlandson, Thomas 204, 205
Rubens, Peter Paul 10–11, *11*, 21, 182, 209, *209*
Rubin, William 157, *157*
The Ruins of the Palace of the Emperor Diocletian ... 172
Rural Architecture in the Chinese Taste 169, *169*
Ruskin, John 74
Rye 77

S, M, L, XL 162, *163*
Sackville West, Vita 18
Sadahide, Utagawa 76, *76*
Saint-Pierre, Bernardin de 15
La Sainte Bible 37, *37*
Salamina 66, *66*
Salas Redondo, Laura 159, *159*
Salome 16, 110, *110*

Salomon, Bernard 105, *105*
Sans, Jérôme 159, *159*
Saudé, Jean 195
Savorelli, G. 185
The Savoy 16
Sayer, Robert 131, 169
Scarsdale, Sir Nathaniel Curzon, 1st Baron 187
Schäufelein, Hans 203
Schedel, Hartmann 8, 9–10
Schoell, Frédéric 72
Schumacher, Patrik 179, *179*
Schuricht, Christian Friedrich 174, *174*
Schweppes Devonshire Cider 270, *270*
Schwertfeger, Johann 32, *32*
Scott, Walter 14, 213
Scott Brown, Denise 178, *178*
Secker & Warburg 145
A Second Series of the Monuments of Nineveh 151, *151*
Second World War 66, 154, 216
Selenographia 12
Sendak, Maurice 18
Senefelder, Alois 14
A Series, Containing Forty-four Engravings ... 185
Serlio, Sebastiano 166, *166*, *167*, 168
Séroux d'Agincourt, J.B.L.G. 142, 150, *150*
Seven Years' War (1756–63) 70
Seymour, Robert 15
Sforza, Costanzo 202
Shahn, Ben 38, *38*, 39
Shahnama 102, 106
Shakespeare, William 14, 114, *114*, *115*, 214
Shaw, Byam 214, *214*, 215, *215*
Shell Guides 18, 61, 65–6, *66*, 78, *78*
Shen Xingyou 128
Shepard, Ernest H. 18
Sherwin, John Keyse 64, *64*
Shiga Shashin 263
Shotter Boys, Thomas 15
Shvabrin, Stanislav 104
Shvetambaras 30
Siebold, Philipp Franz von 57
Siegl, Helen 98, *98*
Siegl, Nicholas 98
Silber & Fleming 266, *266*, *267*
The Silent Traveller in London 79, *79*
Silvestre, Israel 210, *210*, *211*
Simeoni, Gabriele 105
Les simulachres et historiées faces de la mort 10
Sitwell, Edith 18
Skazka ob Ivane-tsareviche 111, *111*
Slevogt, Max 16
Sliegh, John 226
Smallfield, Frederick 226
Société typographique 248
Sōmoku kajitsu shashin zufu 47, 57, *57*
Songs of Innocence and Experience 14
Sorrenti, Mario 254
Sory, Sanlé 244, 258, *258*
Sotheran, Henry & Co. 193

South Africa 80, *80*
South Kensington Museum *see* V&A
Souvenir Programme ... for Ellen Terry 214, *214*
Sowerby, G.B. 55
Sowerby, James 52
Spade, Kate 264, *264*
The Sphere 215
Stanfield, Clarkson 16
Starck, Philippe 20
Stayner, Heinrich 203
Stebbing, Edward 194, *194*
steel engravings 14, *15*, 74
Steiner, Elizabeth 117, *117*
Steingruber, Johann 163, *163*
Steinhöwel, Heinrich 85
Stel, Adriaen van der 50
stencilling 16, 38, *195*, 251
Stephanoff, Francis 212
Stephanoff, James 212
Sterling, John 217, *217*
Sterne, Laurence 13
Stevens, Alfred 226
Stone, John Hurford 72
Stories from Hans Christian Andersen 18
Stories from The Arabian Nights 18, 93
The Story of Art 20, 144, 155, *155*
Stothard, Thomas 14, 74
Struwwelpeter 15
Stuart, James 'Athenian' 13
Stubbs, George 13, 53
Studio Publications 252
Studio Volta Photo 244, 258, *258*
Suhayli, Anvar-i 84
Sukenobu, Nishikawa 244, *244*, 247, *247*
Sukita, Masayoshi 21
Surrealism 18, 78, 112, 114, 157, 196
Sutherland, Graham 16, 18
Sweerts, Emanuel 263
Sweet's Indexed Catalogue of Building Construction 262
Sylph Editions 119

Taccuino, Giovanni 165
Le Tailleur sincère 242, 244
Talbot, William Henry Fox 15
The Tale of Johnny Town-Mouse 85, *85*
The Tale of Peter Rabbit 16–18
Talfourd Press 20
Taschen 20
Tasso, Torquato 13
Tatler 215
Taylor, J. 175
La Tempête 114, *114*, *115*
Ten Poems from Hafez 119, *119*
Tenniel, John 16, *17*
Tennyson, Alfred 16, 104, *104*
The Terra-Cotta Architecture of North Italy 176, *176*
Terry, Ellen 214, *214*
Testino, Mario 254, *254*
Thackeray, William Makepeace 15, 104
Thames & Hudson 18–20, 144, 158, 179

Theatrum Mulierum 242
Theophilia 12
There is No Natural Religion 36, *36*
Thévenot, Melchisédech 12
Thompson, Charles 15
Thornton, Peter 182
Thulden, Theodoor van 209, *209*
Thurber, James 85
Thürmer, Joseph 189
Tiffany 264
Tim Walker: Wonderful Things 259, *259*
Tisdall, Hans 163, *164*, 216, *216*
Titian 10, 147
Topsell, Edward 12
Torah 24
Tory, Geoffroy 126, *126*
Toulouse-Lautrec, Henri de 16
The Tournament 213, *213*
Tournes, Jean de 105
Touron, Cardinal François de 122–3
toy books 16, 18, 91
Tozashvili, Levan 81
A Tracte Containing the Artes of Curious Paintinge Carvinge & Buildinge 127, *127*
travel guides 18, 64–81
Li tre libri dell'arte del vasaio 122–3, *123*
A Treatise on Landscape Painting ... 136, *136*
Trees in Britain 47, 61, *61*
Treuttel et Würtz 150
Trianon Press 38
Tunnicliffe, Charles 47
Tuppo, Francesco del 86, *86*
Turner, J.M.W. 14, *15*, 74, 134
Turner's Annual Tour 14
Tutte l'opere d'architettura et prospettiva 166, *166*, *167*
Tyler, J. 136

ukiyo-e prints 16
'Ulm Aesop' 85, 86
Ungar, Fritz 20
Uniqlo 264
United States Centennial Exposition (1876) 223, 230, *230*
Urformen der Kunst 196, *196*, *197*
Utamaro, Kitagawa 16
Uwins, Thomas 212
Uzanne, Octave 244

V&A 20, 21, 143, 184, 190, 222, 229, 259, 262
Vaguely Lost in Shangri-La 219, *219*
Valadés, Diego 33, *33*
Vale Press 16
Van Gogh, Vincent 16
Vanity Fair 15
Vasari, Giorgio 142, 146, *146*, 159
Vecellio, Cesare 242, 244, 246, *246*
Venice 10, 13
Venturi, Robert 178, *178*
Vers une architecture 177, *177*

Versailles 13, 210
Vesalius, Andreas 10
Vickers, Hugo 217, *217*
Vico, Enea 246
Victoria, Queen 212, 215, 249
Vie de la Mère de Dieu 11
Vinter, John Alfred A. 226
Virgil 12
Virtue, J.S. and Co. 77, 266
Visionaire 244, 254, *254*, *255*
Vita Æsopi fabulatoris clarissimi e greco latina ... 85
Vita et Æsopus moralisatus 86, *86*
La Vita et Metamorfoseo d'Ovidio 105, *105*
Le vite de' più eccellenti pittori, scultori et architetti 146, *146*
Vitruvius Britannicus 14
Vitruvius Pollio, Marcus 165, *165*, 168
Vogel, Hermann 137, *137*
Vollard, Ambroise 94
Volpato, Giovanni 184, *185*
Vos, Maarten de 208, *208*
Vostre, Simon 31
A Voyage Towards the South Pole 64, *64*
Vries, Hans Vredeman de 168
Vues des Cordillères 72, *72*, *73*

Walker, Emery 16
Walker, Tim 20, 259, *259*
Wang Gai 128, *128*, *129*
War and Victory 10, 11
De warachtighe fabulen der dieren 87
Wasmuth, Ernst 196
Water Birds 14
Watts, G.F. 16
We Want the Queen 217, *217*
Weiditz, Hans 45
West, Benjamin 14
When the Wind Blows 18
Where the Wild Things Are 18
Whistler, Rex 18, 264
Whittaker, John 212
Wild, Charles 212
Wilde, Oscar 16, 110, *110*
Wilkinson, Christopher 88
Winckelmann, Johann Joachim 142, *143*, 148, 150, 152
The Wind in the Willows 18
Winnie the Pooh 18, 21
Wölfflin, Heinrich 143, *144*
Wolgemut, Michael 8, 9–10
Wonderful Things 20
wood engravings 15–16, 223
woodblock printing 14, 16, 24
woodcuts 9–10, 11, 16, 44
Woods, Sir William 212
Woodward, J.O. 58
The Works in Architecture of Robert and James Adam 172, *172*, *173*
The Works of Geoffrey Chaucer 8
World's Columbian Exposition, Chicago (1893) 225, 231, *231*

Wyatt, Sir Matthew Digby 222, *222*, 226, *226*, 227

Yang, Gladys 95
The Yellow Book 16
Yingzao fashi 162
Yokohama kaikō kenbunshi 76, *76*
Young, Charles George 212
Young, W.A. 262, *263*

Zaha Hadid: Complete Works 179, *179*
Zainer, Johannes 85
Zenaro, Damian 246
Zenbei, Maekawa 57
Zhar-ptitse i o serom volke 111, *111*
Zinkeisen, Anna K. 270, *270*
Zola, Émile 37
Zucco, Accio 86